The Influence of the Carnegie, Ford, and Rockefeller Foundations on American Foreign Policy

The Influence of the Carnegie, Ford, and Rockefeller Foundations on American Foreign Policy:
THE IDEOLOGY OF PHILANTHROPY

Edward H. Berman

State University of New York Press
ALBANY

Published by
State University of New York Press, Albany

© 1983 State University of New York

Printed in the United States of America

For information, address State University of New York
Press, State University Plaza, Albany, N.Y., 12246

Library of Congress Cataloging in Publication Data
Berman, Edward H., 1940-
  The ideology of philanthropy.

  Includes bibliographical references.
  1. Endowments—United States—Philanthropy. 2. United States—Foreign relations—
1945-   . 3. Carnegie Corporation. 4. Ford Foundation. 5. Rockefeller Foundation. I.
Title.
HV97.C33B47 1983   327.73   82-19494
ISBN 0-87395-725-3
ISBN 0-87395-726-1 (pbk.)

Contents

Acknowledgments vii

Introduction 1

1 Foundations and the Extension of American Hegemony 11

 The Foundations' Overseas Programs: The Control of Culture 12
 The Origins and Ideology of Modern Philanthropy 15
 Some Early Foundation Programs 18
 On Analyzing the Foundations' Hegemony 26
 Foundation Managers, Their Money, and Their Influence 32
 The Foundations in Perspective 37

2 United States Foreign Policy and the Evolution of the Foundations' Overseas Programs, 1945–1960 41

 Background to the Foundations' Overseas Programs: The Evolving
  Foreign Policy Consensus 43
 The War-Peace Studies Project: Overseas Economic Expansion 43
 The War-Peace Studies Project: Continued Access to Sources
  of Raw Materials 46
 The War-Peace Studies Project: Evolutionary Change versus
  Revolutionary Chaos 48
 Mechanisms to Implement the War-Peace Studies
  Project's Conclusions 50
 The World Bank 51
 Bilateral Aid 52
 The Basis for the Foundations Overseas Programs after 1945 55
 The Direction of the Foundations' Overseas Programs 59
 Foundation Programs and Foreign-Policy Determination 62

3 The Implementation of Foundation Programs in the Third World 67

 Support for Lead Universities in Developing Nations 69
 Foundation Work in Nigeria 75
 Foundation Support for the University of East Africa 76
 The Growth of Social Science in Third-World Universities 79
 Programs in Public Administration 85
 Teacher Education Projects 88
 The Foundations and Foreign Students 93
 Forging an Intellectual Network 96

4 The Foundations Define a Field: Foreign Area Studies, Social Science, and Developmental Theory   99

The Growth of International and Area-Studies Programs after 1945   100
Foundation Support for the Social Sciences   105
The Social Scientists' View of Development   111
The Consensus on Third-World Development   118
The Outcomes and Implications of Sponsored Developmental Theory   121

5 Foundation Influence on Intermediate Organizations, International Forums, and Research   127

Foundation Support for Outside Organizations   129
Exchange of Persons Agencies: The Institute of International Education   129
Exchange of Persons Agencies: The African-American Institute   131
Agencies to Coordinate American Universities' International Activities   133
Africa Liaison Committee   133
Education and World Affairs   136
Agencies to Coordinate the Foundations' Developmental Strategies   137
International Council for Educational Development   137
Overseas Development Council   140
Support for Propaganda Organizations   143
Congress for Cultural Freedom   143
Foundation Support for International Conferences and Studies   145
How Carnegie Corporation Brought Africa into America's Consciousness   145
The Bellagio Conferences on Third-World Development   149
Foundation Sponsorship of "Independent" Research   152
The Extension of the Foundations' Hegemony   157

6 Technocracy, Cultural Capital, and Foundation Programs   161

Technocracy as a Developmental Panacea   163
Program Evaluation and the Technocratic Strategy   166
Foundations and the Reproduction and Control of Cultural Capital   169
The Foundations as Class Institutions   174
On the Contradictions of Liberal Philanthropy   177

Notes   181
Index   221

Acknowledgments

I have incurred many debts while working on this book and I should like to mention those individuals who have made my task somewhat easier than it might otherwise have been. The study would have been impossible without access to archival materials in several locations; accordingly, I should like to thank J. William Hess, associate director of the Rockefeller Archives Center; Frank Wolling, manager of the Rockefeller Foundation's Records Management and Library Service; Eldon Jones, archivist and manager of information services at the Ford Foundation; Sandra Markham, manager of the Ford Foundation Archives; Stephen Stackpole, director of the Commonwealth Program at the Carnegie Corporation of New York; Sara L. Engelhardt, secretary of the Carnegie Corporation of New York; and Arline Schneider, archivist at Teachers College, Columbia University.

Philip G. Altbach and Robert F. Arnove read the manuscript at various stages of incompletion, as did Raphael O. Nystrand; their comments were always valuable and supportive. I am grateful to Richard D. Heyman for giving me access to his materials from the archives of the Carnegie Corporation. E. Jefferson Murphy's insights gained from association with some of the institutions considered in this study helped to save me from several egregious errors. The comments of several anonymous readers were also very helpful.

Funds from the Research Committee of the University of Louisville School of Education helped to defray some expenses incurred while examining archival materials and in the preparation of the book's index. A research leave of absence from the University of Louisville enabled me to spend the 1978-79 academic year at Wolfson College, Cambridge University, during which time some of the ideas in this study were formulated.

Some of the material in this book has appeared in different form in the following journals: *African Studies Review*, 20 (April 1977); *Harvard* viii • ACKNOWLEDGMENTS

Educational Review, 49 (May 1979); and *Comparative Education Review*, 26 (Feb. 1982).

My greatest debt, as always, is to my wife, Julia, to whom the book is dedicated. I could not have completed the study without her unfailing support and understanding.

Introduction

This book originated in a 1975 conversation with a friend who had spent two years as a Ford Foundation advisor in Colombia and was investigating the influence of Ford on the development of several Latin American universities. Because some of my earlier work had been concerned with the role of a small New York foundation on educational policy in British Africa during the inter-war period, my friend assumed that I possessed information on the role of the major American foundations in Third World development after 1945. My life since that conversation would have been much less complicated had that information been neatly (or even otherwise) inscribed on note cards in a filing cabinet.

This conversation led to numerous others, and eventually to the archives of the Carnegie Corporation and the Ford and Rockefeller foundations. My focus was somewhat ill-defined when I first worked in these archives the next year. However, the information gained from others interested in the role of American philanthropy, coupled with a number of hunches and random reminiscences collected while a graduate student in the late 1960s, led me to suspect that these three foundations exerted much greater influence in various sectors of American society than generally recognized by the public or acknowledged by foundation representatives.

Perusal of some material in the foundations' archives strengthened the suspicion concerning the foundations' influence in decisions affecting not only United States domestic policy, but the determination of foreign policy as well. I was also struck by the diversity of interests and causes with which foundation personnel were involved, together with their very real attempts to mitigate the less desirable aspects of American life while simultaneously trying to extend its benefits to those most in need. At the same time, however, I could not help but recognize the disingenuousness that so frequently characterized their work. The foundations sincerely attempt to champion the cause of society's disadvantaged through their programs, but only on their terms. A distinct air

1

of *noblesse oblige* permeates their work, a feeling that their good intentions can be translated into beneficial programs if foundation officers are not impeded by those for whom these programs are designed.

During the several years spent collecting and analyzing data on the foundations' activities, I have shared my preliminary findings with almost anyone willing to listen. The reactions have ranged from slightly veiled hostility, to patronizing dismissiveness, to bemused interest, to slight incredulity at the degree of the foundations' influence in culture and polity, to a complete lack of surprise. The latter viewpoint can be summarized as follows: "Why are you so surprised? Everyone knows that institutions like the foundations only undertake activities supportive of the major objectives of this society. Are you so naive as to expect that they would do otherwise or to admit as much?" Since "everyone" but me knew what the foundations *really did* as opposed to what they claimed to do, I assumed that some library research would document the full extent of their activities, thereby obviating any further inquiry on my part.

The trips to the library proved disappointing, however. To be sure, several studies examining particular aspects of the major foundations' work had appeared after 1970 and these did document some of their activities. These basically descriptive studies were helpful in providing background information, but their restricted focus and analytical poverty did little to shed light on the foundations' "real" activities or to help place them in a larger societal framework. The major exceptions were a 1968 series of *Ramparts* articles, a 1972 piece on the Russell Sage Foundation, and, to a lesser extent, the suggestive tone of Waldemar Nielsen's 1972 study.[1] This investigation led me to conclude that while many people *suspected* that the foundations' influence extended beyond their acknowledged activities or numerous programs, there was scant evidence to support this contention. The paucity of serious studies of these major institutions was striking. I wanted to ascertain if indeed there was congruence between the foundations' official rhetoric and the realities of their activities. In this way I hoped to learn what "everyone" else already knew, as well as to investigate more fully my suspicion regarding the generally unrecognized role played by the foundations in the furtherance of state capitalism at home and particularly abroad.

Foundation spokesmen have always stressed the altruistic nature of their institutions, while simultaneously denying that their work furthered any narrowly partisan or national interest. Such claims have been articulated with even greater regularity since the end of World War II. The postwar period was marked by an expansion of the overseas programs of the Carnegie Corporation and the Rockefeller Foundation, as well as the entry into the foreign arena of the Ford Foundation, which Dean Rusk once characterized as "the fat boy in the philanthropic canoe."[2] This foundation litany concerning the exclusively humanitarian nature of their work at home and abroad is simply not supported by internal foundation memoranda, letters, policy statements, and reminiscences left by their officers. These indicate unequivocally how foundation programs were designed to further the foreign policy interests of the United States.

This foundation involvement in the determination and implementation of United States foreign policy did not come as a complete surprise, although its regularity and extent far exceeded what I had suspected. The archival materials, coupled with interviews with foundation personnel and those formerly associated with their overseas programs, gradually helped me to understand the foundations' role as silent partners in United States foreign policy determination and as vital cogs in the ideological support system of state capitalism. Indeed, these two major functions have been inseparable.

The unravelling of these linked functions was more difficult than I initially envisioned. Foundation personnel neither carry rifles into combat in support of United States overseas expansion nor do they actively support counter-insurgency training for American forces. Documentation and description of such activities would be a relatively simple matter. The foundation role in support of United States foreign policy objectives and as an ideological pillar sustaining the world capitalist system is not overt and, consequently, is more difficult to document. The foundations further these goals by encouraging certain ideas congruent with their objectives and by supporting those educational institutions which specialize in the production and dissemination of these ideas. The foundations' contribution to American foreign policy has been mainly in the cultural sphere, and over the years they have perfected methods whereby their educational and cultural programs would complement the cruder and more overt forms of economic and military imperialism that are so easily identifiable.

The support by the foundations for various educational configurations both at home and abroad cannot be understood apart from particular historical circumstances. To divorce their programs from the sociopolitical contexts that led to their formulation would be analogous to studying a major revolutionary upheaval in isolation from the background preceding the outbreak of hostilities. It would also deny future generations part of their history. Such a course would, at the same time, enable the foundations to continue unchallenged their claim that their organizations exist solely for the purposes of human betterment and the pursuit of truth. Such shibboliths support the existing sociopolitical order and contribute to the furtherance of the ideological hegemony of those institutions like the foundations that dominate American society. The continued failure to analyze critically some of the foundations' basic assumptions can only lead to the wider dissemination of a foundation-approved version of reality and its resultant programs, which, like the major thrust of the Progressive reforms early in this century, attempt to meliorate the worst of the social imbalances and to make the domestic society a more comfortable place for most citizens. This vision of reality perpetuated by the foundations, however, also leaves unchallenged the basically inequitable distribution patterns of this society and the position of those who most benefit from its current organization.

There has been insufficient analysis of the manner in which the foundations' activities have supported the existing social order and the furtherance of state capitalism. Few have been concerned with the manner in which institutions like the foundations have helped to perpetuate a version of reality supportive of their own interests. Fewer still have identified the relationships linking the foundations' influence and interests at home with the direction of United States foreign policy since 1945. No serious student of politics, of whatever ideological persuasion, would attempt to disassociate foreign policy formulation from domestic considerations. The influence of the Carnegie, Ford, and Rockefeller foundations in the formulation and implementation of United States foreign policy since the end of World War II has been neglected. This study's focus on the foundations' overseas activities introduces a heretofore overlooked element into the analysis of United States foreign policy: the support provided by nongovernmental agencies in the elaboration and extension of a worldview commensurate with the economic, military, and political hegemony of the United States. The study also documents the important role played by the foundations in their support for certain domestic cultural institutions (particularly universities), whose activities help to legitimate the system of state capitalism.

The foundations' role as silent partners in United States foreign policy cannot be understood without analyzing their underlying assumptions, organizational structures, methods of operation, recruitment patterns, and key personalities. In short, the influence of the foundations cannot be neatly packaged and scrutinized as an isolated phenomenon. From their beginnings the foundations defined specific functions for themselves. These were to be carried out by "responsible" individuals selected by foundation representatives. McGeorge Bundy referred to these individuals as the "learned men" when explaining his foundation's long-standing emphasis on education.[3] These "learned men" are crucial to an understanding of the foundations' great influence at home and abroad. They did not simply walk into foundation offices off the street; rather, they were recruited, nurtured, and trained to run these very powerful institutions. Foundation policy is formulated and implemented most carefully by these individuals. Little is left to chance.

The Carnegie, Ford, and Rockefeller foundations have consistently supported the major aims of United States foreign policy, while simultaneously helping to construct an intellectual framework supportive of that policy's major tenets. Chapter one examines some of the pre-1945 programs that established the directions for the foundations' endeavors after World War II and indicates that the post-1945 foundation support for foreign policy objectives was not *sui generis*. The ideology sustaining foundation programs before 1945 was patent and, as the chapter suggests, established a pattern to be followed after 1945. The architects of post-World War II foreign policy enjoyed close relationships to the major foundations and to large corporations, as this chapter briefly notes. Indeed, many of these individuals regularly moved back and forth between corporate headquarters, foundation offices, and State or Defense department positions. An understanding of what led them to formulate certain policies while in one position helps to account for their decisions while occupying another.

Fifty years ago the Italian cultural Marxist Antonio Gramsci elucidated his theory of cultural hegemony and indicated how society's ruling classes extend their domination through the control of ideas and of culture. The major foundations collaborated with United States government agencies and multilateral aid organizations after 1945 to disseminate certain ideas in the developing nations of Africa, Asia, and Latin America in an attempt to insure their support for United States foreign policy objectives. A section in chapter one links these foundation programs to the control of culture and suggests the viability of the Gramscian model for understanding the foundations' role in the extension of American cultural imperialism.

Liberal capitalism is replete with contradictions, of course, and organizations like the foundations that derive from and are supportive of this system enjoy their share. These contradictions exist on several levels and form a recurring theme throughout this study. On one level, the foundations' location in the *liberal* capitalist state leads them to support projects that appear antithetical to the best interests of state capitalism. This is the result of a modified pluralist orientation within the institutions themselves, a pluralism that leads to shades of opinion/ideology not always as supportive of state capitalism as its more orthodox proponents would like.

On another level, the foundations have long faced contradictions between their public adherence to democratic principles and their support of a carefully selected and nurtured elite to implement their programs at home and abroad. Indeed, the very structures of the foundations reveal this contradiction rather starkly. Both the trustees and the foundation staffs are recruited from backgrounds that can hardly be considered representative of the population at large. This has considerable significance for their programs.

Foundation acceptance and promotion of the principle of elite governance and its effect on the structuring and staffing of the institutions themselves are also noted in chapter one. Although such basically undemocratic elitism is inherent in a capitalist society, where authority and power always flow downward, the Carnegie, Ford, and Rockefeller foundations have gone to great lengths to rationalize the contradiction between democratic principles and elite dominance. One manifestation of this has been the foundation support over the years for certain conservative approaches in American social science, approaches that attempt to argue away the contradiction of elite governance in a democratic society.

The foundations' belief in elite governance is important in its own right and equally for the programs that derive from such a perspective. Just as the Carnegie, Ford, and Rockefeller foundations supported a limited number of elite American universities in the belief that these would train the experts required to manage the increasingly complex domestic society, so did they support comparable universities in the developing nations. Such a course reflects the foundation principle that society is better managed by the few than by the many, and that the decisions made by the elite will generally be in the best interests of the majority. The support for elites in the foundations' overseas programs can only be comprehended as part of an analysis of their support for domestic elites, particularly since the overseas programs were merely adaptations of earlier efforts at home.

It was the Cold War that gave the foundations' overseas programs their coherence, direction, and strategic importance in the furtherance of United States foreign policy. Chapter two, consequently, examines the Cold War context in which the foundations' overseas programs were formulated. Foreign policy planners during this period expressed concern over the possibility that Soviet gains in the developing nations would limit United States corporate access to overseas markets and raw materials sources deemed essential to the domestic economy and national security. While this argument is familiar to those acquainted with the major revisionist historiography of the last two decades, it assumes added significance in view of the attempts by foundation officers to join their programs to the broader foreign policy objectives of the United States government. The analysis in chapter two accepts the broad outlines of this revisionist interpretation of the Cold War, an interpretation that helps to explain the enthusiasm with which many foundation programs were initiated. Many foundation officers participated in the framing of these foreign policy decisions and helped to implement similar programs while working in a foreign aid agency in Washington, D.C. before joining one of the foundations. We shall see the almost symbiotic relationship linking the decision-makers in government agencies, corporate boardrooms, and foundation offices. Their similar backgrounds, common outlook, and shared perspectives on the United States' role in the world helped to insure a broad consensus on the directions to be followed. The foundations' major direct contribution to the evolving Cold War strategy was a sophisticated cultural offensive, designed to supplement the policy of military containment.

The recurrent discussion of the roles of certain individuals is necessitated by the fact that foundation programs evolved from the worldview held by these men and that the foundations themselves are defined by the particular constructs upon which these men agree and decide to act. Fifteen years ago political scientist Philip Green spoke to a similar issue, and his comments are germane in the present context. "To understand foreign policy decisions," he wrote, "we need to understand the attitudes of those who make them, and those who set the context within which they are made. By and large this means that we must understand elites—those who hold formal decision-making posts, key positions of public prestige, influence, and power."[4] It is the argument of this book that foundation personnel have been centrally involved in the foreign policy process since 1945 and that they occupy positions of "public prestige, influence, and power."

This necessary emphasis on the activities of select individuals should not lead us to posit a contest between the "good guys" and the "bad guys" vying for control of the foundations. While the roles of these individuals in foundation direction and in foreign and domestic policy formulation are indeed pivotal, we must not forget that their activities take place within an institutional structure whose goal in the furtherance of state capitalism is unambiguous. There is no doubt that these men (and the foundations remain largely male redoubts) wanted to devise programs to make life better for more people at home and abroad. They sometimes disagreed on the means to accomplish this end, leading to conflicts and apparent contradicitons in their programs and funding patterns. Some were, and remain, politically "liberal," while others are of a more distinctly "conservative" bent. Their differing political perspectives and the resulting differences over program priorities sometimes led to modification of particular activities in certain fields, e.g., the Rockefeller Foundation's reconceptualization during the 1970s of the direction of its developmental effort in several Third World nations. These differences, however, were regularly subordinated to the institutional requisites dictated by the foundations' location in the system of state capitalism, a location that precluded a certain range of activities while regularly encouraging others.

The provision of foreign aid for developing nations' infrastructures and for the strengthening of their educational and cultural institutions became an important consideration for United States policy planners after 1950. Chapter three shows how the foundations, after consultation with representatives of the Washington foreign policy bureaucracy, decided to strengthen a limited number of strategically located universities around the world. Foundation representatives frequently conferred to insure that their efforts would be complementary rather than competitive. Such consultation led the Carnegie, Ford, and Rockefeller foundations to delineate rather concisely those institutional areas where they felt capable of making the greatest contribution. The Carnegie Corporation concentrated on teacher education and the strengthening of libraries, the Ford Foundation on the social sciences and public administration, the Rockefeller Foundation on the social, natural, and biomedical sciences. Foundation officials hoped that the university departments and programs that they supported would provide an evolving indigenous leadership cadre with perspectives on development similar to their own.

Fellowship provisions were an important part of the foundations' institution-building programs overseas. Through these fellowship provisions, a limited number of Africans, Asians, and Latin Americans had the opportunity to study at those same elite American universities that the foundations had earlier supported, and whose intellectual perspectives they helped to shape. The manner in which this was accomplished is examined in chapter three, as are the foundations' objectives in supporting this activity.

The foundations began to elaborate a theory of development at the same time that they began to provide support for educational activities in the developing nations. Their funds also created most of the foreign area studies programs at American universities. Chapter four examines the evolution and explicit ideology of this foundation-sponsored developmental theory and the area studies programs and social sciences departments from which it evolved. This developmental theory to a great extent established the parameters within which developing nations seeking western aid have had to adapt their modernization plans. It was not coincidence that the major contributions to this developmental theory emerged from those same university departments that had received substantial foundation largesse over the years.

Packenham's study of the dominant political development ideas among mainstream American social scientists from 1947 to 1968 notes that the consensus held that modernization could best be brought about by gradual change, orchestrated by a well-educated elite imbued with a belief in the efficacy of democratic ideals as epitomized by the Washington or Westminster model, and dedicated to the principle of sustained economic growth.[5] This consensus resulted to a great extent from the external support provided to a group of carefully selected academics, whose known political persuasions almost insured treatises on development consistent with the viewpoints held by the foundation officers making grants.

Many foundation programs were and continue to be administered by agencies or institutions created by the foundations specifically for this purpose. Such ostensibly autonomous institutions as the Fund for the Advancement of Education, the Center for Advanced Study in the Behavioral Sciences, the International Council for Educational Development, the Social Science Research Council, the African-American Institute, Education and World Affairs, the Overseas Liaison Committee of the American Council on Education, the Overseas Development Institute—to name only several—are closely aligned to the major foundations through program subsidies, overlapping board memberships, and a shared outlook on domestic and world affairs. Chapter five examines this network of institutions supported by the foundations and investigates as well several of the mechanisms and publications funded by the foundations to expound their ideology. The convening of international conferences and the publication of the proceedings figure prominently in this, as does the sponsorship of ostensibly independent research studies. What becomes clear from this analysis is the manner in which such institutions, forums and publications reinforce the perspectives held by the foundations. Such reinforcement serves to legitimate the foundations' activities, since all concerned claim that their independent organizations and publications are free to express whatever views they choose.

Foundation programs at home and abroad have always been undergirded by the belief in the ability of technical expertise to solve the myriad problems associated with societal betterment and Third World development. Chapter six discusses the technocratic consciousness that permeates the work of the major foundations and examines the implications of the foundations' belief that the application of a more sophisticated technology is the surest way to attain the goals that their officers establish. In a "technist" society, as Manfred Stanley defines ours, the expert, particularly the technical expert, is elevated to a position of importance by the larger society. Those who possess expertise are considered superior (and certainly consider themselves so), are listened to, and are envied.[6] The major foundations specialize in the creation of technologically-oriented experts, and such people manage the foundations as well.

A corollary to the belief in the efficacy of technologically derived decisions to effect meaningful social change is the sentiment, commonplace around the foundations, that even more effective programs can be designed if the successes and failures of earlier programs are diagnosed. Thus, the foundations ostensibly place heavy emphasis on program evaluation. Commonsense suggests that a degree of objectivity in the evaluation of a particular program necessitates an evaluator with neither vested interests in the program itself nor ties to the funding agency. The foundations stipulate as much in their grants to non-affiliated outside organizations. However, the foundations' programs themselves, those that they initiate both at home and abroad, are regularly evaluated not by outsiders, but rather by individuals either currently or previously affiliated with one of the foundations directly, or through a subsidized organization. This means that the foundations are in effect accountable to no one and to outside body for their work. The chapter also considers the implications for a democratic society of this lack of accountability by organizations that control to such a great degree the production and dissemination of knowledge and of culture.

The foundations' continuing influence in the production and dissemination of culture is not assured, however. The occasionally contradictory nature of their activities, some manifestations of which are noted in the text, have potentially serious implications for the foundations, as the book's concluding section notes.

1

Foundations and the Extension of American Hegemony

This chapter examines the foundations' origins during the early 20th century and discusses as well the ideology that led the foundations of that period to develop programs supportive of the capitalist system from which they sprang. What emerges from this discussion is an understanding of the continuity that linked the early foundation programs to those initiated after World War II.

Since their inception, the Carnegie, Ford, and Rockefeller foundations have given particular attention to educational and cultural affairs. This has enabled the foundations to play critical roles in the production and dissemination of certain kinds of knowledge and ideas. The influence or control that the foundations have over the reproduction of culture has regularly been used to further United States foreign policy.

Those who control the production and dissemination of culture and ideas influence, to a great degree, the way in which people view the world and the commonsense categories into which they organize their knowledge and by which they conduct their lives. The chapter also discusses how ideological hegemony is used to further interests congruent with the class that controls the means of production, while at the same time limiting concerns that society's dominant class considers less important or threatening to its interests. The structures of the foundations and the manner in which they recruit their trustees and staffs are important elements in understanding the furtherance of their hegemony. The chapter concludes by attempting to locate the foundations in the system of liberal state capitalism and to suggest how this location helps to account for the foundations' important role in the control of culture. At the same time, the contradictions inherent in liberal capitalism are noted, as are the ways in which these contradictions affect the foundations' activities.

The Foundations' Overseas Programs: The Control of Culture

In 1961 President Kennedy asked Philip Coombs to assume the newly created position of assistant secretary of state for educational and cultural affairs. Coombs had joined the staff of the Ford Foundation–created Fund for the Advancement of Education in 1952 and had worked on a number of domestically based educational projects during his ten-year association with that organization. Perhaps the most tangible achievement during his tenure as assistant secretary was the publication in 1964 of a book entitled *The Fourth Dimension of Foreign Policy*.[1] The gist of this Carnegie Corporation-funded volume is that education and various cultural activities are important, if generally unrecognized, aspects of a nation's foreign policy, and consequently they need to be coordinated with the overall objectives of that policy. Similar reasoning lay behind the considerable funding provided by the Carnegie, Ford, and Rockefeller foundations for the expansion of educational institutions in Africa, Asia, and Latin America after 1950.

Investment in education has been the primary focus of organized American philanthropy since its inception. The vast sums given by John D. Rockefeller, Sr. to reconstitute the University of Chicago in the 1890s and to create the General Education Board in the early 1900s initiated a pattern followed to the present. Ford Foundation president McGeorge Bundy remarked in 1968 that "[t]he oldest and strongest of the ties that connect this foundation to other parts of society are those that bind us to the world of education." Foundations like Ford support education because, again in Bundy's words, "we depend on learned men for advice and special study on nearly every subject we take up." Foundation personnel feel that a certain kind of education can train individuals whose contributions are "of central importance to the national well-being."[2] In the post-World War II era, when the "national well-being" was defined globally, the major foundations increasingly supported educational institutions in strategic geopolitical locales in the hopes that these would educate individuals who viewed the United States national interests in ways similar to those held by their foundation sponsors and who would also help to structure a world amenable to these interests.

The long-standing foundation emphasis on the training of carefully selected experts to provide the "advice and special study on nearly every subject we take up" derives logically from institutions staffed by individuals from upper-class backgrounds, who themselves believe that the United States can best be managed by an elite group of well-trained, dispassionate technocrats.[3] This pattern was apparent in foundation support for a limited number of elite American universities as early as the 1930s and inaugurated a trend still followed.

Foundation support for educational institutions and the concomitant emphasis on the training of experts has given the foundations great leverage in the production and dissemination of knowledge. They are critically situated to play pivotal roles in determining what knowledge, what ideas, what views of the world receive support and become incorporated into the society's general discourse. Coser spoke to this point some years ago, noting how the major foundations act as the "gatekeepers of ideas." By this he meant that the foundations, because of the significant resources available for their officers to use at their discretion, were "in positions to foster certain lines of inquiry while neglecting or de-emphasizing others."[4]

The foundations' location in the capitalist state leads them to support educational institutions—particularly universities—at home and abroad to train individuals who not only share their perspectives, but who will use their influence to "sell" it to others who are less convinced of its merits. Gramsci indicated how the world view of a society's dominant class is most effectively disseminated throughout the society not by force of arms, but rather through the acceptance by the majority of the citizenry of a carefully defined set of ideas. To put this somewhat differently: it is more effective to persuade the population at large that the worldview propagated by their leaders is in the majority's interest and is "correct" than it is for the leaders to have to resort to the state's coercive apparatus (the system of justice, the military, the police) to force the majority to accept this.[5]

The act of persuading is largely the responsibility of intellectuals, who, according to Bates, strive to "extend the world view of the rulers to the ruled, and thereby secure the 'free' consent of the masses to the law and order of the land."[6] These intellectuals, or "salesmen" as Bates calls them, thus occupy an intermediate position between the ruling class and the people. Acceptance of the ruling-class version of reality, which has been certified as "true" or has the appearance of commonsense, is dependent on the efforts of these "salesmen." The grants appropriated by the Carnegie, Ford, and Rockefeller foundations help to train these salesmen or intellectuals in the universities that they support at home and around the world. Miliband notes how "the 'engineering of consent' in capitalist society is still largely an unofficial private enterprise, in fact largely the business of private enterprise."[7] The foundations are an important part of this enterprise.

The universities supported by Carnegie, Ford, and Rockefeller in Africa, Asia, and Latin America resemble in many ways a group of American universities that have also benefited over the years from foundation attention. The Ford Foundation, for example, has funded at a significant level programs in the social sciences, public administration, and teacher education in American universities. Similar program emphases, excepting the latter, are discernible in Ford-supported universities in Africa, Asia, and Latin America. Likewise, the emphasis on the basic sciences and biomedical research that has been a staple of Rockefeller Foundation educational programs in the United States is replicated in the Foundation's overseas endeavors, as is the provision for advanced training for especially well-qualified university personnel.

These overseas university programs, like their domestic counterparts, were designed to train a coterie of indigenous experts who internalize certain norms and who are destined to assume leadership positions in their respective societies. From their positions of leadership it is hoped that these foundation-sponsored experts will move their nations along the path to development (often sketched out by other foundation-trained experts) in a way to guarantee political stability, economic growth, and, minimally, a policy of benevolent neutrality toward the Western bloc.[8] This developmental path ideally will be characterized by an open economy linked to one of the world's major currencies and the continued access by corporate enterprise to sources of raw materials considered strategically important to the United States.[9]

The foundation programs in Africa, Asia, and Latin America, in short, were designed to improve conditions there, mainly through the aegis of an enculturated stratum of local nationals, whose subsequent modes of behavior would be supportive of the national-security and economic interests of the United States. The conceptualization of these foundation educational ventures coincided with the demise of the colonial empires of Britain, France, and the Netherlands after 1945. The resultant educational and cultural programs were a reflection of the belief that America's post-World War II interests could be served by aligning the evolving Third-World nations to the United States through the provision of social services (particularly education), which had been limited by the former colonial powers, thereby fulfilling an articulated local need and at the same time weaning these nations away from flirtation with socialist doctrine. The extension of a sophisticated form of cultural imperialism also had the advantage of obfuscating the continuance of discredited and crude forms of economic and military imperialism.

The foundations' educational and cultural efforts abroad, which complemented those of the official United States foreign-aid program, formed part of what Lasch has called the "Cultural Cold War," a well-coordinated attempt to identify and to socialize Third-World leaders who would travel the middle road between communism and fascism.[10] Foundation programs were designed, in short, to train reform leaders.

The 1963 United States Advisory Commission on International Educational and Cultural Affairs, chaired by former Carnegie Corporation president John Gardner, elaborated on the kind of indigenous leader who should be the recipient of America's attentions. The commission noted that in selecting foreign participants for exchange programs, special effort should be made "to seek out and select those candidates . . . who are sufficiently vigorous and restless to help promote *desirable* social and economic change."[11] The programs of the major foundations, as well as those of the United States government, would endeavor to select just those individuals who would help promote the kind of "desirable social and economic change" outlined by the commission. Indeed, the foundations had been doing just this for years.

The Origins and Ideology of Modern Philanthropy

The attempts by the Carnegie, Ford, and Rockefeller foundations to impose a cultural pax Americana in Africa, Asia, and Latin America after 1945 were not sui generis. They built on a long tradition of American philanthropic endeavor abroad.[12] The Rockefeller Foundation, for example, had been involved in extensive medical-education programs in China from 1913, efforts which only ceased after the triumph of the Red Army in 1949.[13] The Carnegie Corporation, following the lead of the much smaller Phelps-Stokes Fund of New York, made its initial grants for African education in 1925, and continued its work in eastern, central, and South Africa until the outbreak of World War II made the continuation of these programs virtually impossible.

The early programs of these foundations not only established precedents for their later overseas activities, but all represented as well adapted versions of programs originally undertaken in the United States. A similar ideology characterized these foundation programs, whether they were undertaken at home early in the century or abroad fifty years later. This common ideology is traceable to the motives that led the foundations' benefactors to leave vast sums to create their organizations in the first years of the 20th century.

The major American foundations were established to accomplish certain ends in the heyday of capitalist accumulation. These included the stabilization of the rapidly evolving corporate and political order and its legitimation and acceptance by the majority of the American population; the institutionalization of certain reforms, which would serve to preclude the call for more radical structural change; and the creation through educational institutions of a worldwide network of elites whose approach to governance and change would be efficient, professional, moderate, incremental, and nonthreatening to the class interests of those who, like Messrs, Carnegie, Ford, and Rockefeller, had established the foundations. The subsequent support by the foundations for various educational confi\guarations both at home and abroad cannot be separated from their attempts to evolve a stable domestic polity and a world order amenable to their interests and the strengthening of international capitalism.

The appearance early in the 20th century of the first of the major foundations coincided with attempts by leaders of the progressive movement to evolve a liberal consensus and to chart a more equitable political and economic path for the United States. The more far-sighted of the progressives recognized that a societal consensus could only be achieved if the extremes of poverty and wealth were somewhat mitigated. This could not come about until the working classes were more firmly integrated into society's political and particularly its economic system and its dominant norms. At the same time there was agreement that the most outrageous abuses associated with the system of industrial capitalism must be curbed. Such a belief led to the gradual abolition of some of the more grievous industrial injustices (e.g., by passage of child labor laws and the eventual acceptance of labor unions) and the extension of social services (e.g., public schooling and a modicum of health care). Simultaneously, progressive reformers attempted to limit the ability of the new monied class to corrupt the political process through passage of antitrust legislation and the institution of governmental controls, over, for example, the nation's railroads and meat-packing industry.[14]

There was no thought in these reform attempts to forsake the advanced technology and evolving corporate structure epitomized by the Rockefeller or Morgan empires. Nor was serious consideration given to a return to a more primitive mode of production and simpler organizational structure represented by the 18th-century crafts industries. Indeed, John D. Rockefeller's Standard Oil Company suggested the vertically integrated corporate structure that would serve as the model for the contemporary multinational enterprise. Henry Ford's innovative assembly-line concept combined efficiency with technical expertise, as well as increasing managerial control over the total production process in a way assured to maximize productivity. Together these represented the wave of the corporate future, in which production would be rationalized, waste would be eliminated, managers would coordinate the workplace, and consumer items would form the staples of the expanding domestic economy.[15]

Rather than advocating the abolition of this system, the progressive reforms represented attempts to harness the positive and eliminate the negative attributes of industrial capitalism. They also were concerted attempts to find a middle ground between the extremes of oligopoly on the one hand and socialism on the other, while encouraging an atmosphere congenial to increased levels of productivity. Socialism appeared a viable possibility to many in the United States early in this century, particularly to many workers, fresh from Europe, who congregated in the large cities. So strong was the appeal of socialist doctrine that in 1912 the Socialist Party's candidate for president polled some one million votes. While socialism obviously was anathema to those like John D. Rockefeller and Henry Ford who had accumulated their fortunes in a close approximation of a laissez-faire capitalist economy, it was no more welcome to the leaders of the progressive movement, who were firmly committed to the principles of a capitalist economic and political order. This is not to suggest that progressives were uniformly unfavorable to all socialist doctrine; intellectuals like Charles A. Beard, John Dewey, and Randolph Bourne were supportive of some socialist principles. Their arguments, however, were overwhelmed by the proponents of the evolving corporate liberal policy, who shared with foundation officials an unequivocal hostility to any manifestation of socialist doctrine.

Tax-saving incentives were clearly on the minds of some of the early philanthropists as they pondered the establishment of their foundations. This is indicated in conversations between John D. Rockefeller, Sr., and his chief advisor on philanthropy, Reverend Frederick T. Gates.[16] But neither the threat of taxation nor the mounting public criticism leveled at these "malfactors of wealth" is enough, according to Karl, to really explain "the degree of systematic organization and attention they gave to the process."[17] By 1905 Carnegie had established the Carnegie Institute of Washington (1902) and the Carnegie Foundation for the Advancement of Teaching (1905), and Rockefeller had founded the Institute for Medical Research (1901) and the General Education Board (1903). These preceded the chartering of two of the great modern foundations, the Carnegie Corporation in 1911 and the Rockefeller Foundation in 1913, as multipurpose institutions dedicated to the general advancement of mankind.

Just as the managers of the evolving corporate structure strove for the rationalization and more efficient operation of the system of production, so did the new breed of foundation executives strive for the rationalization of social services and the more efficient and manageable functioning of the larger social system. The progressive credo—with its emphasis on efficiency, the elimination of waste, the alleviation of mass misery, and the establishment of a more humane, decent, and just society—was internalized by the foundation manager and, on occasion, by his more enlightened corporate counterpart. Indeed, it was almost natural that these men should move between the corporate and foundation worlds because, as a recent observer has noted, "their values were quite similar. They both accepted the prevailing economic, social, and political system as given, and they sought to make the system work smoothly."[18]

A salient characteristic of the Progressive Era was an emphasis on education.[19] A similar emphasis appeared in the work of the early foundations as they supported the nation's colleges and universities in an effort to train professionals and managers to run America's institutions. These initial programs were designed to provide society's future managers with the appropriate expertise and to socialize them into the norms required to run the institutions of the liberal capitalist state.

The early foundation executives understood the roles to be played by their institutions in insuring social change that was gradual, moderate, and unambiguously controlled by society's dominant classes. As Karl and Katz remark:

> Many of those involved understood perfectly well that the new cooperative [economic and social] structures [of the Progressive Era] might provide an alternative to socialism and the welfare State, both of which seemed inevitable in contemporary Europe, in which the American private sector could retain its dominant position in the formulation of public policy. In this effort, it is not too hard to see, the role of the philanthropic foundation might well prove central to the ambitions of the private sector.[20]

Several examples of the early foundations' programs and modi operandi demonstrate just how they sought to insure the private sector's dominant position in public-policy formulation. These few examples will also indicate the linkages between the foundations' early domestic activities and their later involvement as silent partners in American foreign policy.

Some Early Foundation Programs

One of the first projects commissioned by the Carnegie Institute trustees after the foundation's organization in 1902 was the writing of a national economic history. The conclusions of this project were predetermined by the selection of historians and economists who agreed with the comment of economist E. R. A. Seligman, scion of a prominent New York banking family and a consultant to the project, that "the aim of economics is the show the reconciliation of private wealth with public welfare." Such a statement reflected the increasing salience of socialist doctrine during the Progressive Era. Avowed socialists regularly won victories for local and occasionally for state political offices, a trend that was, not surprisingly, worrisome to the capitalist class.[21]

Those who mounted the study prided themselves on their objective, apolitical, and value-free approach to their subject. At the same time, they reproached those writers in the Marxian tradition who, according to members of the study team, allowed their political biases to influence their research and conclusions. However, the clearly articulated, but unacknowledged, ideology of those involved in the study led this Carnegie Institute project to become, as Slaughter and Silva note, "a vehicle for legitimating industrial capital." While providing legitimation for the new system of corporate capitalism, the history also provided a bulwark against a socialist alternative to the evolving system. The tendency on the parts of the Carnegie Institute trustees to support researchers whose political viewpoints mirrored their own, and whose conclusions consequently tended to fall within predetermined parameters acceptable to both foundation patron and researcher, has continued unabated to the present, a trend that will be documented below.

The Russell Sage Foundation, chartered in 1907, was also engaged at this time in a series of projects intended to insure that social change was carried out in a way that would not threaten the evolving system of industrial capitalism and the privileged positions of those who dominated it. These projects involved, on the one hand, the construction of an ideological approach to change that would help to ameliorate the worst excesses of the industrial corporate system without basically challenging the nature of that system and, on the other hand, the creation of a cadre of professional workers who would carry the ideology to the dispossessed.

Slaughter and Silva note how the Sage Foundation played the crucial role in coordinating the disparate charity organizations that had arisen in the burgeoning urban areas to deal with the growing human dislocation brought about by the rapid immigration and industrialization of the late 19th century. Many of the individuals involved in these charity movements had a deep and abiding concern for the plight of the poor. It is equally clear that a major cause of the misery confronting the charity workers was the very system of industrial capitalism that they so vigorously supported, but which shattered the poor immigrants' sense of community. Since the charity workers refused to recognize the roots of this mass misery, their palliatives focused more on attempts to reform the existing system and to adjust their clients to it, than to search for alternative organizational structures that might result in a more equitable society less destructive of the immigrants' communities.

The evolving corporate structure and the concentration of wealth associated with it were generally acceptable to these liberal reformers, although they agreed that ways had to be sought to mitigate its worst excesses. The attempts by the Russell Sage Foundation to coordinate the charity organizations so that they could better serve the needs of the poor were in keeping with this liberal reform tendency. These efforts were directed by a group of upper-class urbanities—lawyers, financiers, university presidents—whose concern for the poor was only approximated by their sense of noblesse oblige.

The need to coordinate and to professionalize the field of social work, so that its pervading ideology would be one of limited reform within a framework of corporate capitalism, led the trustees of the Sage Foundation to begin subsidizing several charity-organization publications with a view to bringing them together into the one influential voice of the newly defined field. The focus of these attentions was a journal entitled *The Survey*. According to Slaughter and Silva, this publication soon became the authoritative voice of the evolving social-work profession. They note how this and other Sage-subsidized journals soon began to offer "detailed and continued instruction in ameliorative reform providing the white-collared with a more palatable solution to the problems posed by rapid industrialization than the drastic structural solutions offered by socialism."

Sage-funded efforts to create a professional, middle- and upper-middle-class force of social workers who subscribed to the major outlines of the system of corporate and finance capitalism were equally important in determining the parameters of social work early in the century. To further this objective, the Sage Foundation made significant grants to budding schools of social work in Boston, Chicago, and St. Louis before 1915. This support was calculated to train workers with the appropriate perspectives on the existing organization of society and to insure that proposed reforms fell within strictly defined margins.

The work of the General Education Board in Negro higher education during the first two decades of the 20th century has been studied by Anderson; and it provides another illustration of the manner in which those who controlled the early foundations attempted to utilize them to impose upon society a particular construct.[22] The board was created in 1903 with a $1 million bequest from John D. Rockefeller; by 1909 he had added over $50 million to this total, and by 1921 the board's endowment was a staggering $129 million. As the name implies, the board had a broad mandate to serve the needs of education throughout the nation. Among those areas of interest defined by the trustees was the particular problem of Negro education in the American South.[23]

By the time the General Education Board came into existence, agreement had been reached on the appropriate education to be offered to southern Negro youngsters. It had been decided at a series of conferences beginning in 1898 at Capon Springs, West Virginia, that southern Negro education would be two-tiered. Education for the majority attending school would be of a narrowly defined vocational nature. The Capon Springs conferees felt that such an education would insure a modicum of skill training for a growing Negro labor force. This restricted educational provision was encompassed under the rubric of the "Tuskegee philosophy," which held that Negro youngsters should be educated in ways to insure their continued docility and attachment to the existing system, and the inculcation of traits that would increase the labor value of the race.[24]

Second, an academically oriented education, preparatory to professional training, would be offered to the future leaders of the segregated southern Negro communities. This training would prepare a limited number of professionals and semiprofessionals who would be qualified to serve the needs of their self-contained communities. This differentiated educational plan hammered out at Capon Springs at the turn of the century was largely the work of a group of northern industrial capitalists, financiers, and liberal philanthropists. The Southern Education Board, primarily an advocacy group for the cause of southern public education, grew out of the Capon Springs gathering of 1901 and assumed as well many of the functions performed by the annual conferences. Its main source of support was the General Education Board. In fact, it was difficult to ascertain where the membership of the one board ended and the other commenced, so interlocked were the directorates of the two organizations.

By 1915 enough questions had been raised concerning the direction of a number of Negro colleges that the General Education Board convened a conference to discuss these institutions. The problem confronting the board was that these colleges were taking an independent course and, consequently, did not fit into the plan worked out at Capon Springs and subsequently elaborated by the Southern Education Board. Anderson indicates that this 1915 conference represented a major attempt by the industrial philanthropists to exert even tighter control over the direction of Negro higher education than had been the case theretofore.

The institution singled out by the board to be the model for higher education for future Negro leaders was Fisk University in Nashville. The direction that General Education Board wanted to insure was indicated by Fisk's president, Fayette McKenzie, who, in Anderson's words, "attempted to persuade Fisk's students to forsake equalitarian principles and to work within the Southern racial hierarchy to improve the region's industrial efficiency and maintain interracial cooperation." Here was truly a meeting of the minds between the representatives of the board and the administration of an influential university. McKenzie was merely giving expression to sentiments generally shared by the board's trustees.

This shared ideology, which consigned the southern Negro to a permanent position of economic subordinancy, led the trustees of the General Education Board to make significant commitments to Fisk. It was also important in encouraging other philanthropists to make donations to Fisk. The magnitude of this support is indicated by the following pledges to a Fisk endowment campaign in 1924: $500,000 from the General Education Board, $250,000 from the Carnegie Corporation, and $250,000 from a combination of other northern philanthropies. The ideology informing this support was unambiguous. Anderson notes that in 1923 the General Education Board "generated a memorandum on the Fisk endowment campaign which emphasized the urgent need to train 'the right type of colored leaders' who would help make the Negro a capable workman and a good citizen."

The vast resources of the General Education Board were used to perpetuate an educational structure for southern Negroes that precluded the social and economic advancement of all but a selected few, whom the foundation managers considered "safe." The viewpoints of the board's trustees and those who implemented their policy held that the existing discriminatory patterns of American society north and south were but minor blemishes on an otherwise well-patterned social fabric. Through their programs they would attempt to make the blemishes somewhat less obvious. One way to accomplish this was through the provision of higher education to a carefully selected group of black leaders who accepted a social structure in which their people would remain a permanent underclass, available to help forward the industrialization beneficial to the few rather than to the many. The General Education Board was only one of several foundations during this period through whose programs this ideology was translated into practice. The Phelps-Stokes Fund and the Carnegie Corporation were also among this group.

The president of the Phelps-Stokes Fund, Anson Phelps Stokes, was among the General Education Board trustees concerned with Negro higher education early in the century. Thomas Jesse Jones, the Fund's educational director, was the author of a 1916 study on Negro education and a collaborator with representatives of the General Education Board concerning the attempts to design an "appropriate" higher education for southern Negroes. The Phelps-Stokes Fund was instrumental after 1915 in furthering the Tuskegee educational philosophy, designed to perpetuate the black man's servile status in the southern socio-economic and political order.[25] The fund was equally instrumental in internationalizing the Tuskegee philosophy, acting as the catalyst in having this ideology and its attendant programs transferred in toto to Britain's African colonies after 1920. In this the fund was aided by the Carnegie Corporation of New York and by one of the Rockefeller philanthropies.

In 1919 the trustees of the Phelps-Stokes Fund agreed to support an investigation of educational conditions in several African territories. Thomas Jesse Jones was selected chairman of this African Education Commission. Working closely with British colonial and missionary officials, Jones and his party toured eight countries in West and southern Africa during 1920 and 1921. The commission's report reads remarkably like Jones's earlier survey of Negro education. The report of the African Education Commission, like that on Negro education, stressed the importance of a restricted educational franchise for the African masses and touched on the need for a modicum of professional training for an African elite. It represented, in short, an Africanization of the Tuskegee philosophy of education and, as such, won the enthusiastic endorsement of the British Colonial Office, whose officials perceived it to be the pedagogical complement to their political policy of indirect rule.[26]

In 1923 the trustees of the Phelps-Stokes Fund agreed to a Colonial-Office suggestion to sponsor a second African Education Commission to examine conditions in East, Central, and South Africa. The International Education Board, one of the Rockefeller foundations of which Anson Phelps Stokes was a trustee, partially underwrote expenses incurred in mounting this study. Given the sponsorship and the personnel involved, this second African Education Commission could hardly have produced a novel document. The only notable difference between the first and second reports was the recommendation in the latter for a network of Jeanes teacher-training institutes in East, Central, and South Africa. There were to be modeled on the parent institutions that played a central role in the perpetuation of the Tuskegee concept of a rurally based and restricted educational franchise in the American South.

The Jeanes school concept in the United States dated from 1907, when, after consultation with the principals of Hampton and Tuskegee institutes, Anna T. Jeanes of Philadelphia established a foundation supporting the broad outlines of the Tuskegee philosophy. Additional financial support for the Jeanes schools in the United States came from the General Education Board, the Rosenwald Fund, and the Phelps-Stokes Fund.

Jones's reasons for advocating a series of Jeanes schools for white-ruled East, Central, and South Africa were twofold. First, he believed that the non-European peoples in these areas were unsuited for a literary education and, consequently, that a reasonable alternative must be sought for them—an alternative beneficial to both the dependent peoples and to their European benefactors. This belief grew out of Jones's southern American experience and was related to the perceived "civilizing" effects of the superior European culture on the more primitive African culture, whether in America or in Africa. Second, his great regard for the civilizing and uplifting impact of British colonialism led him to recognize that the Tuskegee philosophy, and its concomitant network of Jeanes schools, implanted in Africa would provide the British colonial administrators with a tool to control the Africans under their jurisdictions, while at the same time providing a social service that appeared beneficial to the Africans.

Jones began discussions and correspondence with officers of the Carnegie Corporation concerning possible support for a series of Jeanes schools in Africa even before returning to New York from the second African Education Commission tour. In 1925 his efforts proved successful, when the corporation agreed to appropriate $37,500 for the founding of a Jeanes teacher-training school in Kenya. This was the first of many Carnegie grants for African education.[27]

The exportation to Africa of this institutional form, which played a role in extending the hegemony of American industrial philanthropists over a subject black population in the southern United States, established a pattern to be followed by the great foundations in the post-World War II period. After 1945 the ideology of the American corporate state would be carried abroad through the aegis of national and occasionally multinational aid agencies, and, as will be documented in the chapters to follow, foundation-supported universities and their affiliated institutes. African political independence did little to alter the new nation's peripheral locations and continuing economic and cultural dependence on the centers of world capitalism. Indeed, just as the foundations' post-Reconstruction efforts in the American South were designed to attach that region's economy and institutions more securely to the northern-based capitalist center, so have the latter-day foundation cultural efforts in Africa, Asia, and Latin America been designed to insure the continued linkages of selected nations to the United States-based center of the capitalist world.

Another important way in which Phelps-Stokes Fund personnel attempted to legitimate the Tuskegee philosophy in Africa was through the provisions of fellowships enabling a carefully screened group of Africans to study in institutions within the Tuskegee orbit. The Rockefeller Foundation had established the precedent in 1917 for the award to foreign nationals of fellowships enabling them to study in the United States. The Carnegie Corporation and the Ford Foundation subsequently established similar programs.

The fellowship program made available by the Rockefeller Foundation for foreign nationals was only one of several early attempts by the foundation to spread its influence abroad. Brown notes that the first act of the foundation after receiving its charter in 1913 was the establishment of the International Health Commission, whose objective was "to extend world-wide the hookworm and public health programs initiated in the United States."[28] These and the many other health and sanitation programs undertaken by the Rockefeller philanthropies over the years have indeed played a large role in bettering the lot of many of the world's poor. While acknowledging this, we must not be lulled into believing that these worthy programs derived from a totaly disinterested humanitarian spirit on the parts of personnel associated with the foundation. On the contrary.

Brown notes that the General Education Board's public-health programs in the southern United States were undertaken at least in part in the belief that qualitative improvements in the health of southern workers would lead to quantitative increases in their productivity.[29] This equation assumed particular significance in the context of the sizable Rockefeller family holdings in the southern economy at the time when the programs were initiated. A comparable argument can be made when examining the intentions of Rockefeller Foundation personnel involved in the extension of these public-health campaigns abroad. The Rockefeller Foundation programs in the developing nations—be they medical, agricultural, or educational—consistently followed in the wake of commercial activities associated with the Rockefeller family financial empire.[30]

Brown contends that Rockefeller Foundation personnel were conscious that programs with a humanitarian aura about them—such as those in the field of public health—would lead the indigenous population to view sympathetically the activities of other foreign entities in their lands, for example, multinational corporations. Thus, while an argument can be made for the good work accomplished by the foundation's Peking Union Medical College in the period after 1921, to take one example, an equally compelling argument can be made for viewing the college as an important wedge in facilitating greater penetration of Chinese cultural, political, and economic institutions by United States corporations and agencies.

The Peking Union Medical College was modeled along the lines of American medical schools of the period.[31] This resulted in the training of a small number of physicians in the methods of Western science and technology. It also led to the decision, strenuously opposed by the more nationalistic Chinese, to use English as the medium of instruction. The college soon began graduating a Western-oriented elite, who could hardly begin to cope with China's staggering health problems. This emphasis on education for an elite was consistent with the Rockefeller philosophy. At the same time, foundation officers opposed the training of semiprofessional and medical auxiliaries and ignored the potential contribution of China's 400,000 traditional doctors. The practical effect of this decision to train an elite was to make medical care unavailable to the majority of China's rural population, while making accessible to wealthy urban dwellers the most sophisticated Western medical treatment.

The Chinese medical elite served another function, however, in addition to its attempts to meet the country's health needs. Brown argues that an equally important purpose was "to create a system of medicine ideologically and culturally conducive to the development of China and other countries as participants in economic relations with the industrialized Western nations."[32] The foundation-supported medical elite facilitiated the process of cultural mediation between the traditional China and the China that Rockefeller personnel hoped to see modernized along Western lines. Foundation officers recognized the importance of a developed China and the other nonindustrial areas for the continued strength of the capitalist system.[33] Cultural penetration of the nonindustrialized areas was considered an important factor in furthering development—perhaps more important than other means. Rockefeller Foundation president George Vincent stated as much in 1917, when commenting on foundation work in the Philippines. He noted then that "dispensaries and physicians have of late been peacefully penetrating areas of the Philippine Islands and demonstrating the fact that for purposes of placating primitive and suspicious peoples medicine has some advantages over machine guns."[34]

On Analyzing the Foundations' Hegemony

The commonality of outlook that led the foundations to undertake certain programs at home and abroad and to support intermediary organizations to implement these does not necessarily imply an active conspiracy. High-ranking officials did not gather in a New York or Washington office or over lunch in Bogotá, Bangkok, or Brazzaville to devise programs ostensibly designed to link Africans, Asians, and Latin Americans to the world capitalist economy. The arguments developed later indicate that the need for such a conspiracy was obviated by the fact that those who controlled and staffed the major foundations after 1945 shared the beliefs that (1) the exportation of American-style democracy and the continued linkage and incorporation of the peripheral economies of the developing nations to that of the United States would serve the interests of the peoples there better than any other approach, and (2) educational and cultural programs would play important roles in linking Third-World elites to major institutions in the United States and to the norms embodied in them. These men came from remarkably similar backgrounds and shared many values, and they were certain that their approach was correct, not only for Third-World peoples but for the United States as well. They were the liberals of their era, who wanted to see the Third-World nations achieve independence and to take their places among the community of nations. At the same time, they wanted to insure that the leaders of these nations were not seduced by the lure of socialist dogma and that their economies remained open for capitalist penetration.[35]

The programs supported by the major foundations at home and abroad since 1945 have been conceived and implemented by a carefully selected and nutured elite. This reliance on a few individuals for major policy decisions and program implementation is merely the continuation of long-established foundation procedure. In the mid-1930s, and particularly after 1945, the major foundations began funding academic studies that tacitly, and frequently explicitly, supported the theory that elite dominance of American society was not inherently undemocratic. Support for this theory was clearly in the foundations' interests, given the nature of their organizations and their lack of accountability to any public body. While the proponents of this evolving theory of democratic elitism maintained that the theory was nonideological, it was of course, as Bachrach notes, "deeply rooted in an ideology . . . which is grounded upon a profound distrust of the majority of ordinary men and women, and reliance upon the established elites to maintain the values of civility and the 'rules of the game' of democracy."[36]

Foundation support for the theory of democratic elitism, which ostensibly would enable all classes of citizens to rise to positions of influence and responsibility, played a central role in the foundations' emerging hegemony.[37] It appeared to epitomize the democratic ethos: talent and merit would be rewarded wherever they were identified. Achievers from nonprivileged backgrounds would be encouraged, nurtured, and inducted into the decision-making stratum of the democratic state. The theory of democratic elitism gave the appearance of nonpartisanship, of neutrality, indeed of concern only for identifying talent that might serve the interests of the republic, regardless of its origins. The theory appeared to be commonsensical. At the same time, of course, it deflected attention from the existing inequitable social arrangements in the society at large and from the power of institutions like the foundations, which clearly were controlled by and served the interests of certain classes.

Foundation support for the theory of democratic elitism is consonant with both their organizational structures and operating methods, which from their earliest days manifested a belief in the importance of elite-directed planning for the more orderly development of society. The foundations have long accepted the idea that societies are best led by a carefully selected, talented few, whose views and actions will further the existing order. Those not so designated, but who still aspire to leadership positions, are frequently neutralized.

An example of this is contained in a 1921 letter from the director of the Carnegie Institution of Washington, D.C., to the president of the Carnegie Corporation. At issue was proposed Carnegie support for the *Journal of Negro History.* The journal's editor was Carter G. Woodson, an outspoken advocate of Negro rights and frequent critic of those foundations, e.g., the Phelps-Stokes Fund, that supported the gradualist approach to Negro self-determination. Carnegie Institute director Franklin Jameson noted the value of Woodson's journal, and recognized that "it attains as high a level as could be expected." Unfortunately, however, "that level cannot in the nature of things (since in the main it must be done by negroes) attain the level which is rightly expected of the Carnegie Institution." He concluded by recommending that if Carnegie funding was approved, then "the ultimate authority as to what should be done should rest with the Department of Historical Research in the Carnegie Institution."[38]

The major foundations' concern with nurturing carefully selected, talented individuals to maintain society on a steady course was heightened after 1945 by the recognition of the role that the United States had assumed in international affairs. The cold-war consensus held that a monolithic communist threat was directed against the economic and political hegemony of the United States-dominated world capitalist structure. To counter this threat, the United States government sought to increase the levels of well-educated manpower that could contribute to the national-security effort. The Carnegie, Ford, and Rockefeller foundations played important roles in this effort.[39] The government also encouraged reform in the developing nations that would lessen the susceptibility of these territories to communist penetration and propaganda. At the same time, foundation programs were undertaken to create circumstances in the developing world that would insure change that was predictable, manageable, and consonant with the perceived economic and strategic interests of the United States. An important way to help achieve such an outcome was through the control of culture, a commodity that the foundations have helped to dispense as well as to create, and especially through training provided for a select group of foreign nationals.[40] This would be the foundations' major contribution to the expansion of state capitalism.

The foreign policy that evolved from this worldview may indeed have furthered this nation's national interests. At the same time, the statuses, influence, and economic well-being of many Washington policy-makers who approved, designed, and implemented this policy were enhanced. Many of these men had ties to one of the major foundations. As they utilized their economic and political power to set in motion policies from which they benefited, they also managed to convince significant segments of the body politic that such policies served the nation's interests. These men were conscious, as Apple notes in a related context, that "[d]omination can be ideological as well as material, that control and domination are often vested in the commonsense practices and consciousness underlying our lives as well as by overt economic and political manipulation."[41]

The way in which we approach the world, the categories we utilize to determine our daily activities, the parameters within which major domestic and foreign-policy decisions are shaped, are not "naturally" produced. These did not just descend from the heavens one day in neatly defined categories. Rather, they have been consciously determined by individuals and congeries of organizations on the basis of criteria deemed appropriate by those individuals and/or organizations. They are, in short, socially derived phenomena, rooted in someone's or some group's agreed version of reality. The foundations have played crucial roles in providing legitimation for particular social phenomena and thereby have helped to insure the dominance of a version of reality consonant with their interests. They have, at the same time, been instrumental in creating and perpetuating an ideological and cultural hegemony which allows of few alternatives to their sponsored version of reality. Marx and Engels spoke to this point almost 150 years ago, noting, "The ideas of the ruling class are in every epoch the ruling ideas."[42] The major foundations are clearly among those institutions created and utilized by the ruling class.

Ideological and cultural hegemony is not generally attained by default or by uncontested imposition. Rather, it is the outcome of struggle and mediation between various classes at a given time in a society's history. Each class attempts to assure the polity that its perspectives, its ideas are indeed proper and likely to benefit those at whom its pronouncements are directed. While the incorporation of one class's perspectives into a society's collective consciousness is regularly contested, the struggle is not always between equals. In a system of state capitalism, for example, where institutions like the foundations are linked to the state, it is fanciful to deny that the foundations enjoy a distinct advantage in their attempts to impose their ideological and cultural hegemony over, say, the American working class, which enjoys very little state support because of its traditional confrontational position vis-à-vis capital. The state, through its influence, policies, and powers of suasion, in this example acts as mediator, facilitating the imposition of one class's hegemony over another. More simply put: in a system of state capitalism (or in any other system, for that matter), the state supports agencies whose interests are consonant with its own against those that wish to alter or even to supplant it.

Raymond Williams notes that hegemony "is something more substantial and more flexible than any abstract ideology." For this reason it cannot "be understood at the level of mere opinion or mere manipulation." It is, rather, a whole body of practices and expectations; our assignments of energy, our ordinary understanding of the nature of man and of his world. It is a set of meanings and values which as they are experienced as practices appear as reciprocally confirming. It thus constitutes a sense of reality for most people in the society, a sense of absolute because experienced reality beyond it is very difficult for most members of the society to move, in most areas of their lives.[43]

The major foundations have played important roles in creating the sense of reality accepted by many people. They have accomplished this through, for example, their involvement in the development of educational television and their funding for certain programs in selected universities. Sallah notes how "the dominant class uses its privileged access to ideological institutions [among which can be included the mass media and the universities] to propagate values which reinforce its structural position." At the same time, the propagation of values supportive of the dominant class's position serves "to define the parameters of legitimate discussion and debate over alternative beliefs, values, and worldviews."[44] Viewpoints and perspectives that support the position of the dominant class are funded by the foundations, while those that are seen to threaten that position are not.

The intellectuals who operationalize the process of hegemony, Bates's "salesmen," do so by selecting and emphasizing particular kinds of information. In the school, for example, this can take the form of emphasizing certain aspects of a nation's history and deemphasizing or even neglecting others. Or the contributions of particular groups to a nation's development can be minimized while those of other groups are lauded, even though these latter may not have played the fundamental role ascribed to them. Curricula, textbooks, and teachers all participate in the legitimation of this selective version of reality, as of course do the mass media.[45]

Williams terms this socioeconomic and political filtering of information the "selective tradition," and notes that it "is always passed off as 'the tradition', the *significant* past" by the dominant culture.[46] Such selectivity, such definition of what is to be counted as significant and what is to be devalued, is a crucial mechanism in the extension of the dominant culture's hegemony.

The major foundations help to extend the dominant class's hegemony through the control that they exercise over the production and dissemination of culture. Their strategic funding enables them to legitimate particular viewpoints while simultaneously devaluing others. It is questionable if the theory of democratic elitism and linked pluralist theory would have come to dominate post-World War II American political theory had it not been for significant levels of foundation support. At least this is the conclusion of one of the theory's main proponents.[47]

The example of C. Wright Mills's dealings with the Ford Foundation suggests how foundation largesse can be withheld in an attempt to devalue perspectives at odds with those who control the foundations. In a 1961 interview with historian David Eakins, Mills indicated that he had approached Ford for assistance for a study entitled "The Cultural Apparatus." The foundation's sole response to his detailed prospectus and application was, according to Eakins, "a form-letter rejection. The junior officer processing the materials objected to such a reply. His superior's answer was that the foundation had absolutely no intention of risking the support of work that might prove 'another *Power Elite*.'"[48] A second example is equally suggestive.

Seybold documents how in 1951 officials at the Ford Foundation were concerned to discredit academic Marxism, particularly in Western Europe.[49] Such an effort was part of the larger cultural cold war. A consultant's report in that year noted that although "the non-Communist left in Europe is anti-Stalinist," it was at the same time "to a large degree pro-Marxist." Many European intellectuals felt that Marxism as a theory continued to provide a workable blueprint for the organization of society despite its corruption at the hands of Lenin and Stalin. The Ford consultants in turn felt that these intellectuals, who were very influential in their respective countries, needed to understand that there was a reality little to distinguish Marx from Lenin and Stalin. It was the theory itself, not just those who implemented it, that led to corruption. Consequently, the report continued,

A major descriptive analytic study of Marx's political record and the code of his political conduct, undertaken by a scholar or an institution above suspicion of partisanship and known for strength of liberal convictions, might substantially contribute to disabusing the European non-Communist left of its traditional belief in Marx as a great man in the history of radical progressivism. Such a study might help close the present gap between Marx and Stalin and identify the former, as well as the latter, as the "Machiavellian" he was. Marx could be left to the Communists, and the non-Communist left could reinforce its anti-Stalinism by anti-Marxism, thus ridding its ideology of its present paralyzing ambivalence.[50]

By supporting such a study *and* by specifying the particular scholar to conduct it, the Ford Foundation could be assured of conclusions supportive of its ideology, while at the same time arguing that the conclusions reached were independent of the foundation, arrived at objectively and in accordance with accepted canons of scholarship. The appearance of objectivity, of nonpartisanship is another important element in the extension of hegemony.

An important aspect of hegemony is its totality, the degree to which the approved view of the world saturates all facets of the society. In

Gwyn Williams's term, it "incorporates" everything. To be successful, hegemony must be "an order in which a certain way of life and thought is dominant, in which one concept of reality is diffused throughout the society in all its institutional and private manifestations, informing with its spirit all taste, morality, customs, religious and political principles, and all social relations, particularly in their intellectual and moral connotations. . . . This hegemony corresponds to . . . the dictatorship of a class."[51] For Gramsci, the successful ruling class was one that had already established its intellectual and moral leadership before the assumption of political power. The requisite for this is, according to Joll, "a homogeneous social group that is also capable of attracting support from other groups."[52] Such a homogeneous social group has positioned itself in the upper reaches of the American corporate and financial structures, the foreign-policy organizations, and the major foundations, institutions from which its hegemony can radiate. A brief discussion of the structure of the foundations, how they select their trustees and staff, the wealth they control, and their links to policy-formulation groups indicates how this group's homogeneity is insured and its hegemony furthered.

Foundation Managers, Their Money, and Their Influence

Perhaps the most striking feature of the foundations' structures is the relative homogeneity of their trustees and staffs. Although they claim that much of their work is designed to benefit the less fortunate in this society and abroad, their procedures and personnel policies have a distinct air of noblesse oblige about them. The poor, dispossessed, and minority groups in whose names many of their programs are launched infrequently participate in the decisions to initiate these projects.

The boards of trustees of the major foundations are self-perpetuating. They select individuals to serve according to criteria that they themselves establish, individuals who are, according to John J. McCloy, long-time Ford and Rockefeller trustee, "real imaginative [and] public-spirited men."[53] Such procedures insure an upper-class monopoly on these important positions. Whitaker's recent analysis found that over half of the trustees of the thirteen largest American foundations attended Harvard, Yale, or Princeton. The most salient characteristics of this group were that they were white Episcopalian or Presbyterian males, who were between 55 and 65 years of age and who served on the boards of several foundations simultaneously or concurrently.[54] Whitaker could only conclude that the foundation trustees "constitute a wholly unrepresentative influence, and one which supports the established traditions of the power elite."[55]

These findings confirm the earlier conclusions of Lindeman and Whyte and suggest that little has changed in the intervening period, the foundations' public rhetoric to the contrary notwithstanding. Now, as when Whyte observed twenty-five years ago, "the median trustee . . . is a banker or a corporation president." The foundation continues to represent, as Lindeman observed more than forty years ago, "a consistently conservative element in our civilization, and . . . wherever their appropriations are accepted there enters at the same time this subtle influence in the direction of protecting the value system in existence."[56]

Abroad, as at home, the foundations seek out staff to implement projects determined primarily in New York and only after token consultation with people in the areas in which they are to be undertaken. The foundations are convinced that the key to their successful developmental effort in Africa, Asia, and Latin America require, in the words of a Ford Foundation vice-president, that their institutions play "an important role in linking the modernizing elites of the world."[57] Such a view assumes that meaningful change can and should only flow from the top down, that change should be led and orchestrated by an elite with the appropriate and approved training, one that supports the existing social structure. Change, in short, should be evolutionary, predictable, and manageable by society's elites. Society's leaders will decide the agenda to be followed by the majority, who will have little or no voice in determining the nature of the society in which they live. These perspectives are consonant with the foundation-supported theory of democratic elitism.

John J. McCloy's comments on the way in which the Ford Foundation searched for trustees while he was chairman of the board provides an example of what the theory of democratic elitism meant to foundation representatives. After noting that the trustees "were always looking for people in other areas than the Eastern Seaboard, who could reflect or interpret opinion of that area," McCloy listed several individuals who, from his perspective at least, were "not indicative of any one point of view or . . . establishment point of view in any sense."[58] These included J. Irwin Miller, Stephen Bechtel, and Roy Larsen.

Miller was at the time head of Cummins Engine, a company which long has ranked among the *Fortune* list of the 500 largest American corporations; he was also a director of several corporations, banks, and life-insurance companies, as well as a trustee of Yale University. Bechtel headed the world's largest construction firm, which held extensive Department of Defense contracts for work around the world; he was at the same time a director of several major corporations and a trustee of Stanford University. Larsen, in addition to being the chairman of the executive committee of Time, Inc., was later to become chairman of the board of the Fund for the Advancement of Education. He was chosen for the Ford board, according to McCloy, because as "a representative of the media . . . he [would] interpret public opinion," an important factor for an organization increasingly conscious of its public image.[59]

Perhaps McCloy really believed that these influential men (who are representative of the individuals chosen to serve as trustees of the major foundations) did not represent an "establishment point of view"; however, it is difficult to imagine that they represented anything else. As McCloy suggests, if only implicitly, the opinions of these men were ones that mattered on important issues and, consequently, they were recruited by the Ford Foundation. With regard to Bechtel, for example, McCloy noted that he "was a tremendous traveller. He was all over the world and we thought that we could get from him some better concept of the forces that were playing around the world and he seemed . . . an obvious man to take on."[60] How could Bechtel's viewpoint be anything but reflective of his and his class's vested interests? When he went to Saudi Arabia to discuss plans for defense establishments supported by the U.S. Department of Defense, it is doubtful that he sought the advice on the shape the world should assume from the local Bedouin tribesmen. At the same time, however, one suspects that he chatted at length with representatives of the Saud dynasty and the government elite. Whose "concept of the forces that were playing around the world" did he communicate to his fellow trustees at the Ford Foundation when program initiatives were discussed? Somehow it seems difficult to believe that Bechtel could perceive the best interests of an impoverished Saudi.

This self-perpetuating foundation elite makes policy and, of course, has the financial resources available to see that its policy is implemented. These funds in turn are frequently the catalysts for money from other sources. The following figures, chosen randomly for the period under investigation, suggest the degree of influence that the foundations can exercise at home and abroad through their strategic funding.

In 1955 the Rockefeller Foundation trustees appropriated some $19 million in new grants. Because the foundation was structured along programmatic lines (e.g., Biological and Medical Research, Social Science) rather than by geographical areas, it is difficult to state with precision what proportion of this amount was designated for international programs. However, an estimate of one-third of the total, or some $6 million, would appear reasonable.[61] For the 1955–56 fiscal year the Carnegie Corporation trustees voted new appropriations totalling some $7.2 million. Of this amount approximately $1.5 million was designated for programs abroad.[62] These figures were dwarfed by the 1955–56 grants voted by the Ford Foundation trustees, however. For that fiscal year the staggering total of $557 million was appropriated, of which some $25 million was designated exclusively for international programs.[63]

Rockefeller Foundation appropriations for 1960 increased to slightly less than $33 million. Applying the same formula of one-third of the total appropriations designated for international activities means that some $11 million was earmarked for overseas programs.[64] This amount does not include the year's expenditures for the foundation's University Development Program, which was funded for a ten-year period with $100 million, and which will be discussed in more detail in Chapter 3. Carnegie Corporation appropriations for the 1959–60 fiscal year totaled $9.6 million, of which some $1.5 million went to support the corporation's international activities.[65] Ford Foundation grants for this year were significantly reduced from those of the mid-1950s, totaling $165 million.[66] Of this reduced amount, some $65 million was designated for international concerns, an amount that represented a significant proportional increase over the international appropriation four years earlier.

Rockefeller Foundation appropriations for 1966 totaled $41.8 million. Almost $8 million of this amount was designated for the foundation's University Development Program. Assuming that one-third of the remaining $33 million budget went to fund programs of an international nature, we can estimate Rockefeller's 1966 grants for international programs at $19 million.[67] Carnegie Corporation appropriations for 1956–66 increased to $13.3 million, while expenditures for international efforts remained steady at approximately $1.5 million.[68] Ford Foundation trustees voted a 1956–66 budget of $356 million, of which some $118 million was designated for international programs and concerns.[69]

The ability of the Carnegie, Ford, and Rockefeller foundations to allocate these significant resources provides these institutions, and those trustees who control them, with considerable leverage in determining social and educational policy at home and overseas. It also enables them to further their particular hegemony as their grants help to determine social and educational priorities and the commonsense categories by which people organize their lives. The foundations' influence extends far beyond the grants that they award or the institutions that these monies help to shape, however. This influence can be traced to the crucial organizations that determine public policy and to the "think tanks" that frequently help to formulate this policy.

Domhoff has indicated the foundations' influence in a range of organizations that determine public policy. He also comments on the role played by the foundations, and those linked to them, as pools from which to choose experts who serve on important ad hoc policy-formation groups.[70] The ties between the Carnegie, Ford, and Rockefeller foundations and the Council on Foreign Relations, which has played a central if unrecognized role in foreign-policy determination since the 1930s, suggest the form that this influence sometimes takes.

In the late 1930s the Rockefeller Foundation made large appropriations to the council to underwrite a study of the long-term problems growing out of World War II and to plan for the peace to follow. We shall return to this "War-Peace Studies Project" in the next chapter. Since 1945 the Council on Foreign Relations has been financed primarily from two sources, corporate gifts and grants from the Carnegie, Ford, and Rockefeller foundations. In 1961 foundation funds accounted for some 25 percent of the council's operating revenue.[71] This is not surprising when it is considered that in the same year ten of the fourteen Carnegie trustees were members of the council, ten of the fifteen Ford trustees belonged to the organization, and twelve of the twenty Rockefeller trustees were council members.

In 1964, a representative year, the chairman of the council's board of directors was John J. McCloy, who at the same time was chairman of the board of trustees of the Ford Foundation and a trustee of the Rockefeller Foundation. David Rockefeller served as one of the council's two vice-presidents during the year, while Carnegie trustee Henry Wriston served as council president. James Perkins, then Carnegie Corporation vice-president and later a director of the Rockefeller's Chase Manhattan Bank and president of the Ford-supported International Council for Educational Development, was a member of the Council board of directors, as was Carnegie trustee Charles Spofford. A fellow council director was Whitney Shepardson, who had retired from the Carnegie vice-presidency some years earlier. John Dickey, a trustee of both the Ford and Rockefeller foundations, was a member of the council's Committee on Studies, which determined what foreign-policy issues should be considered in any particular period.

Also serving as directors in 1964 were former secretary of the Air Force Thomas Finletter and Allen Dulles, director of the Central Intelligence Agency during the early 1960s. If it is difficult to indicate where the role of the council ceases and that of the government begins in foreign-policy formulation, as several commentators have recently noted,[72] it is equally difficult to distinguish between the men who serve as trustees of the major foundations and those who occupy important positions within the Council on Foreign Relations. Similarly, it is difficult to ascertain when foundation policy is subsumed by the pronouncements of the council, so intertwined are the personnel from the organizations and so similar their outlook on the nature of the world community.

These links between the foundations and the council are paralleled of course by those between the foundations and the official Washington foreign-policy agencies. The men who move among these several institutions come from similar backgrounds and have had comparable educational experiences; consequently, they tend to share a certain view of the world and of the role of the United States in it. Some few individuals within these orgnaizations are recruited from backgrounds not as privileged as that of the majority; however, the socialization processes that operate both at the elite universities where they (as well as most foundation staff) are educated and within their occupational careers all but assure that they will accept, if only tacitly, the norms propounded by those who determine institutional policy.

This foundation—Council—foreign-policy elite has been ubiquitous in official policy positions and as members of ad hoc policy-formulation groups since 1945. Party affiliation is incidental; Republicans among the elite have served in Democratic administrations, while liberal Democratic members have served under more conservative Democratic presidents. This movement across political party lines gives the appearance of nonpartisanship. The idea of "service" replaces that of "politics" and vested interests and reinforces the appearance of political independence, if not of neutrality. This circulation of elites also helps to create the perception that these men arrived at their influential positions without a hint of favoritism, that their ascendency to positions of power and influence was a direct result of their demonstrated competence to manage complex affairs and institutions. Their rise can therefore be understood as a manifestation of the theory of democratic elitism in action. The apparent apolitical and disinterested involvement of this elite is an important element in the extension of the dominant hegemony.

The Foundations in Perspective

Both the supporters and detractors of the foundations would probably agree that these institutions form part of the liberal or progressive wing of the capitalist state. This location accounts for the fact that many of the programs enacted by the foundations in the 20th century have been designed to better the lot of the dispossessed and to bring about a more equitable and congenial domestic polity. At the same time, however, this location also helps to explain why there is no evidence that foundation personnel have given serious thought to the possibility that society's betterment could transpire *except* within the structure of state capitalism. Indeed, it would be surprising if they had, given the foundations' origins, their personnel, and their ideological orientations. The Carnegie, Ford, and Rockefeller foundations, in short, are among the important agencies that further the objectives of state capitalism in the United States.

The situation is similar when the focus of the foundations' activities shifts overseas. There, as at home, many foundation programs are designed in the interests of the recipients, e.g., Carnegie Corporation support for the Centre for Applied Legal Studies in South Africa at the University of Witwatersrand, which attempts to mitigate somewhat the repressive nature that the South African legal system exercises over the majority black population, or the financial support and relocation opportunities made available by the Ford Foundation for Chilean political refugees fleeing that nation's murderous junta.[73] Such beneficial programs and worthwhile intentions notwithstanding, there is evidence to indicate that the major thrust of the foundations' overseas activities is intended to improve conditions in, say, Nigeria, India, or Thailand while simultaneously insuring that these nations' leaders and institutional structures continue to be linked to the world capitalist system, albeit as members of the periphery rather than the center. Again, we should be surprised were the foundations to attempt to do otherwise, despite their oft-repeated public claims that their programs are not intended to serve narrowly national, partisan, or personal interests. As integral cogs in the capitalist system they can do little else but further that system's interests through their programs.

The foundations' influence in foreign-policy determination and in the extension of their worldview into the domestic polity—and beyond— derives from several interrelated factors: (1) their possession of significant amounts of capital, which can be allocated as their self-perpetuating directors deem appropriate; (2) their ability to allocate this capital to certain individuals and groups strategically located in the cultural apparatus (universities, the arts sector, the media, authors, and publishers), who in turn produce works frequently (but not always) supportive of the worldview of the foundations themselves, thereby providing an important source of legitimation for their perspective; (3) their links to and incorporation into the decision-making stratum of the capitalist state; and (4) their shared view that the development of the domestic polity and polities abroad can best be advanced through the aegis of the world capitalist system, dominated by the United States.

Just as the state must rely on the multinational corporation to carry much of the burden for the expansion of surplus capital in hopes of aggregation and increased accumulation, so too it must rely on institutions like the foundations to export the ideology of the capitalist state, while simultaneously using this agency to facilitate the legitimation of the system as a whole. The foundations represented one of the few sources of unencumbered "risk" capital available during the period from 1945 to 1975. These funds could be allocated in a manner determined exclusively by foundation officers. Throughout most of this period the state allowed the foundations to designate their capital, at home and abroad, as they chose.[74] In fact, the state subsidized the foundations by granting them tax-free status. The overseas programs of the foundations complemented to a significant degree the foreign-policy initiatives of the state throughout this period. To be sure, there were occasional differences of emphasis and direction between representatives of the foundations and the state (represented abroad by, for example, political officers in the United States embassy or agents of the Agency for International Development), but these were insignificant compared to the overarching shared concern of both groups: execution of a foreign policy that protected the interests of the United States and of the world capitalist system upon which that policy rested. This shared belief in the general direction of United States foreign policy after World War II—always allowing for minor differences—resulted from, among other things, the fact that many of the same individuals were so directly involved in the political fortunes of the state, the nation's major corporate and financial institutions, and the foundations.

It is important to mention the frequently contradictory nature of liberal capitalism, as well as the apparent and very real conflicts within the dominant class. Theirs is not a unitary perspective on all matters; the most cursory acquaintance with daily political jockeying in Washington, London, or Paris quickly reveals this. Contradictions occasionally surface within the foundations as well. Examples include the funding provided by the Ford Foundation for the avowedly Marxian interpretation of American education authored by Samuel Bowles and Herbert Gintis in 1976, or the Russell Sage Foundation's 1972 support of three leftist sociologists to study that foundation's organization and operations.[75] Other examples might include the funding provided for such "radical" researchers on Third-World development as Denis Goulet, the support afforded several left-wing Latin social scientists, or the support and advice given by the Ford Foundation to enable Tanzania to further its program of African socialism.

Such contradictions are very real and, at least in part, are the result of contestation among foundation staff holding different viewpoints. However real these contradictions are and however much they result in support for programs and individuals that appear antithetical to the overarching ideology of state capitalism and the foundations themselves, we need to understand that such support represents less an ideological reorientation on the part of the funding institutions than an attempt to honor, however minimally, the pluralistic commitment of the foundations themselves. The liberal capitalist state and linked organizations like the foundations do not provide support to individuals or groups that have the potential to mount a *meaningful* challenge to their hegemony, however much project support they might provide to reform-oriented or even occasionally radical opponents.[76] The foundations' much-publicized pluralist orientation needs to be understood in context: differing opinions and persuasions are indeed welcomed—if not actively encouraged—just as long as they are expressed within the parameters determined by the requirements of capitalism. Pluralism, in short, loses its attraction if and when it affords critics the opportunities to challenge the very legitimacy of the system that sustains the foundations.

The foundations' public pronouncements have consistently stressed the value-free and humanitarian nature of their programs, while denying the existence of a covert agenda. More sophisticated or cynical observers might scoff and say that it is naive to take the foundations' pronouncements at face value; rather, they would argue, one must assume that the foundations' activities have long been designed to further certain objectives in addition to those publicly acknowledged. This may indeed be the case. However, we shall recall at the same time that an important way by which one class's hegemony is extended is through the appearance of reality, and not necessarily through reality itself. If one class has at its disposal the means of persuasion, it can sometimes convince people that its worldview is correct, even if that worldview is some distance removed from reality. Through their control of culture and the dissemination of ideology, the major foundations have been strategically located to foster a view of the world that gives the appearance of reality to numerous publics, even while adherence to that worldview does more to serve the interests of the few rather than the many. What we must do is to juxtapose the foundations' public rhetoric, which has helped to define the worldview for so many, against the realities of their activities. These have been designated to further the interests of the recipients, but, as the data presented below indicate, only while simultaneously furthering the interests of the class that controls the foundations.

2

United States Foreign Policy and
the Evolution of the Foundations'
Overseas Programs, 1945–1960

United States foreign policy attained a degree of coherence after the triumph in the late 1940s of those planners favoring a tough stance toward the Soviet Union.[1] The next two decades were characterized by a policy of strident anticommunism, repeated military intervention into geopolitical regions perceived by Washington policy makers and their advisors as falling under communist or anti-American influence, and the significant expansion of American corporate investment abroad. The period also witnessed the proliferation of military and economic aid programs, epitomized by the global network of military alliances on the one hand and the Marshall Plan and various developmental aid activities on the other. At the same time, there was a discernible increase in the number and activity of national and multinational agencies created to dispense aid to developing nations: the United States Agency for International Development being representative of the former, and the International Bank for Reconstruction and Development (the World Bank) of the latter. This period was marked also by the large and well-coordinated developmental-assistance programs of the Carnegie, Ford, and Rockefeller foundations in support of the efforts of the official United States and multinational foreign-assistance agencies.

In 1939 the Rockefeller Foundation made the first of several large grants to the Council on Foreign Relations to finance a series of studies designed to focus on the long-term problems of the war and to plan for the peace to follow. The major recommendations of this "War-Peace Studies Project" subsequently became staples of United States foreign policy. These recommendations led to the following conclusions regarding that policy in the post-1945 world: (1) access to sources of raw materials deemed essential to the expansion of the national economy and security of the United States must be safeguarded; (2) American

41

economic prosperity was dependent on corporate expansion and financial investment overseas, a course which could be enhanced if the living standard of the peoples both in Europe and in the underdeveloped world were raised; and (3) only in a stable, noncommunist, and capitalist-oriented world, where change was effected through nonrevolutionary means, could these goals be assured. In this chapter we will elaborate on each of these and will see as well how the rising tensions associated with the cold war after 1950 insured the immutability of these objectives.

Many of the trustees and staff of the Carnegie, Ford, and Rockefeller foundations had worked in one of the Washington agencies conceptualizing or carrying out this post-World War II foreign policy before joining one of the foundations. After 1950 they began to draft plans for increasing their foundations' involvement overseas. The rationale for these proposed overseas programs was remarkably similar to that issuing from the departments of State and Defense and the first postwar aid agency, the International Cooperation Administration, as justification for a more active American involvement abroad. The similarity of language and of outlook that characterized those in the foreign-policy bureaus and the foundations is not surprising, since these individuals brought along intact their worldview as they moved from Washington to New York foundation offices.

The consensus about the direction of United States foreign policy from 1950 to the later stages of the Vietnam war has been recognized by commentators of various political persuasions. Hodgson, for one, has noted how this "hybrid, liberal conservatism, blanketed the scene and muffled debate." This was as true on the fringes of the "responsible" left (represented by Americans for Democratic Action) as it was in "the boardrooms of Wall Street and the manufacturing industry." Dissent from the foreign-policy consensus was certainly not precluded but, according to Hodgson, it did involve the risk of "disqualifying the dissenter from being taken seriously, and indeed often from being heard at all."[2] Foundation officers, who were prominent architects of this foreign-policy consensus, were clearly not among the dissenters.

Conservative commentator Irving Kristol delineated in 1967 the three major purposes of American foreign policy. In addition to ensuring national security and minimizing the possibility of armed conflict, this foreign policy should, he argued, "encourage other nations, especially the smaller ones, to mold their own social, political, and economic institutions [in ways to insure values] that are at least not repugnant to (if not actually congruent with) American values."[3] Foundation programs in Africa, Asia, and Latin America were undertaken to accomplish just this objective.

The foundations' arguments favoring an increase in their overseas activities were quickly followed by concrete proposals. These generally involved strengthening educational institutions, particularly at the university level, undertakings that foundation officers felt could help to train the developing nations' future leaders. This decision to make significant financial commitments to the training of a limited number of Africans, Asians, and Latin Americans after 1950 was part of the larger foreign-policy objective of countering the Soviet cultural offensive by supporting strategically located cultural and educational institutions around the world. Such programs were designed to encourage, as Joan Nelson put it in her sympathetic study of United States foreign aid, "independence or pro-Western alignment in the foreign policy positions of [the] developing countries."[4]

Background to the Foundations' Overseas Programs: The Evolving Foreign Policy Consensus

In his study of the period immediately after World War II, historian Daniel Yergin notes the "messianic liberalism" that led the foreign-policy establishment to seek ways to create "a world safe both for liberal democracy and liberal capitalism."[5] The outlines of the foreign policy to insure such a world began to evolve from the War-Peace Studies Project, which was initiated in 1939. By the time the last project report was completed in 1945, the Rockefeller Foundation had given over $600,000 toward the study, whose steering committee included Carnegie Corporation vice-president Whitney Shepardson. The conclusions of the War-Peace Studies Project present in outline form the basics of United States foreign policy after World War II. At the same time, the sponsorship of the project by the Rockefeller Foundation and the involvement of numerous personnel then and subsequently associated with one of the major foundations show how foundation perspectives are frequently incorporated into foreign-policy formulation.

The War-Peace Studies Project: Overseas Economic Expansion

The emphasis in the War-Peace Studies Project on the relationship between American exports and overseas investment on the one hand and the domestic economy on the other was simply a reformulation of a staple of American foreign policy dating from the 1890s. From its inception, this Open Door policy sought to utilize the power of the state to make available to American industry and finance capital the markets of nations abroad. The onset of the Depression of the 1930s lent urgency to this equation of exports and domestic growth and stability. Williams, Gardner, and Eakins[6] describe how agreement was reached among the leaders of the corporate, financial, and government sectors of the United States that new methods must be sought to facilitate expansion of the export trade. Failure to do so would almost certainly insure that the United States would succumb to class warfare resulting from the widespread unemployment and appalling social conditions of the period.

The outbreak of World War II, with its rising industrial demands, forestalled such an occurrence, however, as the country returned to full employment and a semblance of economic stability, if not prosperity. The more far-sighted of the corporate and governmental leaders recognized, however, that this boom economy was a short-lived phenomenon and that the ensuing peace and likely reduction of industrial activity might well be accompanied by a sharp recession, with the resultant danger to social stability. It was this realization that was behind the drive to increase overseas trade and investment, the perceived panacea for domestic economic prosperity and related social tranquility.

Members of the War-Peace Studies Project's Economic and Financial Group had reached a similar conclusion even before the United States became a belligerent in the war. Its memorandum to President Roosevelt and the Department of State in mid-October 1940 concluded that the American national interest required, minimally, "free access to markets and raw materials in the British Empire, the Far East, and the entire Western hemisphere."[7] The Economic and Financial Group elaborated on this the next summer. Memorandum E-B34 concluded that significant alterations in the American economic system would have to accompany the country's attempts to limit its economic activity to the Western hemisphere. This was so because, as the memorandum noted, the "economy of the United States is geared to the export of certain manufactured and agricultural projects and the import of numerous raw materials and foodstuffs."[8] The concept of a "self-contained" American economy was rejected, the planners urging instead a worldwide free trade zone open to American manufacturers and suppliers.

Looking back over this period, historian David Baldwin has commented on how those planning postwar foreign policy viewed "economic development abroad . . . as a requisite not only for peace but for prosperity as well. Economic growth was related to higher levels of international trade, which in turn were related to higher levels of production and consumption because of the advantages of international specialization. The goal of economic growth was also seen as a means by which the United States could insure full employment at home."[9] If the health of the domestic economy was dependent on American overseas economic activity, then measures had to be taken to strengthen the economies of the country's major trading partners. A 1945 policy statement of the Import-Export Bank (an agency of the United States government) spoke to this need, noting that loans for economic development were justified because "the best trading partners of the United States are countries which have reached the highest state of economic development."[10]

The reconstruction of Europe through the aid provided by the Marshall Plan should be understood in this context of the necessity of restoring the economic health of an area of great importance to the American export industry and finance capital. Economic assistance would enable the Western European nations to rebuild their industrial infrastructures to prewar levels, thereby revitalizing their economies and reconstituting them as "the best trading partners" for American corporations and financial institutions. At the same time, political decisions led to military measures (e.g., the Berlin airlift, the creation of the North Atlantic Treaty Organization) to insure that the Western European nations retained their autonomy in the face of the increasing Soviet threat to dominate the western as well as the eastern half of Europe. American policy planners recognized that Soviet occupation of Western Europe would effectively remove those nations from the world capitalist economy. Eakins has summed up this concern as follows: "[C]ommunist victories, whether electoral or not, were seen as ending, or at the very least drastically reducing, foreign investment from the West, and thereby destroying the viability of the entire system."[11]

The nations of the developing world presented a different sort of problem for the foreign-policy planners wishing to open the economies of the world to American capital penetration. Here there was little industrial infrastructure or experience upon which to build, many of the nations were still formally linked in colonial status to one of the European powers, and it was recognized that the infusion of large amounts of capital as in Western Europe would not necessarily guarantee the rapid transformation of these areas into trading partners on terms advantageous to American interests. If the underdeveloped areas were to contribute to American economic prosperity as they had formerly benefited the economies of the colonial powers, new methods had to be devised to insure this outcome. American policy planners, like their early- and mid-19th century English counterparts, were less interested in the acquisition of a formal empire than they were in devising procedures and forging links that would bind the underdeveloped nations to American economic interests on terms distinctly favorable to the latter.[12] It was against this background that the debate over the institutionalization of an American foreign-aid program was joined early in 1948, just at the time that the Marshall Plan was coming into existence.

The committee appointed by President Truman in 1947 and charged with making recommendations regarding American foreign-aid assistance was headed by the then-secretary of commerce and railroad heir, W. Averell Harriman. The committee's deliberations were dominated by spokesmen for the business community, particularly by representatives of the powerful and influential Committee on Economic Development.[13] The arguments mustered by this group and its supporters to win Congressional approval for the resultant Economic Cooperation Act of 1948 emphasized the economic benefits that would accrue to the United States from a reconstructed Europe and the increasingly prosperous nations of Africa, Asia, and Latin America.[14] The architects of this policy never doubted that the purpose of the proposed foreign assistance was to benefit American interests. Secretary of State John Foster Dulles put the matter succinctly ten years later when he told a Congressional committee that "not for one minute do I think the purpose [of foreign aid] is to make friends. The purpose . . . is to look out for the interests of the United States."[15] This sentiment has been echoed repeatedly since then, one time being in 1968 when presidential candidate Nixon asked the electorate to "remember that the main purpose of American aid is not to help other nations but to help ourrselves."[16]

The War-Peace Studies Project: Continued Access to Sources of Raw Materials

The steady expansion of the American industrial sector since the beginning of this century and its increasing technological sophistication has led to a growing dependence on sources of raw materials, not all of which are available in the United States. Corporate leaders and military strategists have voiced concern over the years about the possible foreclosure of raw materials sources required by the nation's industries in the one case and its defense establishment in the other.[17]

The importance of continued access to sources of raw materials deemed essential to American industry and national security is a recurring theme in the War-Peace Studies Project, as indeed it has been in official and other policy documents from 1945 to the present. Project memorandum E-B34 for example, issued during the summer of 1941, argued that the failure to integrate the Dutch East Indies, China, and Japan into a postwar economic union would risk "cutting off vital imports like rubber, tin, jute, and vegetable oils," as well as "restricting the normal export of [American] surpluses."[18] This was a formal restatement of the recommendation of Asian specialist Owen Lattimore, who a year earlier had argued that the United States could not let the nations of the Pacific basin be dominated by unfriendly powers because "we secure from it [Southeast Asia] huge amounts of raw material and sell to it huge amounts of finished goods."[19]

Between 1948 and 1952, according to Eckes, Washington policy planners became convinced that, in part, "the prosperity and political stability of the United States and her potential allies hinged on access to vital resources available in peripheral regions vulnerable to Communist aggression."[20] The disruptions occasioned by the Korean War heightened the awareness of the importance of the nations of Africa, Asia, and Latin America as suppliers of raw materials. At the same time, policy planners became increasingly cognizant of the ease with which the nations in these areas could fall within the Soviet orbit. The 1952 report of the President's Materials Policy Commission reaffirmed the importance of these areas for the health of the domestic economy. The report noted that "the areas to which the United States must principally look for expansion of its mineral imports are Canada, Latin America and Africa, the Near East, and South and Southeast Asia."[21] The director of the commission staff was Philip Coombs, who, as assistant secretary of state for cultural and educational affairs in the 1960s and later as vice-president of the Ford Foundation-funded International Council for Educational Development, advocated increased American involvement in the educational and cultural affairs of the nations of Africa, Asia, and Latin America.

The importance of the developing nations as suppliers of vital raw materials was reaffirmed by foundation-supported studies throughout the 1950s. A Carnegie Research fellowship enabled University of Virginia professor John K. King to act as research secretary to the Council on Foreign Relations' study group examining "United States Policy and Southeast Asia" in 1954-55. King published the major findings of this study, with the council's blessing, in 1956, noting, among other things, that the United States was "heavily dependent on materials imported from abroad, especially from the so-called underdeveloped areas, to maintain an expanding and dynamic economy."[22] Two years later an article appeared in the council's influential publication, *Foreign Affairs* (which is generally held to reflect official Washington thinking), arguing that "our purpose should be to encourage the expansion of low-cost production and to make sure that neither nationalistic policies nor Communist influence deny American industries access on reasonable terms to the basic materials necessary to the continued growth of the American economy"[23]

The point of view had been summarized a few years earlier by Paul Hoffman, Marshall Plan director and Ford Foundation president, when he noted that "our own dynamic economy made us dependent on the outside world for many critical raw materials."[24] Any actions threatening to American industrial access to the sources of raw materials vital to the continued expansion of the American economy, he continued, would be viewed as detrimental to the United States.

The War-Peace Studies Project: Evolutionary Change versus Revolutionary Chaos

Packenham's study of the political development ideas that dominated American thinking by the 1950s indicates the consensus among foreign-policy planners regarding the importance of economic and political stability in the underdeveloped world. Indeed, "radical politics, including intense conflict, disorder, violence, and revolution" were considered "unnecessary for economic and political development" and consequently "always bad."[25] This antipathy toward revolutionary change resulted from the conviction that such a course was always subject to communist manipulation and exploitation. The measured and evolutionary development of the new nations was judged by Washington policy makers to be more manageable and in the interests of the majority of the evolving nations' populations. What was generally unspoken, but was no less an important factor in the emphasis on evolutionary development, was the belief that revolutionary change in the emerging nations would endanger regional stability and threaten the continued presence of American corporate interests in the developing nations. Magdoff's estimate that "by 1964 foreign sources of earnings accounted for about twenty-two percent of domestic nonfinancial profits" perhaps helps to explain the interest of American corporations in maintaining regimes in developing nations that were favorably disposed toward private foreign investment.[26]

Foreign-aid assistance was institutionalized after 1950 as part of the attempt to insure gradual and evolutionary change in the nations of Africa, Asia, and Latin America. An important tactical consideration in this assistance was the training of the indigenous reform leader who would eschew revolutionary nationalism in favor of more moderate developmental goals. Washington policy planners hoped at the same time that this training would encourage the leaders of the developing nations to view sympathetically American private investment in their territories.

An official of the Agency for International Development spoke to the importance of training the reform leader when reviewing the history of foreign-aid assistance. "From its beginnings in the early 1950s," he noted, "the university contract program [of the Agency and its precursor, the International Cooperation Administration] was in fact developed to work at one of the great political problems of our time—the necessity of 'evolutionizing' revolution all around the underdeveloped world." The United States government decided, he continued, "to face the fact of revolution among the 'have-nots,' [and] to seek to contain it . . . and the university contract program is one of . . . [the government's] instruments of containment." The attainment of stability in these regions was dependent upon "the character of leadership," which the university contract program was designed to shape.[27]

The increasing level of activity by American corporate and financial institutions in the nations of Africa, Asia, and Latin America, coupled with the growing importance of raw materials available there, meant that American economic interests could only be furthered if United States institutions were left to penetrate these peripheral economies in ways guaranteed to maximize profits. The desiderata from the American overseas investors' viewpoint, consequently, were regimes in the developing nations that provided favorable climates for their private investments, stood as bulwarks against the expropriation or nationalization of their assets, made available sources of cheap and disciplined labor and, where appropriate, guaranteed rights for the continued extraction and exportation of raw materials on terms favorable, or at least not too unfavorable, to their companies. It was hoped that the indigenous reform leader would assure these goals, in exchange for which United States foreign aid would be forthcoming.

Nielsen, in his study of the major foundations, notes that the socioeconomic viewpoint of those who control the foundations is "essentially Lockean—with the protection of private property rights . . . as its central value."[28] The same can be said of the important corporate and financial leaders and the foreign-policy architects as well, men who frequently moved among corporate, government, and foundation positions. This emphasis on private-property rights manifests itself in the foreign-policy sphere through attempts to insure participation on favorable terms for private American enterprise overseas. President Truman summed up this viewpoint succinctly, noting that "the pattern of international trade which is most conducive to freedom of enterprise is one in which major decisions are made not by governments but by private buyers and sellers." He added that America's destiny was contingent on sustaining and expanding the system of private enterprise, objectives which American foreign policies have sought to further.[29] President Reagan's position on this issue has been equally unambiguous, of course, as his pronouncements at the 1981 Cancun economic summit conference made clear.[30]

To be sure, many of the architects of United States foreign policy since 1945 must have found the ideology of communism repugnant on moral and political grounds. Indeed, the strident anticommunism of the cold-war period, which these men helped to articulate, was couched largely in political terms—e.g., the Iron Curtain metaphor, the collectivization of society and concomitant threats to individual freedom and expression. It would be naive, however, to assume that these men, whose wealth, status, and aspirations were inextricably linked to the continuance and furtherance of the system of international capitalism, were not opposed to communism because of the threat it posed to the economic system from which they benefited so handsomely. There was, however, very little public discussion of the vested economic interests endangered by the accession to power of communist regimes or nationalist leaders unwilling to deal with American capitalism on terms favorable to its profit margins. The establishment of a communist regime, a system of state socialism, or the accession to power by a national leader unwillilng to conduct his nation's policies according to the rules of international capitalism was associated by these men with the limitation of markets, the curtailment or severance of access to sources of raw materials, and a general diminution of profits.

Miliband has put this elite's concerns rather more baldly. "The supreme evil" in a developing nation, he notes, "is obviously the assumption of power by governments whose main purpose is precisely to abolish private ownership and private enterprise, home and foreign, in the most important sectors of their economic life or in all of these." This has meant that the main thrust of United States foreign policy since 1945 has been to "prevent the coming into being, anywhere, of regimes fundamentally opposed to capitalist enterprise and determined to do away with it."[31] It would be fanciful to deny the possibility that at least part of the educational and cultural programs of the foundations and the binational aid agencies were intended to socialize Third-World leaders in such ways as to win their support for the continuance of private foreign investment in their countries.

Mechanisms to Implement the War-Peace Studies Project's Conclusions

American foreign-policy planners have sought to carry out the major recommendations of the War-Peace Studies Project in several ways. One of these has involved American financial support for and control of the International Bank for Reconstruction and Development (the World Bank). Another has been the bilateral assistance agreements concluded between the developing nations and the official American aid agency, initially the International Cooperation Administration and currently the Agency for International Development. Trustees and officers of the major foundations have been closely asosciated both with the bank and the aid agencies since their beginnings during the cold-war era. The movement of these men between the multinational bank, the national aid agency, and the private foundations helps to explain to a certain extent the complementary developmental programs that characterize these organizations. A few words about the assumptions underlying the bank and the Agency for International Development will set the stage for an examination of the origins of the foundations' supportive programs in the 1950s.

The World Bank

The World Bank and the International Monetary Fund grew from seeds planted in War-Peace Studies Project recommendation P-B23 of July 1941. This memorandum cited the need for worldwide financial institutions that would help in "stabilizing currencies and facilitating programs of capital investment for constructive undertakings in backward and underdeveloped regions."[32] Further recommendations elaborating on this theme were forwarded to President Roosevelt and the Department of State the next year. In 1944 an international conference was convened at Bretton Woods, New Hampshire, and a monetary fund and a world bank were voted into existence.

The World Bank is ostensibly an independent agency, charged with the responsibility of making loans designed to help developing nations modernize their economies and better the lot of their peoples. In reality, the World Bank, under the guise of international trusteeship, has steadfastly pursued policies that further the purposes of United States foreign policy and capitalist penetration of the less developed countries (LDCs).[33] There has never been a non-American president, the United States controls over one-quarter of the voting rights, and major decisions are regularly subject to approval of the Department of State, although such policy is never spelled out in official bank publications.

The policies and operational methods of the bank were delineated under the presidency of John J. McCloy, who took office in 1947 and whose administrative staff was dominated by American businessmen. McCloy agreed to accept the bank presidency on condition that the United States director (and consequently the bank's number-two man) would be Eugene Black, then vice-president of the Rockefeller family's Chase Manhattan Bank, of which McCloy himself was a director.[34] Black subsequently succeeded McCloy as bank president and joined him as a trusee of the Ford Foundation.

From its chartering in 1946 the American-dominated World Bank has pursued policies in the developing world favorable to American interests. There was from the beginning a marked determination on the part of the American Bank president and his board of governors that the development of the Third World should be accomplished largely through the aegis of private capital investment. Since the bulk of the private capital available for such investment in the period immediately after World War II came from American sources, this policy proved distinctly advantageous to the furtherance of American corporate and financial institutions, particularly those banking concerns that had developed foreign contacts.

Baldwin's analysis of the bank's first twenty years indicates the methods used by bank officials to encourage developing countries to rely more on private investment and less on the public sector in their push for modernization.[35] Bank pronouncements repeatedly stressed the importance of improving the "climate of investment" in the developing nations if bank loans for developmental projects were to be approved. Translated into layman's language, this meant that host governments interested in securing bank loans should, as Baldwin notes, be willing to pay a subsidy, grant tax relief, stifle competition, or undertake other means to insure the profitability of private foreign investment.[36] As a bank historian has put it: "It can hardly be denied that inextricably mixed up in . . . [the bank's] attitudes was a conviction that capitalism was the right way, that private enterprise was best, and, as a rule-of-thumb dogma, that the less State interference, the better."[37]

The 1944 Bretton Woods conference from which the bank emerged was convened to design an economic system congenial to the preservation and expansion of the international capitalist system dominated by the United States. The selection of McCloy and Black, both with close ties to the American corporate and financial structure, insured that this goal would be realized and that the position of the United States as the leader of the capitalist world would be strengthened through the aegis of the nominally international organization. At the same time, the bank was critically located to dictate the terms of Third-World development along lines consonant with the interests of the United States.

Bilateral Aid

The foreign-aid programs, administered by the Agency for International Development and its precursor were undertaken, in the words of Secretary of State Dulles, "to look out for the interests of the United States." A few words about two aid programs, developmental loans and shipment of agricultural surpluses, will suggest how these interests were to be protected.

The developmental loans for African, Asian, and Latin American nations concentrated initially on strengthening these nations' infrastructures. For example, loans for such projects as the construction of roads, ports, processing plants for various raw materials, and telecommunications systems were commonplace after 1950. This concentration on infrastructure projects is not, according to Sutcliffe, accidental. Developmental loans flow to this category of projects rather than to, say, industry or agriculture—from which a large number of local nationals might be expected to benefit—because investment in infrastructure projects does "nothing to compete with foreign capital from the developed capitalist countries which may wish to migrate to the underdeveloped country."[38] At the same time, such investment facilitates greater profitability of foreign capital since it controls, for example, the extractive industries, which need sound and efficiently operating railroads and ports to move the raw materials to overseas processing centers.

The loan agreements to facilitate these projects contain clauses requiring that recipient countries purchase a stipulated percentage of the equipment utilized on the projects from American companies. A presidential commission noted in 1963 that more than eighty percent of all United States economic-aid commitments were then tied to this procurement provision, thereby providing a substantial subsidy for various segments of the corporate exporting sector of the domestic economy.[39] This tying of foreign economic assistance assures continued productivity at home and, at the same time, guarantees a certain amount of overseas employment for American subcontractors.

Certain agricultural commodities have been shipped to developing nations under terms of Public Law 480, passed by Congress in 1948. Under the provisions of this law recipient nations pay for the agricultural produce in local currency rather than in dollars. Such funds are then used within the host country to defray official American governmental expenses, ranging, as Kolko quips, "from embassy overhead to CIA activities."[40] Such an arrangement precludes the necessity of transferring large amounts of dollars abroad to finance governmental activities, thereby reducing the balance of payments deficit. This arrangement also has helped to reduce the perennial American agricultural surplus, thereby lowering governmental expenditures for subsidy payments to farmers and storage operators. Because this procedure has insured large farmers a guaranteed market for their crops, it is not surprising that the influential agrobusiness spokesmen give enthusiastic support to this program. Yet another advantage of this arrangement is the requirement that the majority of such overseas agricultural shipments be carried in American or American flag ships, a stipulation that provides a governmental subsidy to various segments of the shipping industry.

The relationship of the foreign-assistance program to the health of the domestic economy was noted in 1963 by President Kennedy, who commented that "last year 11 percent of our exports were financed under our aid program. And the importance of this aid to our exports is increasing as our developing assistance is increasing, . . . [and] now [is] almost entirely tied to American purchases."[41] Two years later Eugene Black, then World Bank president, Ford Foundation trustee, and prominent Wall Street banker, remarked on the benefits derived by the business community from the foreign-aid program. Foreign aid, he noted, provided a substantial and immediate market for United States goods and services. It also stimulated the development of new overseas markets for American companies. And lastly, it favorably disposed foreign economies toward "a free enterprise system in which United States firms can prosper."[42]

Mr. Black was simply restating in 1965 what had been basic principles of the American foreign-assistance program from its inception. In 1950, for example, the presidentially appointed Gray Commission's *Report to the President on Foreign Economic Policies* mentioned the importance for the United States of sustained economic growth in the underdeveloped nations in the following terms: "economic stagnation, political unrest, and extreme poverty of most underdeveloped countries represent a growing threat to the rest of the free world."[43] The same Gordon Gray who chaired this commission helped to formulate the Ford Foundation's overseas training programs over the next several years.

The Gray Commission report was followed six months later by another document on the same subject. *Partners in Progress* was sponsored by the International Development Advisory Board and chaired by Nelson Rockefeller. Its message was similar to that contained in the Gray Commission report, viz., "strengthening the economies of the underdeveloped regions and an improvement of their living levels must be considered a vital part of our own defense mobilization."[44] Six years later the same theme was sounded by Secretary of State Dulles who, when questioned about the significantly expanded Soviet aid programs, remarked that "we are in a contest in the field of economic development of the underdeveloped countries which is bitterly competitive. Defeat in this context could be as disastrous as defeat in an armaments race."[45]

This belief that the economic development of the underdeveloped regions was ultimately beneficial for the United States was paralleled by the belief that the problems of underdevelopment could only be alleviated within a capitalist framework. The 1963 report of a presidential commission chaired by General Lucius Clay noted that while "we cannot insist upon the establishment of our own economic system" in the developng regions, the United States should refuse its aid to those nations that pursued policies inhibiting capitalist development. In the words of the report: "We believe the U.S. should not aid a foreign government in projects establishing government-owned industrial and commercial enterprises which compete with existing private endeavors."[46]

The report's comments on Latin America are instructive and illustrative of the overall direction of American foreign-assistance programs of the period. They also suggest the almost messianic fervor with which these programs were championed. "Impediments to the growth of private enterprise must be identified and treated, the shallowness and harm of doctrinaire biases against responsible private enterprise exposed, new sources of credit opened to medium and small Latin American businessmen, and foreign investment encouraged." The report goes on to equate capitalism with freedom and democracy, socialism with totalitarianism and anarchy: "Latin America must be encouraged to see its essential choice between totalitarian, inefficient, state-controlled economies and society on the one hand and an economically and politically freer system on the other, realizing that a society must begin to accumulate wealth before it can provide an improved standard of living for its members."[47]

These emphases on private enterprise, foreign investment, and capital accumulation resemble markedly those contained in the articles of agreement of the World Bank.[48] Such similarity is to be expected because the bank and the foreign-aid programs of the United States were really cut from the same cloth. Nor is it mere coincidence that one of the nine members of the Clay Commission was Eugene Black, at the time president of the World Bank. Of significance also is the fact that two other commission members were trustees of the Rockefeller Foundation, while yet another was closely identified with the foreign-policy and - aid establishment and the foundations supporting them through his contacts with the Council on Foreign Relations, the foundation- and government-sponsored Development Advisory Service at Harvard (about which more in Chapter 3), and other influential foreign-policy groups, including the Central Intelligence Agency.[49]

The Basis for the Foundations' Overseas Programs after 1945

The rising tensions of the cold war led foundation personnel to consider the relationship of their overseas activities to American foreign-policy objectives. In a 1948 interoffice memorandum, Bryce Wood of the Rockefeller foundation noted how the Soviets were making great advances because of their "possession of a successful scheme for development." He lamented that the Western nations, particularly the United States, had "not worked out any counter plan beyond a 'finger in the dike' technique," and went on to suggest the establishment by the foundation of a study center to formulate developmental plans for the nations of Africa, Asia, and Latin America.[50] His colleague Philip Mosely wrote early the next year of his hope that the current United States "concentration upon European needs would be followed by a broader program of developing the resources, material and human, of the underdeveloped areas," activities in which institutions like the Rockefeller Foundation could make an important contribution.[51]

Ford Foundation discussions about its overseas work at this time also bore an unmistakable cold-war imprint. An important 1952 policy document indicated that the foundation had decided to concentrate its overseas programs initially in the Near East and Asia because these areas "consist of many newly emergent nations precariously situated along the periphery of the Soviet-Communist orbit." The failure of democracy in these areas would mean "that world Communism would be immeasurably . . . strengthened and the danger of a third world war sharply increased." The role to be played by the foundation in the furtherance of United States foreign-policy objectives was clearly noted in the report. If India "goes the way of China, the whole of Asia will be split in two and perhaps lost irrevocably to the free world." This would be "a disaster of catastrophic proportions." To help avert such a disaster, Ford decided "to help develop the potential leadership of India and Pakistan,"[52] in hopes that these men would then tilt toward the West, thereby contributing to regional stability.

The author of this document was Carl Spaeth, who before World War II had worked for the Rockefeller family's Creole Petroleum Oil Company in Venezuela and had acted as assistant to Assistant Secretary of State Nelson Rockefeller during the war. He understood that United States interests in the developing nations were threatened by more than the Soviet Union. "[E]ven in the absence or relaxation of a Soviet threat," he wrote, "these newly independent nations would be confronted with the possibility of economic and political collapse that . . . could endanger the peace of the free world." This in turn could lead to "the feeling of common cause against the West [and] if converted into agressive force, might at a future time produce a unified and hostile Asian-Near East bloc."[53] Ford programs were designed to lessen this possibility.

Ford Foundation's John Howard amplified on the impetus that the cold war gave the foundation's programs when reflecting several years ago on their origins. He recalled that foundation president "Paul Hoffman decided . . . early [on] that he wanted to develop the International program in the Foundation and he had chosen India as [a] sort of . . . keystone of that overseas activity." India "and in general South and Southeast Asia" were chosen because the area was "the underbelly of China. It was more [of] the Cold War philosophy." India was an attractive field for Ford activity because it was "a leading democracy" but it was "more attractive because it was next . . . to China and China wasn't going down the democratic path and India was."[54] Howard, who had worked on the Lend Lease program during the war and the Marshall Plan and the Mutual Security Assistance Program afterwards, was centrally involved in the Ford Foundation's overseas programs for a decade and a half.

Ford personnel evolved their programs after consultations with those officially responsible for foreign-policy formulation and implementation. Ford director of research Cleon Swayzee wrote in 1953 how he had "discussed our plans with the appropriate agencies in Washington." He could report that everyone there was enthusiastic and "all have offered to assist in every appropriate way, but felt, as we do, that care should be taken to avoid any government identification with these projects."[55] At a meeting several months later of the newly organized Board of Training and Research, Swayzee amplified on Ford's relationship to American foreign-policy objectives. The 15 September 1953 meeting was chaired by Gordon Gray, whose presidentially appointed commission of 1950 had written the *Report to the President on Foreign Economic Policies*. The minutes of that meeting record that "Mr. Gray inquired as to whether our concern was the training of persons to advance United States foreign policy, or what was our basic starting point. Mr. Swayzee indicated that the training was to advance, either directly or indirectly, United States interests abroad."[56]

Carnegie Corporation officials were also contemplating the extension of their overseas programs during this period, and their reasons for doing so were similar to those motivating their Ford and Rockefeller counterparts. Restricted by its charter to work in former British territories, the corporation during the 1950s decided to undertake major initiatives in English-speaking Africa. Alan Pifer explained the basis for the corporation's increased attention to Africa in a 1957 background paper for a Carnegie-sponsored conference. He cited the importance of the three questions of economic development, political development, and race relations as the United States confronted the reality of African independence. There was

> nothing new about any of these [areas of concern]. . . . What is new is that the great revolution of our times, the rise of the colored peoples (in which Asians have taken the lead) has now for the first time made the African peoples important in the struggle between Communism and democracy. This and the growing need for Africa's mineral and other natural resources would seem to account for America's awakening interest. It is why Africa . . . is today being "discovered" by Americans.[57]

The same theme was sounded two years later in a letter from American Council on Education president Arthur Adams to Carnegie Corporation president John Gardner. The issue prompting this communication was the council desire to control a Carnegie-funded organization (the Africa Liaison Committee) that wanted to coordinate the increasing American university activity in Africa. Of more importance were the reasons cited by the council president for American interest in Africa. One of these was that "the present all-out world struggle between communism and democracy surely will soon have Africa as one of its major areas. The nearly two hundred million people in the African countries are a major prize, to say nothing of the as yet untapped and largely unknown mineral resources they may possess." It is important, he concluded, that "Africans in the rank and file may understand the difference between Communism and democracy," and an increase in our program activity there will help to accomplish this.[58] Shortly after receiving this letter, the Carnegie Corporation agreed to the council request that the Africa Liaison Committee be formally associated with it.

By the mid-1950s, then, representatives of the Carnegie, Ford, and Rockefeller foundations had decided to increase their overseas commitments. The overarching reason for this common decision was, as John D. Rockefeller III wrote to Rockefeller Foundation president Dean Rusk in 1954, so that "the interests of our country would be served."[59] Carnegie's Alan Pifer said essentially the same thing in 1957, declaring that "one cannot help escape [sic] the conclusion that the basis for our concern with Africa in the future is going to be self-interest."[60] Ford Foundation vice-president Donald Price recognized in 1956 that "appropriate activities supported by a private American foundation could contribute to African confidence in the United States and the free world."[61] One way in which the foundations could contribute to American foreign-policy objectives was, as Price had written to Carnegie president Gardner in 1954, by having Ford-supported researchers "put such knowledge [of world affairs] more effectively at the disposal of those who are responsible, in government and private life, for representing the United States in international affairs."[62]

The major concerns tht the foundations' international programs should address were succinctly summarized in the following statement published in the Rockefeller Foundation *Annual Report* of 1956.

The officers and trustees of the Rockefeller Foundation are deeply impressed with the thought that the prospects for peace and orderly economic growth throughout the world during the next quarter-century can be decisively affected by what happens in the independent nations of Africa, the Near East, and Asia. If they succeed in establishing constitutional systems with friendly and easy exchange with the rest of the world, increasingly productive economies to supply their needs at rising levels and to play an active role in world trade, and educational systems which can train their leadership in adequate numbers, then peace and stability will have gained tremendous support.[63]

Rockefeller's Charles Fahs elaborated on this statement five years later with some specifics on how the foundation's programs could support United States foreign-policy objectives. In a memorandum to foundation president George Harrar (former president Dean Rusk having just gone to Washington to become Secretary of State), he noted that "foreign policy is the promotion of our national interests abroad and aid is an integral part of foreign policy administration. . . . [T]here is no advantage in trying to separate aid policy from the rest of foreign policy. . . . The trouble is not that aid has been used for political purposes, but that it has been ineffective in achieving them." All of the agencies involved in foreign-aid administration need to understand that "competition with the Soviet Union is a game that has to be played on all the squares of the board and with a mixed and highly flexible strategy." The United States has the advantage of having available both public and private aid agencies to further its policies. "We cannot solve all the problems of education, health, food, and economics in even a few countries, but if we stick closer to our political goals we have a good chance of surviving this difficult period successfully."[64]

The Direction of the Foundations' Overseas Programs

These general policy statements were soon followed by specific proposals designed to expand the foundations' overseas activities primarily in two directions. The first of these involved the establishment of agricultural research and experimentation centers in Mexico, the Philippines, India, and Nigeria. It was at these centers that the major breakthroughs occurred in the development of hybrid seeds, thereby enabling the indigenous populations to achieve dramatic increases in their agricultural yields. This "Green Revolution" received its impetus and initial support from the Rockefeller Foundation, although the Ford Foundation later contributed significantly to its furtherance.[65] The second program thrust involved foundation support for the expansion of the education sector in selected African, Asian, and Latin American nations, with particular attention given to the extension and strengthening of post secondary institutions.

In their university initiatives in these nations the Carnegie, Ford, and Rockefeller foundations worked closely with representatives from the local universities and education ministries, the United States Agency for International Development, and the World Bank. Indeed, it was frequently the case that AID and the bank became interested in a particular university after one of the foundations indicated its intentions to develop programs there. While minor disagreements among representatives of these organizations were not unusual, the relationships were on the whole generally constructive, if not always cordial. An important reason for this professional cooperation was the general agreement among these agencies concerning the importance of strengthening the developing nations' universities along predetermined lines. A representative of AID acknowledged his organization's primary objective in supporting university development in a way that foundation personnel could second. The agency made its commitment to university development overseas because of the conviction that "the character of leadership in the emerging states was to be a prime factor in success or failure. Our ability to deal intelligently with this leadership, and its capacity to lead, were obviously indispensable to the attainment of stable development."[66]

Rockefeller Foundation personnel were equally concerned about the quality of leadership in the emerging states. As early as 1949 a Rockefeller officer had suggested focusing on a few universities in the hope that these would train local leaders and would act as regional training centers. "We might get more for our money," wrote L. C. DeVinney, "if we would pick one or two or three places that look pretty strong compared with the others, and focus our money to build up some of these."[67] The foundation's 1955 decision to appropriate five million dollars annually for five years to expand its University Development Program recognized the importance of the indigenous leaders of Africa, Asia, and Latin America for stability and orderly growth. Foundation president Rusk, in a 1955 memorandum explaining the program to the trustees, wrote that the "primary emphasis of the expanded program would be upon training and providing expert guidance and advice for the use of indigenous resources."[68]

The 1956 Rockefeller Foundation *Annual Report* elaborated on this objective, noting that foundation "funds can be of great significance if applied at the point where the Foundation believes that it can make the best contribution, namely, in the training of professional leadership." To accomplish this, "support is being provided to key institutions in key countries to assist in more advanced training within the local scene [*sic*]." The foundation's officers identified two ways in which this training could be provided. On the one hand, "scholarships and other forms of study grants are being provided in considerable numbers," while on the other "the Foundation's own staff is used to give direct assistance to the organization of advanced training centers."[69]

Ford Foundation personnel displayed a similar interest in strengthening the capacity of a selected few African, Asian, and Latin American universities. Their efforts in Nigeria, Colombia, Thailand, Ethiopia— to name only several—are particularly noteworthy and represented attempts, as a Ford vice-president put it, to link "the modernizing elites of the world."[70] At the same time, Ford was instrumental in the creation of institutions only tangentially linked to a university, but whose purpose was also the training of national leaders. One of these, to be examined more carefully in Chapter 3, was the National School of Law and Administration in the Congo, which opened in 1961.

Another important Ford concern involved the training made available to American scholars to enable them to better understand the complexities of these new national polities with which the United States would have to deal. Ford officials assumed that the knowledge gained by these scholars would be shared with those officially responsible for United States foreign policy. The rationale for this and the other foundation programs designed to further American scholars' understanding of the nations of Africa, Asia, and Latin America will be examined in Chapter 4 and need not detain us at this juncture. However, brief mention should be made of an episode that illustrates how Ford officials felt that their training programs for American scholars could further United States interests abroad.

Ford's John Howard recalled the concern among his colleagues upon discovering that agents from the Central Intelligence Agency regularly solicited information from Ford-supported field researchers working in Third-World nations. Foundation president Rowan Gaither, in particular, felt that this policy was shortsighted. Consequently, according to Howard, he "went down to Washington and raised hell" with the CIA people, who "promised to behave themselves [and] not to do this." Memories around the agency were short, apparently, because the problem soon resurfaced. This time foundation president Henry Heald "went down [to Washington] and he [too] raised hell." Director of Research Cleon Swayzee was dispatched to CIA headquarters to reinforce Ford's position and to show as well how another tack could better serve the nation's foreign policy interests. "Swayzee went down . . . and just said, 'Jesus Christ! If the cover blows on any one of these things everything we're doing will be jeopardized.'" And in a calmer vein: "[t]he more specific function we had was to tell them to lay off the fellows . . . the whole notion that we tried to impress on the CIA was that . . . it was much more in the national interest that we train a bunch of people who at a later time might want to go into the CIA . . . than it was for them to have one guy they could call their source of information."[71]

Carnegie officials also focused on educational institutions when they reconceptualized the corporation's overseas programs after World War II. They too were concerned to train foreign area specialists whose knowledge would serve American foreign-policy objectives. Their grants for this purpose commenced in 1947, and by 1952 the trustees had appropriated $2,500,000 to enable thirteen universities to upgrade their capabilities in European, Japanese, Near Eastern, and Southeast Asian studies.[72]

Carnegie sponsored a number of "reconnaissance" trips to Africa between 1947 and 1952 in an effort, according to a corporation historian, "to assess conditions and needs and make recommendations regarding possible Corporation projects there."[73] Alan Pifer joined the Carnegie staff in 1953 and the longstanding corporation interest in educational affairs became more pronounced, particularly in the developing nations of Africa. Five years later Carnegie supported a conference examining the relationships between the United States and Africa, and the conference report, written largely by Pifer, indicates the direction that Carnegie programs would take in future. "For the development of Africa in every field," concluded the Final Report of the 13th American Assembly, "literacy and schooling are critical. American aid should give priority to strengthening African technical and higher education and the training of African teachers. . . . We not only recognize the need for education of Africans, but also for education of Americans about Africa."[74]

Support for African studies programs was only one way for Carnegie to increase Americans' knowledge about Africa. Another involved Carnegie grants that enabled influential Americans to travel to Africa to assess at first hand the importance of that continent for the United States. To this end the corporation granted $45,000 to the Council on Foreign Relations in 1957 to support the African travel of individuals designated by the council. Among those who traveled to Africa at Carnegie expense between 1959 and 1961 were David Rockefeller of the Chase Manhattan Bank; Thomas Finletter, Secretary of the Air Force in the Truman administration; and Paul Nitze, an investment banker who in 1962 became assistant secretary of defense for international security affairs. Others who undertook these "fact-finding" missions were William A. Burden, who in 1961 became United States ambassador to Belgium; Max Milliken, former deputy director of the CIA and head of the foundation-supported Center for International Affairs at the Massachusetts Institute of Technology; and Charles Spofford, who became counsel to the government of Ghana in connection with the massive Volta River dam project, whose major contractor was the Aluminum Company of America.[75]

Foundation Programs and Foreign-Policy Determination

The architects of American foreign policy since 1945 have moved between Washington policy-making centers and New York foundation suites with a high degree of regularity. Most have also doubled as heads of major corporations or financial institutions or as prominent corporate lawyers. The Rockefeller Foundation alone has seen three of its top officials become secretaries of state since 1952: John Foster Dulles resigned as chairman of the Rockefeller trustees in 1953 to move to Washington, setting a precedent for Cyrus Vance, who did likewise in

1977. In 1961 Rockefeller Foundation president Dean Rusk resigned his position to become John F. Kennedy's chief foreign-policy architect. Ford Foundation personnel also have been closely identified with the United States foreign-policy establishment, although no secretaries of state are numbered among its alumni. Trustees or officers of the Ford Foundation who have figured prominently in American foreign policy since 1945 include Paul Hoffman, one-time president of the Studebaker Corporation and director of the Marshall Plan and of the first United States aid agency; John J. McCloy, assistant secretary of war, first high commissioner to Germany after World War II, president of the World Bank, chairman of the Rockefeller family's Chase Manhattan Bank, and a trustee of the Rockefeller Foundation; McGeorge Bundy, scion of a famous Boston family, dean of Harvard College, and national security advisor to President Kennedy and, briefly, to President Lyndon Johnson; Robert S. McNamara, one-time president of the Ford Motor Company, secretary of defense under presidents Kennedy and Johnson, and president of the World Bank.

There is no reason to think that the perceptions held by these men of the role of the United States in world affairs altered perceptibly as they moved from New York-based foundations and/or corporate offices to Washington policy-making positions. Furthermore, there is evidence to indicate that their collective view of United States foreign policy (which did certainly allow for minor differences or emphases) since 1945 envisioned a stable world, policed by United States military force, in which American corporate and financial enterprise played an expanding role. The consensus among corporate and financial leaders and Washington foreign-policy planners held that the health of the domestic economy necessitated access to overseas markets and sources of raw materials for the continued expansion of the domestic economy, that the economies of Western Europe urgently needed reconstruction, and that the nations of the Third World should be more tightly integrated into the American-dominated economic structure.

To achieve these goals the United States launched the Marshall Plan for the reconstruction of the economies of Western Europe, undertook a foreign-aid program designed to help the economies of the emerging nations develop along lines compatible with capitalist interests, supported several multinational institutions (e.g., the World Bank) designed for the same purpose, and began increasingly to support national leaders in the developing world who were supportive of American economic and strategic interests in their territories. When the trade-aid-persuasion-support policies of the United States failed to perpetuate the favorable relationship between the United States and a developing nation, military intervention was undertaken to win by force that which could not be gained by more peaceful means. Successful examples of this included interventions in Iran, the Dominican Republic, Guyana, and the Lebanon, while less successful undertakings included those in Cuba and Vietnam. Such interventions were generally undertaken with reluctance, however, since the use of force signaled the failure of the more subtle diplomatic approach to foreign-policy execution.[76]

The attempts to encourage and if necessary to force the developing nations to follow policies beneficial to American interests did not necessarily mean that those who designed such policies were hostile to or even neglectful of the aspirations of the developing nations. On the contrary, it can be argued that the architects of the policy of capitalist expansion into the developing nations believed that such a course would enhance the well-being of the peoples there. There was agreement among these men that capitalism was the best means of producing rapid economic growth, a desideratum in its own right. In capitalism's wake came a host of other good things—so the conventional wisdom of the day had it—including, above all, representative democracy and individual freedom.[77]

From the perspective of the foreign-policy elite, then, the expansion of capitalism into the underdeveloped regions produced two positive results: (1) it was good for American enterprise, which benefited from expanded markets, which in turn contributed to the continuing prosperity of the United States; and (2) it offered the greatest hope for rapid economic growth and its ancillary political and social benefits in the developing lands. These positive aspects of capitalist expansion were, from the policy architects' viewpoint, even more obvious when compared to the distinctly negative qualities of state socialism. They believed that the most altruistic thing that American foreign policy could accomplish was to introduce the developing nations to the beneficient effects of liberal capitalist development, while at the same time discouraging their flirtation with the soul-destroying system of state socialism.[78]

The importance of the foundations as recruiting grounds for the foreign policy establishment, whether in Democratic or Republican administrations, has led Halberstam to characterize them as "the shadow-cabinet world."[79] Given this close association between the foundations and the foreign-policy decision makers, it should not be surprising that the foundations' overseas programs were coordinated with the evolving United States foreign policy.

At the same time that the foreign policy architects were forging the consensus around the policy of imperial liberalism,[80] the trustees of the Carnegie, Ford, and Rockefeller foundations were agreeing to the considerable expansion of their programs into the developing nations. They did so, in the words of then-Rockefeller Foundation president Dean Rusk, because of their belief that such programs would help to sustain the "orderliness of economic growth," an objective "that engages directly the self-interest of the economically more advanced peoples and calls for their understanding and assistance."[81] This was the same Dean Rusk who, as assistant secretary of state for Far Eastern affairs in the early 1950s, argued in favor of the United States policy of containment of the Soviet Union and China and who, as Secretary of State a decade later, played a central role in this country's policy in Indo-China. The movement of America's decision makers like Rusk between the government agencies, the corporate and financial centers, and the major foundations helps to explain how the ideology of the one was so often shared by the others.

By the 1950s there was broad agreement among these men regarding the appropriate shape of the world and an understanding that they would utilize the institutions they controlled to further agreed-upon ends. The distinction between public and private agencies or profit and nonprofit institutions soon blurred, as all were enrolled to play their parts in American foreign policy. There was agreement that the foundations had an important role to play in the furtherance of American destiny both at home and abroad. The community of interests linking the foundations to the implementation of United States foreign policy was indicated by the Ford Foundation director of research, who commented that the purpose of Ford's programs in Africa, Asia, and Latin America was "to advance, either directly or indirectly, U.S. interests abroad."[82]

The identification of several individuals linking the foundations, influential policy-formulating organizations like the Council on Foreign Relations, and official policy agencies is not meant to suggest the absence of conflict over major issues within these institutions or among these people. The ruling class is not united on all matters. Disagreement is frequent and occasionally intense, if indeed not rancorous. For example, United States foreign-policy formulation after 1945 regularly has been marked by disagreements between those favoring a policy of free trade and those insisting on the protection of domestic markets through the use of restrictive tariffs. The debates between the internationalists and the isolationists form a staple of introductory analysis of foreign-policy conduct, while the struggle between those advocating a hard line toward the Soviet Union and those of a more accommodationist disposition has been the subject of several recent scholarly studies.[83] Such conflict over policy matters frequently is resolved by compromise, and it is not unreasonable to suggest that these compromises sometimes result in contradictory policies. Similar situations and similar outcomes can also be seen within the foundations.

These debates and resultant contradictions must be kept in perspective, however. The decision-making stratum within the United States foreign-policy establishment historically has come from upper-class backgrounds. The same is true of the major foundations. Those recruits not from upper-class backgrounds are subjected to powerful socialization processes, both through their university training and particularly through their work experiences. However much debate takes place over foreign-policy issues and particulars of foundation programs, it is doubtful if this debate seriously questions the underlying principles of American foreign policy or the system of state capitalism that this policy attempts to further. To put this another way: it is probable that, internal wrangling notwithstanding, the shared fundamental interests of foundation personnel and foreign-policy architects insures that the programs of the foundations are supportive of the long-range objectives of the foreign-policy establishment. This establishment has, since 1945, followed a policy that assures continued American access to overseas markets and sources of raw materials in independent nations characterized by stability and predictability.

The necessity for the United States to follow such a course has not lessened in recent years, and has been noted by numerous commentators. The worldwide recession of the 1970s, sparked by the 1973 war between Israel and her Arab neighbors, made these overseas markets and mineral resources even more important, according to Mary Kaldor.[84] Barraclough amplifies on this, noting that "the rich countries need the poor countries, or at least their markets and resources, quite as much as the poor countries need the rich."[85]

Foundation officers have always recognized the importance of these markets and mineral resources for the continued health of the United States and the world capitalist economy, and, as the next chapter shows, they designed their overseas programs with this in mind. The cornerstone of these overseas activities was the development of educational institutions, particularly universities, in those areas that foreign-policy architects determined to be of strategic economic and geopolitical importance to the United States.

3

The Implementation of Foundation Programs in the Third World

By the 1950s general agreement had been reached among foundation officials, business leaders, and Washington policy makers regarding the importance of the developing world for the United States. There was also emerging at this time a consensus in the United States regarding the path that development in the nations of Africa, Asia, and Latin America should follow. The foundation-encouraged developmental model that soon became incorporated into the conventional wisdom placed heavy emphasis on sustained economic growth, augmented by substantial transfers of Western capital and advanced technologies. This view was summed up succinctly in W. W. Rostow's popular *The Stages of Economic Growth: A Non-Communist Manifesto*, published in 1960. Rostow wrote this book during a "reflective year" away from his academic responsibilities, made possible by a grant from the Carnegie Corporation.[1]

An important aspect of this developmental model emphasized the role of the leadership cadres in the new nations. It was to this group that United States developmental theorists and policy makers looked for the qualities that would help them to transform agrarian, peasant societies into minireplicas of Western, consumer-oriented, modernized states. The fellowship programs of the foundations and the official aid agencies were intended to provide educational opportunities for these Third-World leaders to study at carefully-selected American (and occasionally European) universities, where they would develop these qualities. The foundation-sponsored developmental literature of the period and the foundations' field projects clearly reflect the crucial role that fell to this new Third-World elite.

In this chapter we shall examine foundation support for a limited number of universities and affiliated institutes in strategically located Third-World nations. Foundation personnel were in general agreement that nation building in Africa, Asia, and Latin America required, in the words of Rockefeller Foundation vice-president Kenneth Thompson,

67

"indigenous institutions . . . to prepare the missing leaders."[2] The Rockefeller Foundation's success in strengthening a number of American institutions to prepare the domestic society's future leaders, coupled with its establishment of several international agricultural institutes after World War II, suggested to Foundation personnel the viability of similar undertakings in Third-World nations. Carnegie and Ford officers concurred in this assessment.

The foundations concentrated on particular program areas within these lead institutions in Africa, Asia, and Latin America. A major emphasis was in the development of the social sciences. The Ford and Rockefeller foundations shared the work in developing the social science competencies of selected Third-World students. There was particular concern with training in economics, especially as it related to human-resource theory. This approach was emphasized in two ways: (1) departments of economics and affiliated research institutes were staffed in their formative periods by foundation-selected North American academics convinced of the importance of this theory for developing nations; and (2) the most promising of the foreign nationals were awarded foundation fellowships enabling them to travel to selected American universities for advanced training in economics. The fellowship provisions made available to foreign nationals were an integral component of the institution-building model developed by the foundations, as this chapter will indicate.

The Ford Foundation's interest in the field of public administration in the United States was paralleled by its work overseas. This concern generally took two forms, (1) foundation personnel were involved in strengthening the administrative infrastructures of the lead universities that they supported in Third-World nations; and (2) schools or departments of public administration, sometimes within university settings and sometimes not, were established and guided through their formative periods. The National School of Law and Administration in the Congo, which opened with some two hundred students in 1961, is representative of the latter approach.

The work of the Carnegie Corporation was particularly noteworthy in the field of teacher education, although other foundations, particularly Ford, did make a contribution in this area. The corporation set out in the late 1950s to establish links with most of the post secondary teacher-training institutions in English-speaking Africa. This was accomplished by seconding professors from American and British universities to African teacher-training institutions. There they worked with local counterparts to construct curricula, to improve teaching methods, to search for more efficient ways of supervising student teachers, and to rationalize the relationships among teacher training, rapidly expanding school populations, and the requirements of developing economies increasingly responsive to the dictates of manpower planning schema. At the same time, the corporation provided fellowships to enable promising African teacher-educators and administrators to study at certain American universities.

Foundation personnel envisioned that those institutions receiving their support would in turn provide assistance to less-favored Third-World universities. Rockefeller's Kenneth Thompson wrote of the responsibility of "first generation university development centers helping second-generation centers."[3] That is, once a foundation-supported Third-World university, say X, reached a level of development determined by foundation representatives, it was expected that X would stand in a similar relationship to another university as that which had previously characterized the relationship between the several foundations and university X. Arnove has commented on this "networking" principle and notes how it enables the foundations' influence to transcend institutional and even national boundaries.[4] Such institutional networking allows the foundations' direct presence to be reduced, thereby lessening the likelihood that disgruntled local nationalists can sustain the charge that the foundations are purveyors of cultural imperialism.

This "networking" principle also enables the foundations' ideology to move rather freely within, say, Latin America and to give the appearance of having a life of its own, of having evolved in response to local needs. While the foundations' ideology circulates around Latin American intellectual centers, foundation officers return to New York and observe their work being carried out by a surrogate Latin American institution. The chapter concludes by mentioning several examples of this "networking" principle in action.

Support for Lead Universities in Developing Nations

The decisions by the Carnegie, Ford, and Rockefeller foundations to concentrate their funds and energies on a limited number of institutions in Africa, Asia, and Latin America was not haphazard. The Rockefeller Foundation's L. C. DeVinney suggested to his colleagues as early as 1949 that "we [the Foundation] might get more for our money in the long run if we would pick one or two or three places that look pretty strong compared to the others, and focus our money to build up some of these."[5] The next year Charles B. Fahs reminded fellow Rockefeller officers that now Americans were "committed to putting into effect programs to make the world healthy, prosperous and free." The foundation's major contribution to these objectives should be in training personnel in the underdeveloped countries who can "help their own peoples to understand the changes through which they are going and which lie ahead."[6]

After extended discussions during the early 1950s, the officers of the Rockefeller Foundation reached agreement on the importance of increased support for their program activity in the developing world. In his official request to the trustees in 1955, foundation president Dean Rusk wrote that the "well-being of mankind" depended on the ability of the newly independent nations "to erect a structure of government and public order under which peaceful development may proceed; whether public office can become a public trust separate from private interest; . . . whether they will be 'open societies', in the humanistic tradition of the West, or closed by dogma or ideology." The laudable objectives were jeopardized, however, by the reality that these nations "lack the capital, trained leadership, educated people, political stability, and an understanding of how change is to be digested and used by their own cultures." These problems could be largely overcome if trained leadership became available, and it was to just this end that the foundation could contribute. Consequently, "the primary emphasis of the [recommended] program would be upon training and providing expert guidance and advice for the use of indigenous resources. A substantial increase in fellowship and grant-in-aid funds would be needed."[7]

The trustees responded to this appeal by voting to appropriate five million dollars annually for five years. The foundation's 1956 annual report noted that this money would focus on "the training of professional leadership." To accomplish this, "support is being provided to key institutions in key countries to assist in more advanced training within the local scene [sic]. Scholarships, and others forms of study grants are being provided in considerable number"[8]

Rockefeller officers next turned to the implementation of their expanded program and found broad areas of agreement, particularly around the importance of concentrating on a few universities. Early in 1956 Norman S. Buchanan argued for focusing attention on specific program areas within the selected Third-World universities and upgrading these in hopes that the higher quality might "rub off" on other parts of the university. Such an approach would mean that "far more attention [than in earlier university work] would have to be given to university organization, university administration, and perhaps even university finances and management of resources." He had few doubts regarding the difficulty of such an approach, nor any about its potential importance: "If Rockefeller Foundation could do this, the consequences for human well-being would be exceedingly large."[9]

Another Rockefeller officer argued for developing "a model institution incorporating all our interests," including the social sciences and humanities, agriculture, and the natural and medical sciences. He recognized that the foundation would have to provide personnel "to develop key departments and training programs," but felt that this was what the organization did best, a sentiment shared by his colleagues. While "money for buildings, scientific equipment and so on" was important in the process of institution building, this should be left to other donor agencies. The Rockefeller Foundation should continue to emphasize the development of human resources because it had long experience in doing so and, as Morison concluded, "if we invest more in staff and brains, our dollars will therefore be able to exert an extraordinary leverage."[10]

It took several years of discussion before Rockefeller officers worked out the details of their training programs for indigenous leaders. Vice-president Kenneth Thompson, who headed the university development activities, wrote to the social science staff late in 1960 of his belief "that the issue of developing a few first class universities in the non-western areas will be at the heart of our discussions over the next several years."[11] The foundation's *Annual Report*, published several months later, provided a clearer indication of an evolving program focus. "The great majority of future leaders, investigators, and teachers in any country must necessarily receive their basic training at national universities," the document noted. "Private foundations operating overseas have a unique opportunity to help create patterns by which the limited numbers of highly trained individuals in Less Developed Countries can most effectively contribute to research and to the training of younger people."[12] Late in 1961 foundation president Harrar drafted a memorandum in which he summarized for the trustees the officers' sentiments about Rockefeller's role in the developing nations. There were no surprises. The foundation should support "a few selected universities" because these tend "to be the principal training ground for the individuals who provide leadership in government, business, industry, education, the professions, and humanities."

Harrar went on to express the long-standing foundation principle that its greatest influence on the direction of a given society could be exercised through the training provided to carefully selected future leaders. In this document he asked the trustees to authorize the expenditure of an amount not to exceed $100 million for this work over a ten- to fifteen-year period, with the understanding that monies allocated in 1955 would be subsumed within this amount and be designated for this University Development Program.[13] The trustees, according to vice-president Thompson, "accepted the proposal without blinking."[14]

More internal discussion led to the decision to support five university development centers: the University of Valle in Colombia; the University of East Africa, a regional arrangement involving the national universities of Uganda, Kenya, and Tanzania; the University of Ibadan in Nigeria; University of the Philippines; and a consortium of three Thai universities centered in and around Bangkok—Kasetsart University, Mahidol University, Thammasat University. All of these institutions had received considerable Rockefeller attention since the 1955 foundation decision to extend its work in certain developing nations.

Ford Foundation officers at this time also demonstrated their belief in the importance of education for the controlled development of the nations of Africa, Asia, and Latin America. The foundation, which began its programs in earnest only in the early 1950s, lacked the deliberative and planning mechanisms that characterized the Rockefeller approach. As a result, the foundation's approach to university development was considerably more eclectic and less comprehensive, especially in the early phases, than that of the Rockefeller Foundation. Ford personnel, however, shared the Rockefeller belief in the importance of strong educational institutions to train society's leaders, a belief which shortly was translated into programs both at home and abroad.

Ford representatives traveled widely during the 1950s in search of locales to initiate their programs still in the formulative stage. In 1956, for example, Ford officers John Howard and Melvin Fox accompanied Boston University professor and former State Department official William O. Brown on a "fact-finding" mission to West Africa. This was followed two years later by a second team with a similar purpose.[15] These and comparable missions by Ford representatives to Asia and Latin America led to the conclusion that the foundation could make the greatest impact on Third-World development by supporting educatinal activities in a limited number of post secondary institutions located in areas of geostrategic importance to the United States.

The decision by the Ford Foundation to concentrate its African programs—to use one regional example—on the training of elite cadres in public administration, agricultural economics, the applied sciences, and the social sciences, and to strengthen African universities and other postsecondary institutions for this purpose, was a logical extension of similar emphases in the foundation's domestic work. The foundation's concern for nurturing an academic elite, which would play the leadership role in the domestic polity, found its best expression in the work of the Ford-created and supported Fund for the Advancement of Education.

Ford and fund officials felt that they could nurture, through training offered in elite American universities, a group of potential leaders whose outlook and values would insure their support of the dominant American social, economic, and political institutions. These Ford-nurtured leaders, Bundy's "learned men," would then assume their places as executives of major American institutions, where they would continue to uphold the interests of society's dominant classes. The assumption was that those trained in a particular way at specific institutions were best suited to run the key institutions of American society. Ford thinking held that this approach was technocratic, nonideological, and only designed to assure that society's future leaders received the most appropriate training for the difficult tasks before them.[16] From Ford's perspective there seemed little reason to doubt the efficacy of exporting a similar theory and modus operandi to developing nations.

Ford's international activities during the 1950s evolved along two complementary lines. On the one hand, the foundation sought to create, in the words of foundation vice-president Don Price, "an adequate corps of academic and professional experts" with "knowledge of the languages, cultures, and political and economic development of Asia, Africa, and Eastern Europe." Such people were considered indispensable in helping "to provide the educational foundation for our new national interests in these areas,"[17] to which Latin America would soon be added. We shall examine in Chapter 4 how the Carnegie, Ford, and Rockefeller foundations set about to create this "corps of academic and professional experts" at home.

At the same time, Ford officers were identifying key African, Asian, and Latin American institutions for foundation support. The decision to underwrite the development of particular universities or postsecondary institutions grew out of the numerous "fact-finding" missions undertaken by Ford representatives after 1955. Although Ford lacked the Rockefeller experience in institution building, particularly overseas, the decisions reached by the two organizations regarding this work were remarkably similar.

Foundation personnel identified existing Third-World institutions which, according to their criteria, possessed trusted and politically astute indigeneous leaders, a minimal number of qualified professionals in key departments, an assured level of governmental support, the rudiments of an administrative infrastructure, and a general institutional willingness to adhere to broad policy guidelines laid down by the donor organizations. Personnel in the foundations' New York offices assumed responsibility for the overall planning and implementation of policies designed to bring the universities to predetermined levels. The Ford and Rockefeller foundations supported field offices to coordinate activities on a daily basis. Personnel were seconded or recruited from New York and attached to these offices while they worked on an intimate basis with their indigeneous counterparts, be these in the academic or in the administrative spheres. Frequently, these foundation personnel spent periods ranging from one to three years as members, or more frequently as heads, of academic departments, as deans, and as heads of or advisors to key administrative units within the universities. The logistical complications attendant upon the organization of these sizable ventures necessitated the frequent movement of personnel between the lead universities and the foundations' New York offices. When the overseas university heads arrived in New York for periodic consultations, foundation officers arranged for them to meet with representatives of other aid agencies, e.g., the World Bank or the Agency for International Development.

Carnegie Corporation personnel shared the Ford and Rockefeller belief in the importance of educating the future leaders of Africa, Asia, and Latin America both through the provision of fellowships and the strengthening of local universities. The charter provisions that limited the corporation's work to former British possessions led Carnegie officers to further concentrate on particular African nations. This requirement that its work be sharply focused enabled the corporation to concentrate its programs to maximum advantage. For example, by 1969 the corporation had provided some form of support, according to Murphy, for a significant proportion, "well over half," of the prominent educators in Anglophone Africa.[18]

Carnegie officials noted the importance of strengthening certain African lead institutions as early as 1954. In a wide-ranging document circulated around the corporation office in that year, Alan Pifer laid out the general principles governing the British Dominions and Colonies Program, from which African work was funded. Throughout this document Pifer underscored the importance of support for such institutions as the Rhodes-Livingston Institute in Rhodesia, Uganda's Makerere College and affiliated East African Institute for Social Research, Kenya's Royal Technical College, University College Ibadan in Nigeria and its affiliated West African Institute of Social and Economic Research, and the University College of the Gold Coast. Another marked emphasis throughout this document was the repeated recommendation that the corporation support African studies in the United States.[19]

The concern with world stability and the need to incorporate peripheral areas into the American-dominated capitalist system led the foundations to concentrate their university programs in areas considered of strategic and economic importance to the United States government and American corporations with overseas investments. Foundation involvement in Africa illustrates this. The Ford Foundation's most significant postsecondary African educational undertakings were in Nigeria, Ethiopia, Congo/Zaire, and in a combined university scheme linking the East African nations of Kenya, Uganda, and Tanzania. Rockefeller funds were concentrated in the East African-interterritorial project, in Nigeria, and more recently in Zaire. The work of the Carnegie Corporation was most pronounced in Nigeria, in the University of East Africa, and to a lesser extent in Ghana, Sierra Leone, and the linked University of Botswana, Lesotho, and Swaziland. Two examples will illustrate the purposefulness of the foundations' decisions to strengthen certain lead universities.

Foundation Work in Nigeria

Carnegie, Ford, and Rockefeller personnel early recognized Nigeria's importance in terms of regional stability, political influence, and as an area for potential investment by American corporations. They regularly discussed their respective interests there.[20] The rapidly increasing commercial relationships between Nigeria and the United States suggest the degree of perspicacity in this assessment. Equally important at present, but not something that foundation personnel could have foreseen when making their initial commitments to Nigerian higher education, is the fact that Nigeria ranks second (or third, depending on which monthly figures are used) as a supplier of crude oil to the United States.

The foundations' assessment of the importance of Nigeria was matched by their expenditures there. Between 1958 and 1969 the Ford Foundation spent approximately $25 million in Nigeria, a figure representing almost two-thirds of its total West African expenditures during this period. Of this amount, almost $8 million went to underwrite university development and some $5 million of that was concentrated at the University of Ibadan. If we include in this total the $2.3 million designated for economic development planning (most of which was sponsored by the University of Ibadan) and the $3.9 million spent on training in public administration (most of which took place within a university setting), the total expenditure on university education in Nigeria by Ford was approximately $15 million, by far the most significant share of the total Nigerian expenditures.[21]

The Rockefeller Foundation allocated some $9 million to the University of Ibadan in the decade from 1963 to 1972 as part of its worldwide University Development Program.[22] The concentration of Rockefeller money at a few university centers in strategic locales around the world not only enabled the foundation to exert great leverage in the direction followed by these universities, but also helped the foundation, as a ranking Rockefeller official put it, to preempt "the most promising talent." This latter objective was important because the United States should attempt "to force [aid from the communist bloc countries] into relatively unproductive fields." This could be achieved by "preempting the most promising talent and the projects which have the highest marginal utility for us." The Rockefeller Foundation investment in university education, perhaps most marked at Ibadan by its fellowship provisions, was clearly considered to have high marginal utility.[23]

The total Carnegie expenditure in Nigeria between 1953 and 1973 was approximately $2.2 million, of which some $500,000 found its way directly to the University of Ibadan.[24] This relatively small amount allocated by Carnegie is at least partially a reflection of the corporation's smaller resource base compared to that of Ford and Rockefeller. The total amount of the Carnegie appropriation for its Nigerian work is less important, however, than the impact that such monies had on institutional decisions to concentrate on one program area while forsaking another. Money promised by Carnegie to create or support an institute of education at the University of Ibadan, to use one example, can be crucial in the internal university decision-making process regarding institutional priorities. It would be reasonable to assume that a university principal could be more easily persuaded to earmark internal university resources for an institute of education if he was assured of outside funding to cover, say, 50 percent of the total cost of this project. Another project lacking such outside funding guarantees—but no less important to the university or the furtherance of its mission—would have difficulty winning a comparable degree of support. To put the matter more bluntly: an outside funding agency such as Carnegie Corporation can exert great leverage in determining the priorities of recipient institutions, and this can be accomplished with relatively small grants.

These rough figures on foundation appropriations to the University of Ibadan do not include the approximately $19 million that the university received in the 1968-77 decade from Ford to support the International Institute of Tropical Agriculture. The initiative for and most of the early funding for the institute, as well as much of its subsequent support, came from the Ford and Rockefeller foundations.

Foundation Support for the University of East Africa

Carnegie, Ford, and Rockefeller personnel turned their attentions to the East African territories of Uganda, Kenya, and Tanzania in the early 1960s. In fact, Carnegie had demonstrated an interest in the work of the East African Institute of Social Research even earlier, an interest shared by the Ford Foundation.[25] In 1961 the Rockefeller Foundation made a small grant to enable four representatives of the proposed University of East Africa to travel to New York for consultations at the foundation and with officials of the International Cooperation Administration and the State Department as well.[26] The federated university for which they hoped to gain support was to be a union of Uganda's Makerere College (the oldest and most prestigious in East Africa), Kenya's Royal College, Nairobi, and Tanganyika's new University College at Dar es Salaam. The three foundations played a significant role in moving the University of East Africa from the planning stages to a functioning institution in 1963. The embryonic nature of the institution also meant that each of the foundations could focus on particular areas within the developing university.

In January 1963 a Rockefeller officer was approached about the possibility of the foundation hosting a conference to discuss the needs and directions of the University of East Africa, whose formal opening was only months away. The initiative was taken by Cornelis W. de Kiewiet, then president of the University of Rochester and head of the Carnegie-created Africa Liaison Committee, a coordinative body for American educational undertakings in Africa.[27] The Rockefeller Foundation agreed to host the conference in the late summer at its villa above Lake Como in northern Italy. De Kiewiet then took the lead in getting together representatives of the three foundations and the Agency for International Development to discuss their respective areas of interest in the new university, as well as to evolve a consensus on the approach to university development that they would present to representatives of the three East African governments and other potential donor agencies at the conference.[28]

The conference on the needs of the University of East Africa was convened, after several delays, in late October 1963 at Villa Serbelloni. Joining the representatives from the Carnegie, Ford, and Rockefeller foundations and the Africa Liaison Committee were representatives from the three East African governments and colleges, the British Department of Technical Cooperation and the Inter-University Council, the World Bank, the Agency for International Development, and several British foundations. American foundation personnel, working through de Kiewiet, made clear that they favored a strong university with constituent colleges rather than the loosely federated structure that was favored by several of the African representatives.[29] Foundation officers were concerned that support for semiautonomous colleges would lead to duplication of expensive services in a region woefully lacking in capital. At the same time, they recognized that their funds would be able to exert a greater degree of leverage on the direction of university development if they could work through a centralized rather than a diffused administrative structure.

The foundations made clear to the conferees the areas in which they would like to work. The Rockefeller Foundation would concentrate on attempts to Africanize the university faculty, with special attention given initially to the faculty of social science. It was hoped that a concentration on the social sciences would help, as the Foundation's 1963 *Annual Report* put it, to "stimulate teaching and research on the problems of economic development." This report went on to indicate how the foundation planned to remake the social science faculty: "two members of the Foundation staff have been assigned to Makerere, one serving as Chairman of the Department of Economics and the other directing research on East African economic development problems at the East African Institute of Social Research. Assistance has also been given to research at Royal College [Nairobi]."[30] The foundation's 1964 *Annual Report* elaborated on the support being provided the University of East Africa, noting how the foundation "has assisted arrangements between American universities and the University of East Africa to augment senior teaching and research staffs."[31] The expense involved in this was significant: approximately $1.5 million over a three-year period was allocated by the Rockefeller Foundation. Fortunately, the foundation could count on the Ford Foundation to assume part of this burden if need arose. Less than two weeks after the conference concluded, Rockefeller's John Weir wrote that

> in respect of Africanization, I can tell you confidentially that Frank Sutton [of Ford] and I discussed what role the Ford Foundation might play in this program, and he said that in addition to some of the capital needs that he had indicated for Ford Foundation support, he would be happy to pick up a piece of the Africanization costs if they proved to be larger than the Rockefeller Foundation could handle.[32]

A Ford Foundation appropriation several months later not only indicated that Sutton was true to his word, but also highlighted Ford's other interests in East Africa. Some $74,000 of that $478,000 grant was designated for Africanization of the University of East Africa's administrative staff. Other line items included $50,000 for social science research, $84,000 for support of the College of Social Studies, and $15,000 for central university planning.[33] Ford support for the social sciences, both within several of the university departments and through the East African Institute for Social Research, grew significantly in subsequent years.[34]

Carnegie's Stephen Stackpole indicated the corporation's "interest in the immediate future . . . in the field of education— both departments and institutes—and that we would hope to find ways of assisting the University to develop new programs in this field and new forms of relationships between institutes in East Africa and universities in the UK and in the U.S."[35] Support for departments and institutes of education in African universities formed the cornerstone of Carnegie policy throughout the 1960s and well into the 1970s, as will be noted later in this chapter. This was augumented by support for educational research, particularly as it related to the training of teachers and child development studies.[36]

The conferees left Villa Serbelloni with a clear understanding of the areas for which they would be responsible and with the feeling that the development of the University of East Africa was assured. Carnegie's Stackpole remarked on "the degree of understanding which the British and Americans had of each other's policies and on the part of the Americans at least of some of the problems of East Africa."[37] What he failed to mention was how the several preconference gatherings by foundation representatives in Washington and New York had paved the way for the generally cooperative and cordial atmosphere that characterized the deliberations.

The federated University of East Africa began to fall apart within several years of this conference. Foundation personnel were disappointed over the political wrangling that led to the university's dissolution. At the same time, however, they recognized that their earlier support for the university might now enable them to influence the direction of the programs at three independent institutions rather than at the federated University of East Africa.

The Growth of Social Science in Third-World Universities

The Ford and Rockefeller foundations placed such great emphasis on the development of the social sciences at the lead universities they supported because of their belief in the ability of the social sciences to bring about, in Schroyer's words, "rationallly managed" social change.[38] Rockefeller Foundation personnel had long been aware of the potential of the social sciences to effect change in the developing world favorable to the industrialized nations, particularly to the United States. In a wide-ranging discussion preliminary to the foundation's mid-1950s decision to expand its overseas work, a foundation officer noted the role of the social sciences in helping to "serve the orderly evolution of the unindustrialized countries without damaging their cultural and political integrity."[39] Many in the foundations agreed with the assessment that if Third-World peoples could be "acquainted with the accumulated lore of 'Western' social science," they could "be helped to avoid mistakes in social policy, to develop more efficient administrative agencies and to promote more quickly and more thoroughly a sense of civic responsiblity."[40]

The assumed links between social science and enlightened public-policy determination became an article of faith in United States government and foundation circles after 1945.[41] This had important implications for the discussions of Third-World development priorities that took place in United States policy centers. The conventional wisdom regarding development in the Third-World nations during the 1960s held that the key lay in the creation of technocratically oriented elites, who could apply their social science competencies to the alleviation of the problems of underdevelopment. Such a view was an important factor in the decision that led the Ford Foundation to become the largest financial supporter of social science research in Latin America.[42]

None of the social sciences was considered more important than economics in the accepted developmental literature. Arnove's comments are significant in this context, and no less to the Rockefeller than to the Ford Foundation that he discusses.

> The Foundation's fascination with social science research in large part has consisted of support for a certain breed of economists whose quantitative approach to development is safe and respectable. This favoring of economists, particularly in the early sixties, has accorded well with the Foundation's approach to treating development in terms of economic growth, technological competence, and improved managerial competence.[43]

This approach has enabled the foundations to argue the "value-free" nature of their involvement, based as it is on the "apolitical" concepts of efficiency, growth, and technique. Such an approach has also had the advantage of insuring change that was, from the donors' perspective, orderly, predictable, and generally supportive of Western interests in Third-World nations.

This belief in the ability of the social sciences in general and economics in particular to hasten societal development along acceptable lines was among the factors that led the Ford Foundation to a long-term commitment to developmental planning in Pakistan during the 1950s. Working through Harvard's Graduate School of Public Administration, Ford granted more than $4 million over a decade in an effort to train Pakistani economists and developmental planners in the most "modern" techniques of forecasting and planning.[44] This belief also led the Ford and Rockefeller foundations to invest heavily in the expansion of, for example, the Nigerian Institute of Social and Economic Research and its related departments of economics, political science, and sociology at the University of Ibadan. At the University of East Africa, generously funded by both foundations as well as by the Carnegie Corporation and several multinational and binational aid agencies, the institutional bases for social science research were the East African Institute of Social Research in Uganda and the Institute for Development Studies in Kenya. In East Africa as in Nigeria there was a heavy emphasis on the development of the departments of economics, political science, and sociology.[45] In both locales there was also a marked enthusiasm for the application of the principles of the manpower-planning approach as the key to development. This approach, grounded in the department of economics, was viewed by its foundation sponsors as one of the keys to the orderly growth of educational systems and subsequently of nations in Africa, Asia, and Latin America.[46]

The manpower planning approach to development also had a demonstrated success in the form of the Ashby Commission study of Nigeria's postsecondary educational requirements, which the Carnegie

Corporation had sponsored in 1959.[47] Ford Foundation personnel were supportive of this approach because of their addiction to the application of social science research techniques, which they claimed were value-free, to developmental problems. Another attraction of this approach to development was that it left major decisions in the hands of a group of experts, whose methodologies and data were often so arcane as to prove beyond question by laypersons. This emphasis on human-resource development and its application by technocratically oriented elites accorded well with the foundations' collective view that society's experts were best suited to determine society's agenda and to implement the programs required to move the institutions along the agreed course.

The fledgling social sciences departments in the Third-World universities were linked to the Western, capitalist developmental model, which in turn had been legitimated by foundation-sponsored American academics as the most efficacious route for the developing nations to follow, in two main ways. First, the universities' social science departments were staffed in the formative days after their establishment by foundation-selected and subsidized expatriates whose political and consequently intellectual orientations were supportive of the ideology undergirding this model.[48] Second, Third-World fellowship recipients were sent for advanced work in the social sciences to elite American (and occasionallly British) universities, whose proclivities toward the system-maintaining technological-functionalist and behavioralist view of society were pronounced.[49]

The influence of the foundations on policy determination is suggested by the comment of Kenneth Thompson, the Rockefeller vice-president who coordinated the foundation's overseas university centers during the formative period in the late 1950s and 1960s. He noted, for example, how the Rockefeller-supported "Development Economics training program, undertaken by the School of Economics in the University of the Philippines for members of the government economic civil service, has made a difference in the quality of the operation of the economic secretariat." Additionally, the "School of Economics' research program . . . had led to significant governmental policy changes." At the same time, "a faculty member is currently on leave serving as chairman of the National Economic Council and has drawn heavily on his colleagues for relevant policy-oriented studies."[50] The foundations' influence in determining intellectual perspectives consonant with their outlook, especially in the social sciences, is perhaps even more discernible when data from two African settings are examined. Rockefeller's Thompson noted that no less than two-thirds of all the faculty teaching in the University of East Africa "have been Rockefeller Foundation scholars and holders of Special Lectureships established with Rockefeller funding." And when the sample is limited to upper-level administrators and senior professors, the percentage of university personnel financed by the Rockefeller Foundation for part or all of its training rises to 80.[51]

A similar pattern was discernible at the University of Ibadan. By 1975 the Rockefeller Foundation had supported 114 Nigerian fellows from Ibadan, of whom 73 were then on the university staff. Throughout the period that the Nigerians had been supported for their graduate studies, the foundation had also provided the equivalent of 107 man-years of teaching for the University of Ibadan by carefully selected non-Nigerians. Foundation personnel were indeed cognizant of the crucial role played by its funding patterns, as is evidenced in an internal report prepared in 1975. That document commented on the major impact [of the foundation] on the instructional program," and on the fact that "Nigerian staff development has been given the highest priority in the social science program." Indeed, "the Economics Department . . . is staffed largely by individuals who have received training awards from the Foundation."[52]

Perusal of the list of Rockefeller Foundation fellowships awarded to Nigerians and East Africans in the social sciences between 1955 and 1975 reveals a concentration of grants for study at a handful of elite American universities. Fellowships to study economics, for example, were most frequently made to students attending Stanford, Harvard, Michigan, and Chicago. Arnove's work on the Ford Foundation's Latin American fellowship recipients in the social sciences reveals a similar pattern; Latin American students supported by Ford for graduate social science work have been clustered at Harvard, Chicago, and Stanford.[53] This concentration of fellowship recipients at a handful of elite American universities, whose key social science personnel had established parameters in economics, sociology, political science, and developmental theory, accorded well with the conventional wisdom regarding development in the Third World.

While there can be little doubt that those students educated at Stanford, Chicago, Michigan, and Harvard received high levels of instruction, it is equally obvious that they were being trained in methodologies and ideologies grounded in the Western, capitalist-oriented theory of development. This in turn led to a restricted view of the "right" and "wrong" way of looking at particular problems. Such a perspective, long encouraged by foundation policies, frequently precluded the possibility of formulating unconventional approaches to developmental problems susceptible to no other solutions. In the field of economics, for example, this policy led the foundations to place almost exclusive emphasis on the conservative manpower-planning approach to development and to admit of no alternative approaches.[54]

The foundations' support for the social sciences in the developing nations was premised on the belief in the close affinity between the social sciences and policy formulation.[55] Foundation personnel also felt that the socialization of key Third-World nationals into the norms of Western social science could play a determining role in helping to insure that those individuals would follow development paths that, minimally, were not overtly antagonistic to the interests of the United States. These concerns that the nations of the Third World develop in predetermined ways had less to do with the benefits of such development for Third-World populations than with the perceived advantages accruing to the United States from such a course. This was so because, as Myrdal notes, "the direction of . . . [Third World] reforms have become politically important to the contending power blocs."[56] One final example will illustrate how foundation-supported approaches in the social sciences were used to train national leaders who would align their nations with the United States.

Ford's interest in Indonesia dated from the early 1950s, when Cornell University and the Massachusetts Institute of Technology were granted funds for field projects.[57] Several years later Ford began to provide significant funding to link the economics department at the University of California, Berkeley, with the fledgling Faculty of Economics at the University of Djakarta. Junior Indonesian faculty were sent to Berkeley for graduate study while Berkeley professors moved into temporary positions in Djakarta. John Howard, the director of Ford's International Training and Research Program during the period, summed up Ford's objectives in a few words: "Ford felt it was training the guys who would be leading the country when Sukarno got out."[58]

By the early 1960s the Indonesian Communist Party was exercising increasing influence on government policy and on Sukarno, developments of growing concern to leaders of the nation's armed forces. The armed forces had close ties with the CIA, and both groups were determined to rid the archepelago of the unpredictable Sukarno and to eliminate all vestiges of the communist cancer. The army struck in the autumn of 1965 and there was little doubt as to the outcome. The new regime under General Suharto quickly reestablished contacts with the American political and commercial sectors, contacts that had been under severe strain during Sukarno's last years.

The Ford-funded and Harvard-based Development Advisory Service began to train a limited number of Indonesian economists in the methods of developmental planning even before the 1965 coup had toppled Sukarno. By the late 1960s the upper echelons of the Indonesian planning agencies were overwhelmingly staffed by Indonesian economists who had been trained either at Berkeley or by Harvard's Development Advisory Service. The economic stabilization and development plans that emanated from these several planning aggencies over the next few years bore the mark of that training.

The Ford Foundation's emphasis on training an elite cadre of Indonesian economists who would implement policy acceptable to the foundation sponsors had succeeded. Gustav Papanek, long a Ford associate and director of the Development Advisory Service, inadvertently summed up the manner by which Ford influence was incorporated into the Indonesian decision-making structure. He noted how "all of those people [formerly associated with the Development Advisory Service] simply moved into the government and took over the management of economic affairs, and then they asked us to continue working with them."[59] In this way Ford's interests could be incorporated into planning activities on a regular basis and the interests of the United States would be furthered.

This section needs to be concluded with a caveat that, once again, suggests the potential contradictory nature of the foundations' activities. The foundations' emphasis on a selective approach to the social sciences in their overseas work could not *guarantee* that students would be passively socialized into the norms embodied in the foundation-sponsored approach. There was always the possibility that certain students— be they Africans, Asians, or Latins—would reject, modify, or selectively choose particular elements from among those ideologies emphasized. Indeed, there was also the possibility that some might internalize approaches, e.g., Marxism, that the Western-oriented social sciences depreciated.[60] This could be the case despite the careful selection process that so frequently characterized the university admissions procedure. Such contestation over acceptance of particular ideologies need not always have been overt to have been quite real. It is doubtful if many Third-World university students—with the possible exception of some in Latin America, where protest literature is much more widely accepted and internalized—mindful as they were of the importance of gaining academic credentials for career mobility, would overtly challenge the domain assumptions of their instructors (and the curriculum), because they would (reasonably enough) fear that such challenges might threaten their successful completion of the degree course. The foundations' many advantages in propounding a particular worldview were very real, but they could not at the same time be taken as ironclad assurances of success. It was indeed possible that some students could utilize their academic opportunities to transform an experience with a sometimes subtle capitalist intent, i.e., their social science training, into an outcome that challenged the legitimacy of the overall approach and the system upon which it rested.

Programs in Public Administration

The foci of the Ford Foundation programs in public administration were at Ahmadu Bello University in Nigeria, the University of East Africa, and most importantly, at the National School of Law and Administration in the Congo. In terms of strategic location, political potential, and mineral wealth (particularly the rich copper-, cobalt-, and uranium-producing province of Katanga/Shaba), the Congo appeared significant to Ford officials during the late 1950s and early 1960s, as their internal memoranda indicate. This perception of the Congo's geopolitical and economic importance for the United States was shared by State Department officials, with whom Ford officers regularly consulted concerning their ventures there. These shared assumptions were only strengthened by the chaos into which the Congo was thrown when the Belgian government decided to grant political independence in the most precipitous manner in 1960.

Consultations in 1959 and early 1960 between the United States ambassador to Brussels and the director of Ford's International Affairs program resulted in a joint Ford-State Department program to support the visit to the United States of carefully selected and prominent Congolese. These visits represented "a deliberate official effort to make contact with Congolese leaders of today and tomorrow," to acquaint them with the major American aid organizations (the International Cooperation Administration, the major foundations, the American-dominated World Bank), and official government bodies (the State Department, the United States Information Agency), and the "well-established private banking and business institutions with definite interests in Africa and especially the Congo."[61] The outbreak of the Congolese civil war shortly after the granting of independence brought this effort to a standstill.

Another collaborative project between the Ford Foundation and the State Department was soon mounted in the Congo itself. The National Institute of Political Studies in Leopoldville was the result of conversation among foundation officers, State Department representatives, and the director of the Center for Socio-Political Research and Information in Brussels. The institute, which in 1960 received a five-year Ford grant of $232,000, was designed to serve as a focal point for research on Congolese society and as a dissemination center for information relating to the developmental problems in the country.[62].

This institute was not nearly as important for the subsequent political development of the Congo, however, as Ford's next undertaking there, the establishment in 1961 of a National School of Law and Administration.. Designed to train a cadre of public administrators, the national school concept grew logically from Ford's interest in training a limited number of administrators who would play central roles in their nations' affairs. The success of the National School in performing this function is suggested by Ashley, who notes that "by 1968, the 400 odd graduates of the school made up an elite corps of civil servants who are now holding important administrative and judicial posts throughout the Congo."[63]

The first director-general of the school was a Congolese, but the available evidence suggests that much power was exerted by the first secretary-general, James T. Harris. According to Ashley, Harris was "a Foundation specialist who had formerly served with the American Society of African Culture and had been president of the U.S. National Student Association."[64] Harris had been recommended for the Congo post by David Heaps, who joined the foundation staff in 1960 and with Harris played a central role in the fortunes of the national school. Before coming to the Ford Foundation Heaps had worked for a number of international organizations, including four years spent as program consultant to the Paris-based Veterans Federation, which, according to one of Heaps's Ford colleagues, was funded by the CIA.[65] The connection with organizations funded by the CIA may have been a link bringing Heaps and Harris together, for, according to sources who played a large role in exposing these links during the 1960s, Harris had long been an important and valued CIA operative.[66] There are no available data to indicate that he contineud in that role while serving at the National School. This may be a moot point, however. It is doubtful that Harris would have hesitated to cooperate with the agency when filling such a sensitive position in an area where the CIA was very much involved at the time, even if he were no longer on the agency's payroll.

Between 1961 and 1970, when it phased out its program, the Ford Foundation granted over three million dollars for the work of the National School of Law and Administration.[67] This was supplemented by a small amount to enable "particularly promising students or Government functionaries, capable of furthering their public service to the Congo," to travel to the United States for advanced training.[68] Because of the influence it exerted in American foreign-policy matters, the foundation could also exert a certain amount of leverage on the International Cooperation Administration and the Agency for International Development concerning the allocation of their funds for the work there. In this connection the comments of a high Ford official are germane: after noting that foundation representatives regularly consulted with federal agencies regarding the foundation's overseas work, James L. Morrill commented that the United States government and the foundation "had, of course, very similar objectives."[69]

Ashley, one-time Ford program officer and a sympathetic observer of the foundation's overseas activities, sums up as follows the role played by the Ford-funded Congolese venture in the furtherance of American foreign-policy aims during the turbulent 1960s:

> From the standpoint of the U.S. government, Ford activity in the Congo has been useful in furthering foreign policy objectives. The United States has been successful in its main political objectives of helping to create an independent Congo not subject to Communist influence. It has been able to do this by relying on the United Nations for peacekeeping and on the Ford Foundation for helping to initiate the key institutions for the training of administrators. . . . Ford assistance has therefore been an important element in furthering U.S. interests in Africa.[70]

Ford officials were acutely conscious that the fluid nature of events in the Congo in the years immediately after independence meant that other world powers—not all of which were communist by any means— would attempt to gain influence there, just as the United States, acting at least partially through the aegis of the Ford Foundation, was hoping to further its influence in that strategic nation. The French were particularly worrisome. David Heaps, who at the time was largely guiding the fortunes of the National School in its relations with Congolese authorities, noted that his success in recruiting several French faculty for the school was potentially threatening to American influence in Leopoldville. The time had come to find a way, he wrote to New York headquarters, "of preventing . . . [the French] from becoming too helpful. . . . There is [now] some danger in having too much French influence. . . . We are now discouraging the French from expanding their efforts [at the school]."[71]

American concern over events in Zaire has not lessened since the days of initial Ford activity there. The continuing support provided by Washington for the repressive and corrupt Mobutu regime and the alacrity with which the United States joined other Western nations to repel the 1978 "invasion" of the mineral-rich Shaba province by "communist" insurgents, suggests the importance attached to Zaire by American interests.[72]

The Ford Foundation consistently has stressed that its interest in training administrators and civil servants in Africa derives solely from its concern to educate public servants capable of providing basic administrative services in areas woefully lacking any semblance of an independent civil service. Given the economic interests of the United States in the developing nations where Ford (and Rockefeller and Carnegie) programs have been concentrated and the role of the United States government in furthering these interests, one wonders if perhaps the following assessment by Gouldner is not closer to the mark:

It is central to the effectiveness of a society using a system of "indirect rule" that its organizational instruments be reliably controllable from the outside. The society thus depends greatly on *appropriate socialization and education of the administrative* and political classes. These develop expert skills, and create a readiness to credit the hegemonic class, to define it as a "responsible" and effective stratum dedicated to the commonwealth; they define its role as legitimate and also generate loyalty to the social system.[73]

The outside interests in our study are American (and other capitalist) corporate and financial institutions with significant (and increasing) investments in developing areas. The "expert skills" are learned in foundation-sponsored programs, and the new administrative and political classes indicate to the society at large the benevolence of their rule while minimizing the debts they as a class owe to the outside interest, who benefit more than do the local nationals.

Teacher Education Projects

Carnegie Corporation's work in Africa moved along different but complementary lines to those of the Ford and Rockefeller foundations during the 1950s and 1960s. Carnegie's emphasis on higher education, which became noticeable after Alan Pifer joined the staff in 1953, was further delineated to focus on teacher education. Corporation officials recognized the need for a reputable educational institution to carry out its projected African work, and in the late 1950s just such an institution came forward.

As early as 1948 faculty and administrators at Columbia University's Teachers College began discussing the importance for the college of increasing its international activities. These discussions reveal that Teachers College faculty were as interested in courting the major foundations as the latter would soon be in working with the college. A meeting in the spring of 1948 brought together representatives of the General Education Board, the Carnegie Corporation, and Teachers College to discuss the feasibility of the college's hosting a conference the next year on the Educational Problems of Special Culture Groups.[74] A memorandum by one of the college negotiators spoke directly to the interests of the college in encouraging this and other undertakings with the foundations. Agreement to sponsor the proposed conference would enable Teachers College "a) to cooperate with foundations on a project they are interested in; b) to develop personal contacts with key foreign educators so that they will invite TC faculty to visit them abroad; c) to demonstrate TC's capacity to do a job that will encourage future grants from the Foundations."[75]

Ten years later this same Teachers College faculty member discussed with Carnegie officials the possibility of corporation support for an extensive teacher-education project linking several African institutions to Teachers College. The timing was propitious, since Carnegie officials were looking for ways to expand their African programs. In late 1959 Stephen Stackpole, head of Carnegie's Commonwealth Program, explained to corporation staff the potential in a Carnegie arrangement with Teachers College.

We have been looking for some opportunity to relate an American institute with one or more institutions in Africa. Here is a very promising situation in a field which is at the center of our knowledge and interest where an American institution, which has something special to offer and which has already been involved in problems of African education, is prepared to build up a long-term relationship with a group of African universities.

Equally significant was the opportunity to involve the University of London's Institute of Education in the project. This was important because it was "the one institution in England to which all the African institutions have looked for guidance and which is not only in a position to reconcile American and British concepts of education but growing out of its relation with Teachers College is interested in doing so."[76]

In 1960 Teachers College received the first of several substantial grants from Carnegie for a cooperative Afro-Anglo-American program in teacher education. The main purposes of the program were (1) to facilitate training opportunities for African teacher educators and administrators at Teachers College; (2) to build up an African education unit at Teachers College; (3) to forge links between Teachers College and teacher-training facilities in Sierra Leone, Ghana, Nigeria, Uganda, and Rhodesia; (4) to provide a vehicle whereby Americans desirous of teaching in Africa could be prepared for this task at Teachers College and at the University of London's Institute of Education; and (5) to provide a mechanism whereby Teachers College, and by extension American educational principles and the values implicit in these, could gain entry into an evolving network of teacher-training institutions in ex-British Africa. Carnegie's Alan Pifer argued the importance of American involvement because "in all of Africa educational expansion is the key to economic development and political stability," important elements in the United States' foreign-policy equation. And, he went on to note, "no aspect of education is more critical at this stage of development than teacher training."[77] To safeguard its interests, in short, the United States needed to be involved in the affairs of the developing nations, and the corporation could do so through its educational programs.

Carnegie's involvement in Africa dated from the 1920s and rested on similar premises. At that time officers of the corporation worked closely with personnel from the Colonial Office and the quasi-official International Missionary Council to strengthen various aspects of education in Britain's African colonies. An important part of this work involved the transference to Africa of some of the more salient features of the restrictive and racist educational structure erected for Negroes in the southern United States, known as the Tuskegee philosophy. Such cooperative efforts continued throughout the 1930s, albeit in somewhat attenuated fashion, until the outbreak of World War II.[78]

The postwar period saw a revival of Carnegie's relationship with the British educational establishment, particularly in the form of arrangements with the London-based Inter-University Council for Higher Education in the Colonies. The council, as the name implies, served a coordinating and centralizing function for the expanding network of institutions of higher education which had been established in Britain's colonial territories. Carnegie provided funds for much of the council's work.[79] When Carnegie officers decided in the 1950s to expand significantly their work in Africa, the long-standing relationship with influential British educators and colonial officials proved invaluable.[80]

Carnegie's mode of operation was characterized by the heavy reliance placed on key individuals to carry out corporation-funded projects. This principle was as applicable to the Carnegie programs overseas as it was at home. The central figure in facilitating the corporation's expanding influence in African teacher education was Karl W. Bigelow, who had his initial contacts with the corporation while working on a Carnegie-funded conference at Teachers College in 1949. Three years later the corporation sent Bigelow to Africa to familiarize himself with the English educational system there. An intermediate stop to attend a Colonial Office conference at Cambridge University brought him into contact with most of the important British educators and civil servants concerned with African education. The Carnegie Corporation, which according to Murphy "had no specific program objective in mind" when it funded Bigelow's 1952 trip, was carefully nurturing the man who would carry the burden of its African educational work for some time.[81]

Carnegie staff were not alone in their appraisal of Bigelow's potential for implementing agreed-upon programs. In 1958 a Ford Foundation official chatted with Carnegie's Alan Pifer about the corporation's evolving teacher-education plans in Africa. Later that year, another Ford official, aware of Bigelow's Carnegie association, met with the Teachers College professor in London and was favorably enough impressed to recommend foundation support for some of his African travel.[82]

Shortly thereafter the Ford Foundation decided to leave teacher-education projects—except for a sizable project in Northern Nigeria during the 1960s and some curriculum development work in East Africa—for the Carnegie people and other agencies to coordinate. A

Carnegie-sponsored meeting in London in 1960, attended by representatives of Teachers College, the Colonial Office, the corporation, and the colleges or universities at Ibadan and Zaria in Nigeria, and in Ghana, Sierra Leone, Rhodesia and Nyasaland, and Uganda assured that the role of the Carnegie Corporation in African education would be significant for the foreseeable future.[83]

Carnegie Corporation coupled its support for the Teachers College-based Afro-Anglo-American program with the development of institutes of education in a number of Britain's former African colonies. These institutes were designed to link the education faculties of the evolving African universities with the ministries of education responsible for their nations' expanding primary and secondary systems. Although the corporation had demonstrated an interest in supporting the institute concept as early as 1954, it was not until the early 1960s that a serious commitment was made. Significantly, it was through the work of Karl Bigelow and the Afro-Anglo-American program that corporation officials came to understand the impact that their funds could make on the embryonic institutes of education.

They did not let the opportunity escape them. In 1960 the Carnegie trustees approved a $56,000 grant to strengthen the work of the institute of education at the Nigerian College of Arts and Technology at Zaria. Two years later $54,000 was granted to University College, Ibadan for a similar purpose, while Kenya's Royal College received almost three times that amount. Large grants for the work of African institutes of education continued throughout the 1960s: the University of East Africa received $130,000 for this purpose in 1964, and the next year $404,000 was divided among Nigeria's Ahmadu Bello University, Uganda's Makerere College, and the University College, Dar es Salaam to establish or strengthen their institutes of education. During the next seven years the corporation granted some $1.6 million for the work of several institutes of education and their related activities.[84]

As Carnegie officials recognized that American ties to the newly independent African nations needed to be strengthened, they began to search for the means, which they thought would be perceived by Africans as being nonpolitical, to insure these connections. The Afro-Anglo-American program, which eventually linked the educational systems of the new African nations to the educational concepts, practices, and institutions of the United States, increasingly was viewed as a vehicle to accomplish this end.[85] The support provided for the work of the institutes of education was another. Carnegie officials felt that these program thrusts were mutually supportive, if not inseparable.[86]

Carnegie was able to influence significantly the direction of African teacher education both through its direct subsidization of institutes of education and, more subtly perhaps, through its support for programs at Teachers College, whose faculty viewed African educational development in ways similar to those held by corporation personnel. The role of Teachers College in the reproduction of an ideology supportive of a certain kind of educational development in Africa should not be minimized. By 1975 personnel from institutes of education at universities in most formerly British colonies had been exposed to American pedagogical concepts through their study there. Raymond Williams has noted how such "educational institutions are usually the main agencies of transmission of an effective dominant culture, and this is now a major economic as well as cultural activity."[87] The support provided to Teachers College by Carnegie Corporation suggests, minimally, that Carnegie personnel felt that the courses of study at Teachers College would not challenge the assumptions of the dominant culture, in which both institutions played important roles.

The hopes for advancement at home by those African educators enrolled at Teachers College—as well as their subsequent power, prestige, and influence—depended to a great extent on the successful completion of their graduate training. In view of this, it is doubtful if many challenged the "commonsense" categories that defined their educational experiences in New York. Rather, it seems likely that most, aware that persistent dissent from the intellectual orthodoxy as defined by Teachers College faculty would jeopardize their academic standing and subsequent careers, internalized many of the lessons taught during their graduate days. If we accept the argument that schools process knowledge as well as people and that an institution like Teachers College had an interest in stressing only that knowledge consistent with its role as an integral institution in the dominant culture, it can be seen that the knowledge disseminated to African graduate students did not always consider African interests to be of paramount importance.

Movement of personnel between African institutes and Teachers College for advanced degree work was an important part of the Carnegie-sponsored Afro-Anglo-American program. In this way large numbers of influential African educators studied at first hand American educational practices and ideas. At the same time they could not help but be influenced by the values of the corporate-capitalist system from which these derived. Karl Bigelow, the architect and director of the program, elaborated on the influence that Teachers College, and indirectly the Carnegie Corporation, had gained in African education through its long-standing fellowship provisions. In his 1972 report on the conference of the Association of Teacher Education in Africa—the Carnegie-funded successor to the Afro-Anglo-American program—Bigelow noted that of the twenty-seven official African participants at the 1972 conference, one-third had Teachers College associations, primarily through earlier fellowships funded by Carnegie. He also noted that Teachers College was associated with all twenty African institutions comprising the association's membership.[88]

The Foundations and Foreign Students

The provision of fellowships enabling foreign students to study in the United States has long been an integral part of the Carnegie, Ford, and Rockefeller foundation programs. The Afro-Anglo-American program was a latter-day variant on earlier models. Foundation officials early recognized the importance of these programs in socializing future African, Asian, and Latin American leaders in ways that would make them sympathetic to the interests of the United States and her allies. Such programs provide effective, but generally unrecognized, mechanisms to further the foundations' cultural hegemony. This is accomplished when the foundations ask the outside agencies or participating universities to assume administrative responsibility for the funded program. This arrangement deflects attention from the role of the foundations themselves and enables their personnel to retain an air of disinterested concern over the programs' directions, while at the same time denying any influence. The influence is no less real for being indirect, however, for the foundations long ago devised methods whereby students benefiting from their fellowships studied certain subjects at universities whose faculties could be counted on, minimally, to provide the "correct" perspectives.

As early as the mid-1920s the Carnegie Corporation made sizable grants to enable the Phelps-Stokes Fund to bring to the United States African students for study at those institutions adhering to the Tuskegee philosophy.[89] This support continued through the 1930s and was supplemented by funds enabling British colonial civil servants to travel to the United States to view institutions practicing the Tuskegee philosophy and to study in approved universities. Similar grants to the British Inter-University Council after 1955 were important in providing educational opportunities for future faculty in colonial universities. Carnegie officials initially had little success in sending these fellowship recipients to American universities; their subsequent efforts would be more successful, however.[90]

The influence of the Rockefeller Foundation's fellowship programs at the universities of Ibadan and East Africa has already been noted. Other Rockefeller philanthropies also had provisions for fellowship awards to foreign students. One of these was the International Education Board, established in 1924. An important focus for the board was "improving the stateside training of foreign teachers, including many missionaries from the Far East."[91] The board provided financing for the International Institute at Teachers College, Columbia University, whose programs exposed many foreign students to the educational work of the Rockefeller's General Education Board in the American South, which, like many of their homelands, was considered an underdeveloped area.

The International Institute, and through it the International Education Board, had a major impact on foreign students from around the world, but this was nowhere more pronounced than on the Chinese. Cleaver notes that over two hundred Chinese teachers graduated from the International Institute between 1925 and 1928 and that part of the curriculum examined "how Chinese education should be reshaped." One of the institute's graduates assessed the role that such foreign study played in shaping the Chinese elite, noting how "the returned students occupy practically the entire state—in the diplomatic corps, in the faculties of universities and colleges, and in the military forces."[92]

An early Ford Foundation program provided scholarships for foreign student leaders to study in the United States. The Foreign Student Leadership Program, initiated in 1955, designated the National Student Association as the agency responsible for the selection of "responsible" foreign student leaders to participate. By this time the National Student Association worked closely with the CIA.[93] Ford Foundation officers provided the reasons for supporting this program in the docket excerpt prepared for the September 1955 meeting of the board of trustees. "The proposal is based on the belief that training in responsible student self-government on the American pattern would stimulate the development of similar activities . . . overseas." While Ford officials did not hold "exaggerated hopes" for "what any of . . . [the subsidized] students could accomplish as individuals after their return," they felt certain that "some continuing relationship would develop between the National Student Association, American universities, and student groups in the underdeveloped countries."[94] This was an important consideration in winning the cultural cold war.

Ford officials were conscious of the potential long-term benefits of this program. Those students "trained in the United States," the docket excerpt continued, "may be expected to exert . . . influence over student affairs for several years after their return, some may make [educational work] their permanent career, and others would undoubtedly become important leaders in community and civic affairs." The potential importance of this group of foreign student leaders in furthering American foreign-policy objectives was explicated the next year in materials prepared for distribution to American universities participating in the Foreign Student Leadership Program. National Student Association officials wrote that the "FSLP students are not just any foreign students. . . . The students who will come to your campus will be selected because they are judged to be qualified to absorb what we can offer and take back home what is useful."[95]

The foundations' fellowships programs were from the beginning marked by attempts to place grantees in institutions that foundation officers perceived as academically rigorous, influential, and safe. They recognized that a large proportion of fellowship holders would return to their countries and become university faculty members, politicians, and leaders in the private sector. Accordingly, great care was taken to place them in university settings where they would be socialized into norms deemed appropriate by foundation personnel.

There was no apparent coercion involved in these fellowship programs. The foundations have not overtly manipulated potential fellowship recipients. Such blatant methods are unnecessary because of the understanding on the part of fellowship aspirants that their identification with certain methodological approaches or areas of investigation or their demonstration of certain behaviors will serve to stigmatize them as "irresponsible" among the funding agencies, thereby eliminating any possibility of receiving a grant.

Lasch addressed this problem from a slightly different angle over a decade ago. Then he spoke to the problems for intellectuals when they raise potentially embarrassing questions that funding agencies prefer to ignore.

> Young scholars in the sensitive fields are likely to believe that if they write with excessive candor about certain realities of political and international life, doors will close to them: certain grants will be out of reach, participation in certain organized research programs denied, influential people alienated, the view propagated that the young man [sic] *is unbalanced or unsound.*

This perception of the realities of the funding competition will lead some young scholars to "adapt to this situation with such concessions as they believe are necessary. And the scholars who adapt successfully are likely to be highly influential in their fields in the next generation."[96] This is no less true of overseas fellowship recipients.

One final example will suffice to illustrate how the foundations' fellowship programs shape intellectual perspectives and help to determine how people view the world and decide what is "right" and what is otherwise. The Rockefeller Foundation's *Annual Report* for 1960 noted foundation support for a Carnegie Endowment for International Peace program begun the year before.[97] This program, designed to train diplomats for the developing nations in the practices and procedures of modern international relations and diplomacy, had three discernible aspects: (1) a fellowship program for twenty-five diplomats to study at Harvard, Columbia, or the Graduate Institute of International Affairs in Geneva; (2) in-service seminars, held in Washington, D.C., embassies and coordinated by the School of Advanced International Studies at Johns Hopkins University; and (3) an in-service training program in New York City for United Nations representatives from the developing countries. The committee to select applicants included Hamilton Fish Armstrong, editor of the Council on Foreign Relations' journal, *Foreign Affairs*; Robert Bowie, director of the Harvard Center for International Affairs; Paul Nitze, president of the Foreign Policy Educational Foundation and former Assistant Secretary of Defense for International Security Affairs; and Schuyler Wallace, director of the School of International Affairs at Columbia University.[98]

Bowie had headed the State Department's policy planning staff for Secretary of State Dulles before going to Harvard; he later served as deputy director of the CIA's National Intelligence Branch in the Carter administration. Wallace was director of the Social Science Research Council from 1952 to 1958 and was an associate of the Ford Foundation before being tapped to head the Columbia division. These men not only were members of the foreign-policy establishment, but they were key architects and implementors of the post-1945 policy of cold-war liberalism. The program for which they selected participants could only reflect their shared ideology regarding the role of the United States in global politics and the relationships between the United States and the developing nations of Africa, Asia, and Latin America.

The foundations' fellowship programs have been characterized by recipients who undergo a rigorous screening process not only by representatives of their indigenous institutions, but by foundation personnel as well. Once the selection process is completed, award winners are sent to carefully selected, elite American universities, where they are grounded in the domain assumptions of their particular disciplines. This is not to suggest that they are never exposed to intellectual perspectives considered as unorthodox; clearly they are. However, care is taken to assure that the few unorthodox approaches examined in, for example, their courses in Third-World development are more than counterbalanced by exposure to the voices and perspectives of developmental orthodoxy. The control that the foundations exercise over so many institutions and awards supports Gouldner's contention that "the old society is held together not by force and violence, or expedience and prudence. The old society maintains itself . . . through theories and ideologies that establish its hegemony over the minds of men."[99]

Forging an Intellectual Network

The developmental aid provided by the foundations was designed to reproduce certain characteristics in Third-World educational institutions. The administrative infrastructures, the academic programs, the methodologies emphasized, the professional norms—these were to be developed along lines similar to those that marked certain elite American universities. The foundations accomplished this by supporting programs that linked several American universities to the Third-World institutions to be remodeled. Several of these linkages have been mentioned: Harvard, Chicago, and Stanford played central roles in the remodeling of several Latin American education faculties and departments; the Harvard School of Public Administration was instrumental in shaping the perspectives of Pakistani developmental planners; and the Harvard-based Development Advisory Service performed a similar role in Indonesia. Another striking example was the ten-million-dollar grant given by Ford in the early 1970s for a program of scholarly collaboration between the universities of California and Chile.[100] These efforts reflected the importance that foundation personnel attached to fostering "a network of professional and personal contacts throughout the world," as Ford vice-president Francis Sutton put it.[101]

The Asian Institute of Management in the Philippines illustrates the way in which the networking principle functions and how the foundations' influence is extended without direct foundation involvement.[102] In 1963 the Ford Foundation granted $250,000 to enable three Filipino business schools to cooperate in business education. Several years later it was decided to combine the efforts of two of these schools and to seek funding from several organizations, including the Agency for International Development.

The institute today is staffed by Filipinos, although visiting faculty, particularly Americans, are common. The influence of the Harvard Business School is reflected both in the institute's organizational structure and in its adherence to the well-known Harvard case-study method. Equally significant is the fact that the first two presidents were professors from Harvard. Faculty regularly travel to selected American business schools for further study; indeed, "almost all the faculty have advanced degrees largely earned in the United States."[103] The institute's leaders feel that the undertaking is important enough to be extended beyond their national borders. They are, consequently, "reaching out to many areas in . . . search for students, and generous scholarships and loan facilities are made available not only to Filipino students but also to other Asians."[104]

Rockefeller vice-president Kenneth Thompson has noted how "first-generation university development centers," such as the University of Valle and the University of East Africa, help "second-generation centers," such as the Federal University of Bahia (Brazil) and the University of Zaire, respectively.[105] Indigenous faculty and administrators from the universities of Valle and East Africa help to develop the newer universities in Bahia and Zaire in much the same manner that Rockefeller Foundation personnel from New York and American universities earlier fostered the development of the former institutions. This networking arrangement does not preclude the direct intervention by foundation personnel into the affairs of one of the "second-generation" universities, however. The Ford Foundation is a significant contributor to the Federal University of Bahia, and the Rockefeller Foundation representative at Bahia has played an important part in the determination of that university's programs.[106] This activity is paralleled by Ford Foundation efforts at the Center for Educational Studies in Mexico, which in addition to receiving Ford grants in excess of $500,000, has a special relationship with the Stanford School of Education, where center staff can study for advanced degrees.[107] The Stanford School of Education, in turn, forms part of the foundation's "resource base" in education and received close to $1 million during the 1970s to provide training for Ford-recruited graduate students in education.[108]

The foundations over the years have assiduously strengthened a number of strategically located Third-World institutions in ways that link them to American universities.[109] Staff from these Third-World institutions currently are working to strengthen other Third-World educational institutions along similar lines. The foundations' presence has decreased considerably in recent years, but their influence continues unabated through the work of surrogates socialized into norms that the foundations have determined.

4

The Foundations Define a Field: Foreign Area Studies, Social Science, and Developmental Theory

At the end of World War II only a handful of American universities had programs in international affairs and even fewer had developed offerings in non-Western studies. Those few in existence in 1945 had been established largely with funds provided by the Rockefeller Foundation.[1] Twenty years later international-affairs and area-studies programs were entrenched in major university centers from New York to California. The faculty for these programs generally divided their time between the area-studies or international-affairs programs and one of their university's social science (and occasionally humanities) departments. These scholars in turn formulated the major tenets of the conventional theory of development for the nations of Africa, Asia, and Latin America. The Carnegie, Ford, and Rockefeller foundations played the catalytic and sustaining role in these activities after 1945. Their reasons for doing so were inextricably linked to rising cold-war tensions, as was their support for the expanding field of national security studies at the same time.[2] The foundations only began to reduce their level of support when the federal government decided to underwrite these programs more generously after 1960.

In this chapter we examine the reasons for the foundations' decision to expand the capabilities of selected American universities in international studies, and detail how their grants created the new programs that set the standard for a thriving and influential field. The foundation grants for these programs were coupled with funds to support certain social science disciplines that were deemed indispensable to the development of viable foreign area-studies programs. These included sociology, political science, and economics. Foundation personnel believed that

99

the dynamics of the nations of Africa, Asia, and Latin America could best be understood by American academics who combined a thorough knowledge of the society in question, through a study of language and culture, with one of these social science disciplines. They were concerned, as a Ford Foundation officer put it, about "the abysmal lack of knowledge" available to American decision makers concerning these areas, which were of increasing importance in United States foreign-policy determination.[3] The American university programs were intended to alter this situation and, in the words of another Ford officer, they were also "to provide the educational foundation for our new national interest in these areas."[4] As in most of their work, the foundations achieved their objectives through a combination of their direct efforts, subsidization of outside agencies that implemented their programs, and strategic grants to faculty and student researchers.

These attempts to improve the capacity of selected American universities in foreign area studies coincided with foundation efforts to strengthen the educational infrastructures of a limited number of African, Asian, and Latin American nations. Foundation officers were aware that their increasingly heavy involvement in the educational affairs of developing nations was based more on their shared perceptions of what was required than on any explicit theory about the development process. This awareness led the foundations to support the efforts of a number of American social scientists, who were affiliated with the evolving international and area-studies programs, in their elaboration of a theory of development for the nations of Africa, Asia, and Latin America. The resultant developmental theory was, not surprisingly, supportive of the thrust of the foundations' overseas activities. The theory also provided legitimation for the foundations' programs abroad, while simultaneously reinforcing the developmental effort of United States governmental agencies, whose personnel frequently consulted with foundation officers. The chapter examines the evolution and content of this foundation-sponsored developmental theory. It concludes by raising some questions about the theory's implications for Third-World nations, whose developmental plans have to a large extent been framed in categories established by this theory.

The Growth of International and Area-Studies Programs after 1945

The Carnegie, Ford, and Rockefeller foundations played their leading roles in creating the major international and area-studies programs at American universities because, in the words of a Ford officer during the period, they recognized "the need to improve the capabilities of the United States in meeting its responsibilities in world affairs—more especially for maintaining the strength of the non-Communist nations and for assisting the social and economic development of the new emerging nations."[5] The first major effort to this end was in 1945 when the Rockefeller Foundation granted $250,000 for the creation of a Russian Institute affiliated with Columbia University's new School of International Affairs. Other large Rockefeller grants to Columbia soon followed, as did several from the Carnegie Corporation, which in 1947 made a series of grants to enable several universities to further their efforts in international affairs and area-studies programs. The most significant of these was a $740,000 grant to Harvard University for the establishment of a Russian Research Center.[6] By 1952 the two foundations had granted several million dollars to strengthen international and area-studies programs. Significant as these efforts were however, they were dwarfed by the subsequent Ford Foundation appropriations for the same purpose.

Ford's interest in strengthening American competency in international affairs was first mentioned in a 1952 internal document that suggested possible program areas for the recently reorganized foundation. Although the study focused on Ford opportunities in Asia, it soon became the basis for most of the foundation's overseas activities. Carl Spaeth, the report's author, recognized that "America's power to overcome Asian misunderstanding and to contribute to the shaping of events in these areas can only be in proportion to the extent of her knowledge of the characteristics of the region in which she operates, and the availability of competent, trained personnel to carry out her intentions there." He concluded by noting that "the development of American knowledge about Asia and an increase in the number of men skilled in dealing with her problems could well prove to be the key to the [problems] of Asia and its relation to world peace."[7] The resultant funds to train these specialists were channeled through the foundation's International Training and Research Program. By the mid-1960s the Ford Foundation had allocated the staggering sum of $138 million to a limited number of universities for the training of foreign-area and international-affairs specialists.[8]

There was agreement among foundation personnel that these specialists should make available to foreign-policy decision makers their knowledge of the nations that they studied. The national security of the United States demanded no less. Consequently, the foundations frequently acted as the intermediaries between area specialists and government agencies in matters pertaining to national security. One example of this was discussed at a 1953 meeting of Ford's Board of Overseas Training and Research. The draft minutes of that meeting record that "the feeling was expressed that long-term studies undertaking to evaluate the vulnerability of . . . [India, Indonesia, and Iran] to Communist influence were greatly needed and should be undertaken. . . . [Mr. Gray] suggested that the staff work out appropriate and adequate liaison with the government [to carry out such studies]." Professor George M. Kahin of Cornell University submitted a proposal that detailed how such a study would be conducted in Indonesia.[9]

Several years later Charles Fahs of the Rockefeller Foundation commented on the important role to be played by foundation-supported international-affairs specialists in the furtherance of United States foreign-policy objectives. In a memorandum to Rockefeller president Harrar, Fahs argued that "wherever possible, programs should be subcontracted to non-governmental agencies, e.g., universities. An effort is long overdue to correlate overseas contracts with area study competence in the contracting institutions in order to assure greater knowledge of the local situation."[10]

The Ford Foundation almost singlehandedly established the major areas-studies programs in American universities. Between 1959 and 1963, for example, Ford made direct grants of approximately $26 million to support non-Western language and area-studies programs at fifteen universities: Boston, California, Chicago, Columbia, Cornell, Harvard, Indiana, Michigan, Northwestern, Pennsylvania, Princeton, Stanford, Washington, Wisconsin, and Yale.[11] These same universities are the leaders in the production of Ph.D. degrees and, because of their prestige, generally manage to place their graduates in the upper echelons of the American corporate, political, and academic strata, from which their graduates' ideas frequently dominate their respective fields.[12]

The area-studies programs were designed to develop American scholars' expertise in specific areas, e.g., Africa, Latin America, the Near East, South Asia, the Soviet Union and Eastern Europe. The foundations also supported the growth of more general programs in international affairs during the 1950s and 1960s, and the funding was equally generous. The most important of these included Harvard's Center for International Affairs, the Center for International Studies at the Massachusetts Institute of Technology, the Center for Strategic Studies at Georgetown University, the Institute of International Studies at Berkeley, the Stanford University Institute for Communications Research, and the Center for International Studies at Princeton University. Nor were these programs limited to the United States. The Graduate Institute of International Affairs in Geneva has been supported from its inception largely by the Rockefeller Foundation. The Royal Institute of International Affairs in London and St. Antony's College, Oxford, have also been sustained over the years by funds from the Carnegie, Ford, and Rockefeller foundations.[13]

The links among the foundations, some subsidized university centers, and foreign-policy formulation are suggested by noting just a few of the key individuals associated over the years with these foundation-supported international programs. The first director of MIT's Center for International Studies was Max Milliken, a former assistant director of the CIA. An equally influential member of the center staff was W. W. Rostow, who subsequently became a key foreign-policy advisor to President Kennedy and Johnson and an architect of the Vietnam war. Individuals associated with Harvard's Center for International Affairs over the years have included Robert R. Bowie, head of the State Department's policy planning staff; Henry A. Kissinger, secretary of state in the Nixon administration; McGeorge Bundy, national security advisor to presidents Kennedy and Johnson and later Ford Foundation president; and James A. Perkins, vice-president of the Carnegie Corporation and a director of the Rockefeller's Chase Manhattan Bank.

Fellowship provisions were from the beginning an important component of the foundation effort to enlarge the pool of knowledge about foreign areas. The Carnegie and Rockefeller foundations made their contributions to this end, but again it was the Ford Foundation whose activities were so remarkable because of their scale. As early as 1953 Ford's Board of Overseas Training and Research announced grants totaling $488,150 to "enable 97 young Americans to begin or continue studies concerning Asia, the Near and Middle East." The announcement went on to indicate that "the purpose of this program is to stimulate increased knowledge [of these areas] and to help meet the urgent needs . . . for large numbers of men and women well qualified in business, education, . . . agriculture, labor relations, and the professions."[14] Ford officials regularly stated their conviction that fellowship recipients would contribute to the national interest by making their knowledge available to those responsible for foreign-policy formulation.[15]

This Foreign Area Fellowship Program was administered for its first decade by staff of Ford's International Training and Research Program. In 1962 program administration was entrusted to a joint committee of the American Council of Learned Societies and the Social Science Research Council, which in turn delegated responsibility to a number of area committees, e.g., the Joint Committee on Latin American Studies, the Joint Committee on African Studies. Massive Ford support accompanied this transfer. Beckmann estimates that between 1953 and 1965 the Foreign Area Fellowship Program granted approximately $10 million dollars to 1214 scholars, primarily for advanced graduate study dealing with particular geographical locales. Former fellowship holders are strategically located not only in the major international and area-studies programs in American universities, but are commonplace in less prestigious institutions as well. Their publications contribute to the nation's knowledge about the non-Western world and help to shape the population's general perception of that world.[16]

Just as the foundations take great care in the selection of those foreign nationals who will study in the United States, so do they—and the joint councils that now administer their programs—exercise similar care when selecting among applicants for award of the prestigious Foreign Area Fellowships. Such careful selection does not, however, guarantee the passive socialization of apprentice American scholars into desirable norms. It is probably the case that many, if not most, will follow academic careers characterized by intellectual orthodoxy and acceptance of the society's overall political objectives; this at least is the conclusion drawn by recent investigations.[17] It is equally possible, however, that a certain number, but statistically a small proportion, will become detached from academic and political orthodoxy. This contradiction has potentially important political considerations, not the least of which is its ability to undermine the confidence of some intellectuals and decision makers in the continuance of the American imperial mission.

Foundation-sponsored training of future American scholars—whether administered directly or through a more specialized agency—could no more insure that the recipients would internalize certain norms and support predetermined ends than could similar undertakings in Third-World universities.[18] Indeed, the more pluralistic nature of American universities—compared, at least, with those of Africa, Asia, and Latin America—and the wider range of dissent tolerated in this society, makes it likely that some young scholars formerly supported by foundation largesse will become critics of their former patrons and will communicate their views to a wide range of students and fellow scholars. Their critiques have the potential to challenge the legitimacy of foundation activities, their prominent roles in American society, and the material base upon which they rest.

Yet another contradiction needs to be mentioned at this juncture. In recent years the foundations and organizations like the World Bank have provided research support for scholars whose political perspectives were considerably to the left of their sponsoring agencies. This is a marked departure from the practice of the 1960s and early 1970s. A well-known example of this new direction at home was the support provided by the Ford Foundation for the Marxian interpretation of American education by Bowles and Gintis.[19]

The funding of so-called radical researchers has extended to scholars studying international problems as well, particularly those of Third-World development.[20] Paulston notes that "educational agencies such as the World Bank, the Ford Foundation, the Rand Corporation, et al., have recently sought the aid of neo-Marxist scholars in efforts to diagnose what went wrong with reforms grounded in the liberal world-view, a perspective that by definition avoids recognition of power and conflict and is thus unable to explain its failures."[21]

Support for scholars working in the Marxist tradition does not necessarily imply sympathy for the politics of the researchers by the sponsoring agency, nor does it mean acceptance of the conclusions reached. There are several possible reasons for this support.

One reason, perhaps related to the point made by Paulston, is that funding agencies have determined that support for these scholars is important because their research frequently generates information that more orthodox research methods fail to uncover. Knowledge of the Third World is important to United States foreign-policy analysts, regardless of its source, as foundation personnel have long recognized.[22] As Arnove remarks, the information generated by researchers on Latin America—whatever their political persuasion or methodological orientation—"enables the United States to understand better and, perhaps, respond more effectively to Latin American thinking and actions."[23]

A second reason might be that some, although not all, who sit in the State Department, the World Bank, and the foundations are bothered by their liberal consciences. Perhaps they have trouble reconciling the knowledge that their aid programs in reality do little to alleviate the plight of the world's dispossessed, while at the same time providing legitimacy for a basically inequitable economic and social order from which they benefit. A third reason could be that some within the foundations feel that a grant here or there to an unorthodox or even "radical" researcher might serve to defuse the potential criticism that the foundations only encourage research congruent with their interests, while regularly proclaiming the opposite.

Foundation Support for the Social Sciences

Rockefeller support for the social sciences dates from the 1920s and was at first channeled through the Laura Spelman Rockefeller Memorial, which in 1929 became the Rockefeller Foundation's Division of Social Science.[24] During this decade the memorial also supported the establishment of the Social Science Research Council, which in turn administered the memorial's fellowship program in the social sciences. The memorial's officers reached agreement by 1925 on the importance of strengthening a limited number of American universities as centers of social science research. They soon decided to do the same for several European universities.[25] Their goal was to link a number of prominent universities that shared a common approach to social science research.

The foundation's work in Africa, Asia, and Latin America after 1945 drew heavily on this legacy.

In the early 1930s, officers of the Rockefeller Foundation's Division of Social Science began to search for ways to use the social sciences to alleviate—or at least to rationalize—the social disruption occasioned by the nation's economic collapse. This led to the 1935 decision to focus the division's activities on three areas: international relations, economic stabilization, and public administration. John Van Sickle, associate director of the Division of Social Science, urged that the foundation support research that could point the way toward economic stabilization before it was too late. "Existing insecurity and catastrophic decline in standards with mass unemployment constitutes a serious threat to the existing system," he wrote at the end of 1934.[26] "There can be no question that the very existence of the social order is at stake. Unless a satisfactory solution can be found soon, men and women will demand a change."[27] As the Depression deepened, Rockefeller Foundation officers intensified their search for solutions, not all of which could be termed enlightened. In 1937, for example, foundation president Raymond Fosdick wrote plaintively to an acquaintance: "In a chaotic world like this, have the social sciences a contribution to make to the problem of human control? If so, what is it, and how do the social sciences propose to go about it?"[28]

The efforts to strengthen a few university centers of social science research, coupled with the hope that the results of that research could contribute to the alleviation of society's problems, were important among the factors that led the Rockefeller Foundation to support academics who had the promise of elaborating social science theories that would contribute to societal stability. The next twenty-five years marked the formative period in the development of three of these social sciences: sociology, political science, and economics. Funding from the Carnegie, Ford, and Rockefeller foundations played central roles in encouraging certain trends within these disciplines, which in turn were important in the subsequent formulation of developmental theory for Third-World nations.

Gouldner has written at length about the evolution of the structural-functionalist school of sociology and has indicated how its proponents came to dominate academic sociology in the United States. He notes the ideological underpinnings of this school of sociological analysis, arguing that "with the Depression and the growing salience of Marxism in the United States, there was greater pressure to develop and fortify the intellectual alternatives to Marxism, and to expel Marxism from consideration as a sociology much as any other." In view of this, Gouldner argues, the early work of Talcott Parsons, the father of structural-functionalism, was neither value-free nor nonideological; rather, it was a particular response to the significant social crisis precipitated by the Depression.[29]

Andreski elaborates on the ideological orientation of functionalism, noting that "it propagates a conservative ideology in the name of science." But the deceptiveness of the doctrine is deepened, Andreski argues, by the fact that it "bestows its blessing on every system which exists, so long as it exists; which means that it throws its weight on the side of the powers that be, whoever, wherever, and whenever they might be."[30] Gouldner agrees with this assessment, but only up to a point. Functionalism, he notes, "is not really committed to social order in general, but only to preserving *its* own social order. It is committed to making things work despite wars, inequalities, scarcity, and degrading work, rather than finding a way out."[31]

This functionalist orientation, with its emphasis on equilibrium, order, stability, and moderation, was well suited to the maintenance of the policies of corporate liberalism at home and imperial liberalism abroad, which characterized the 1950s and 1960s and which shared the concern for consensus and stability at home and for evolutionary development and controlled change abroad. The major foundations regularly supported the work of this school of structural or technological functionalists, not least because of their shared ideology. Many of the academic "stars" of the functionalist persuasion received funding to enable them to apply their perspectives to developing nations as well as to the United States. In this respect the work of such scholars as Edward Shils, Reinhard Bendix, Daniel Lerner, S. N. Eisenstadt, Seymour M. Lipset, and Marion Levy, among others, on developing nations takes on particular significance.[32]

The works of these men not only set the standard for academic research by American political sociologists, but their collective influence meant that alternative perspectives on development frequently had difficulty in securing comparable funding. While the foundation grants occasionally were made directly to the researchers, they were usually channeled through the Social Science Research Council, which administered research funds through its several committees. Indeed, the council probably could not have survived without this foundation money. Between 1956 and 1969, for example, the Carnegie, Ford, and Rockefeller foundations provided over three-quarters of the council's revenue.[33]

The council and its committees have always been dominated by academics whose work was considered to be in the mainstream of their respective disciplines, as Seybold's study documents. Functionalism occupied this position within academic sociology, while behavioralism did likewise in political science. Because the foundations were interested in encouraging certain perspectives and because of the council's financial dependence on the foundations, the research supported by council grants generally reflected perspectives similar to those held by foundation officers. We can speculate as well that the more entrepreneurial of the researchers applying for grants administered by one of the council's committees understood the importance of couching their applications in terms likely to draw a sympathetic response from those of the dominant school who judged their proposals' merits.

The behavioralist approach in American political science, with its concomitant pluralist and quantitative emphasis in the study of politics, was becoming more pronounced at the same time that functionalism was gaining ascendency in the field of American sociology. The strength of the behavioralists derived at least as much from the strategic financial support that they received from the major foundations to work out their theories and disseminate them through various publications as from the inherent merits of their ideas.[34] Data collected by Peter J. Seybold and Donald Fisher, among others, indicate that the foundations supported behavioralism at least in part because it provided a foil to use against other, "radical" theories which had gained prominence during the Depression and which, especially in the mid-1950s work of C. Wright Mills and his followers, were influencing an increasing number of scholars. Funding for the practitioners of the behavioralist approach within political science was also channeled through the Social Science Research Council.

Horowitz notes that the focal point of behavioralism is "the study of power, and the disbelief in its undemocratic and sinister concentration in American society."[35] The behavioralist-pluralist approach is marked by its emphasis on observable behavior, its collection of vast quantities of data on groups ranging from fishmongers of southern France to the aborigines of central Australia, and the construction of sophisticated models designed to test hypotheses relating to the functioning of political systems. Behavioralism has long been supportive of the concept of consensus politics and elite leadership in the United States. Its proponents have expended considerable effort collecting data on every conceivable group save the American elite, and its emphasis has been steadfastly antagonistic to the viewpoints of the power elitists or conflict theorists, who argue that it is the concentration of power in the hands of certain classes in American society that accounts for disparities in income, education, general living standards, and life chances. The behavioralists-pluralists counter by contending that everyone has an equal chance to get ahead in the open marketplace of contemporary American society, and that no single group or coalition of groups enjoys a controlling advantage in that marketplace.

It was no coincidence that the major foundations' collective interest in behavioralism crystallized just at the time that competing social science theories were challenging the continuing dominance of America's elites. Since the behavioralist approach did not raise fundamental questions regarding the existing social order, as did the work of the power-elitist school, it is understandable that such mainstream behavioralists-pluralists as Robert Dahl, David Truman, V. O. Key, and Gabriel Almond attracted significant foundation support, thereby explaining at least in part how the behavioralist approach soon became the authoritative voice of American political science.

A new direction in American economics was also becoming more noticeable during the 1950s. It was not long after Theodore Schultz's presidential address on the theme of Investment in Human Capital at the 1960 meeting of the American Economic Association that the theory of human capital became, according to Karabel and Halsey, "clearly ascendant in academic and policy circles, especially in the United States."[36] With Schultz setting the pace at the University of Chicago and Gary Becker doing similarly at Columbia University, there developed an influential group of economists who viewed the theory of human capital as the panacea for developmental problems both at home and abroad. Briefly stated, these economists viewed human beings as a form of capital, in which certain investments could be made, thereby guaranteeing predictable outcomes. Education was soon identified as a largely underutilized form of investment. More appropriate educational investment would insure significant returns beneficial both to the individual and to the society.

Implicit in this approach was the assumption that these individuals in whom an investment had been made would work in societies characterized by rapid economic growth and open political structures. Given the American penchant for equating development, whether at home or abroad, with economic growth and stability—a theme to which we shall return below—such an assumption was almost predictable. The Carnegie, Ford, and Rockefeller foundations generously subsidized the work of the leaders of this movement, including Schultz, Becker, and Denison at home, and the work of Frederick Harbison and Charles Myers abroad.[37]

The work of the human-capital theorists was no less ideological than that of their functionalist and behavioralist colleagues. Karabel and Halsey have remarked on the distinctly "pro-capitalist ideological sentiment" of human-capital theory and have noted how closely it affirmed the American way of life and the ideology of corporate liberalism at home. The fact that the theory supported the dominant American ideology of the day, they continue, coupled with "its ability to align itself with the increasingly powerful interests of the higher education industry, were doubtless factors in its attractiveness to holders of research funds, quite apart from its intrinsic merits as an intellectual tool of analysis and its precise quantitative methods."[38] Bowles and

Gintis elaborate on this assessment, noting how the intellectual framework of human-capital theory "provides an elegant apology for almost any pattern of oppression or inequality (under capitalism, state socialism, or whatever), for it ultimately attributes social or personal ills either to the shortcomings of individuals or the unavoidable requisite of production. It provides, in short, a good ideology for defense of the status quo."[39]

By the early 1960s, then, just at the time when the Carnegie, Ford, and Rockefeller foundations were making serious commitments to the growth of area-studies programs in several major American universities, the social sciences in those universities were increasingly being dominated by intellectual perspectives that were basically conservative and oriented toward maintenance of the existing social arrangements in the United States. It was not mere coincidence that these particular perspectives were in ascendency; the available data indicate that they had been handsomely subsidized by the same foundations whose funding was now building the area-studies programs. This arrangement should cause little surprise: the evolving liberal theory, like all ruling ideologies, was designed to support extant interests, all disclaimers to the contrary notwithstanding. The elaboration of this theory in a manner that suggested its autonomous development was an important mechanism to support and subsequently to disseminate the dominant ideology.

This attempt to design an intellectual support system for the existing societal organization at home was significant, if predictable, in its own right. Of importance also was the fact that these same foundation-sponsored disciplines of sociology, political science, and economics were, together with language study, to form the core of the area-studies programs. These three disciplines would also provide the data from which models for Third-World development would be constructed. The restructuring of Third-World educational institutions was to form a crucial component of these developmental models.

The increasingly technical and quantitative approaches that characterized sociology, political science, and economics served to obfuscate the more fundamental structural imbalances threatening the fabric of American society and the true nature of developmental problems in the Third World. The social scientists-cum-technicians argued that their sophisticated methodological approaches were designed to address just such questions and represented the sole guarantee against ideological biases creeping into their research. Implicit in this argument was that other approaches were ideological, polemical, unscientific, and consequently unprofessional, and that they, the mainstream social scientists, were the champions of value-free inquiry dedicated to an unfettered search for the truth. At the same time, they could point to support from the major foundations as evidence for their claim that their work represented disinterested and dispassionate inquiry. Very little attention seems to have been given to the ideological orientations of the foundations themselves or to the assumptions underlying the social scientists' approaches in their respective disciplines.

While the social scientists argued that they were interested only in the value-free and nonideological research and data that their sophisticated methodological models helped to collect, they failed to recognize, or at any rate to admit, that the questions they posed were designed to produce only a limited range of possible answers which tended to confirm their hypotheses. Andreski feels that the undue emphasis that these social scientists placed on methodological concerns was purposeful. "By averting the eyes from the explosive issues of the day," he argues, "methodological purism acts in fact as a prop of the *status quo* whatever it might be, which largely explains the worldly success of its devotees and the wide appeal of their creed."[40] A search for the truth predicated on certain givens, givens that circumscribe the range of possible answers, is of course no less ideological than the most clearly articulated ideology. Gunnar Mydral has commented on this with his usual lucidity:

> A "disinterested" social science has never existed and never will exist. For logical reasons, it is impossible. A view presupposes a viewpoint. Research, like every other rationally pursued activity, must have a direction. The viewpoint and the direction are determined by our own interest in the matter. Valuations enter into the choice of an approach, the selection of problems, the definitions of concepts, and the gathering of data, and are by no means confined to the practical or political inferences drawn from theoretical findings. The value premise that actually and of necessity determines approaches in the social sciences can be hidden . . . In fact, most writings, particularly in economics, remain in large part simply ideological.[41]

Given the valuations or, as Gouldner calls them, the background assumptions of the mainstream social scientists and their foundation sponsors regarding the organization of the domestic society and the course that social change should take abroad, it would be surprising if the theories that they espoused for Third-World development were any less ideological than those that characterized their investigations of domestic phenomena. It is to an examination of these theories that we now turn.

The Social Scientists' View of Development

American ideas about the modernization or development of the nations of the Third World were inextricably linked to the need, identified by

Tipps, to find "long-range solutions to the threats of instability and Communism in the Third World."[42] Arthur Schlesinger, Jr., noted that the social scientists and Washington policy makers they advised hoped "to persuade the developing countries to base their revolutions on Locke rather than on Marx."[43] W. W. Rostow argued in a similar vein in his influential book *The Stages of Economic Growth*. "The ideological dimensions of the Cold War heighten a sense of choice concerning the appropriate political and social techniques for modernization," he wrote. The lines needed to be firmly drawn because of "the existence of the international Communist movement, with its explicit objective of takeover within the underdeveloped areas." He considered "the most important single item on the Western agenda" to be the ability to "demonstrate that the underdeveloped nations . . . can move successfully through the preconditions into a well-established take-off within the orbit of the democratic world, resisting the blandishments and temptations of Communism."[44]

Packenham's study of the political development ideas holding sway among mainstream American social scientists during the period from 1947 to 1968 notes that the consensus held that modernization could be brought about by gradual change, orchestrated by a well-educated elite imbued with the efficacy of democratic ideals as epitomized by the Westminster or Washington model and dedicated to the principle of economic growth.[45] An examination of the literature of the mainstream social scientists, most of whose work was supported by grants from the Carnegie, Ford, and Rockefeller foundations, reveals that the modernity advocated for the developing nations had, as O'Brien notes, a distinctly American face.[46] This is hardly surprising because, according to Horowitz and Katz, of "the automatic assumption [on the part of American social scientists] that social science did indeed have values: the values of the 'American century'."[47] But by some distorted quirk of logic, many social scientists argued that their approach to developmental theory, embodying as it did "the values of the 'American century'," did not constitute an ideology! Perhaps they truly believed that the Western world at least had reached, as the title of Daniel Bell's book put it, *The End of Ideology*.

Foundation support for political development theory in the Third World was channeled through the Committee on Comparative Politics of the Social Science Research Council, which according to Seybold, was dominated by political scientists of a distinctly behavioralist and pluralist orientation.[48] In 1960 the first of a series of influential books collectively entitled "Series in Political Development" appeared, and was followed within the next few years by several others that set the standard for political development theory in the United States.[49] The secretary of the Committee on Comparative Politics, whose major responsibility was coordinating grant applications and recommending research to be funded, was Bryce Wood, a former assistant director of the Rockefeller Foundation's Division of Social Science at the time when the foundation embarked on its substantial program to build centers of social science excellence in Third-World universities in the late 1950s.

The books in the political development series, together with several other series in the field which appeared in the 1960s, are noteworthy for their emphases on evolutionary change, political stability, institution building, and the mobilization of elites to effect the desired changes. The emphasis on elites derived from the need to mold and patronize a class that shared the American values of order, stability, and evolutionary change and that would run their polities in ways to insure these outcomes. O'Brien speaks to this point, noting how American political scientists of the period stressed "the need to create an international community of political elites, a 'world culture' in which modern (American) values became widely if not universally shared."[50] The degree to which the foundation shared this perspective was spelled out by the Ford Foundation vice-president who noted that the key to successful developmental efforts in the Third World required that the foundations play "an important role in linking the modernizing elites of the world."[51]

An unarticulated assumption running through this literature was that the masses in Africa, Asia, and Latin America shared the general American values of industrial democracy, political stability, economic growth, and social progress a l'Américain. In reality, of course, there are no empirical data to indicate that the masses indeed did so, but this lack did not deter the mainstream social scientists from constructing intricate models premised on the assumption that these values were truly universal.[52] This assumption is more understandable, however, when we recall that one of the tenets of the dominant American ideology in the post-1945 period held that "the United States should, at all times, exert its influence and power in behalf of a world order congenial to American ideals, interests, and security. . . . It can do this without egotism because of its deep conviction that such a world order will best fulfill the hopes of mankind."

The viewpoint was expressed by Harvard historian William Langer in a foundation-supported study issued in 1960. Langer had worked with the Office of Strategic Services during World War II and for the CIA in the early 1950s. He also worked closely with Ford Foundation officials to help them define their overseas programs during this period.[53] Social progress, industrial democracy, political participation, economic growth, stability—these were very much the developmental goals that the United States wanted to encourage during the 1960s "on behalf of a world order congenial to American ideals, interests, and security."

Several commentators have suggested that some of the influential social scientists concerned with developmental problems in the Third World were less concerned with ascertaining the desires of the people in these areas than insuring that their particular visions of development were imposed on the populations in question—by whatever means might be required. O'Brien, for example, mentions Lucien Pye, long-time member of the Social Science Research Council, as an exponent of the concept of incremental, controlled development imposed by American-backed indigenous elites.[54] Another, perhaps more influential, advocate of this view is Samuel Huntington, Harvard professor, member of the National Security Council in the Carter administration, and Vietnam War planner. Huntington is also the coauthor of *The Crisis of Democracy.* This book, one of several commissioned by the Trilateral Commission, was published in 1975 and attracted considerable attention because of its uncharacterically blunt attack on the "excesses of democracy" and the "reassertion of democratic egalitarianism" in the United States. The remedy for these unhealthy trends, according to Huntington's analysis, was a return to a more manageable and efficient system of elite governance.[55] The work of Huntington, Pye, et al., has been supported by one or another of the major foundations over the years, either through the Social Science Research Council or, more recently, the Council on Foreign Relations' 1980's Project or the Trilateral Commission.[56]

Sandbrook's comments on two representative works of American political development theory of the 1970s are instructive for the light they shed on the manner in which the foundation-supported conservative ideology encompassed within this theory became the received wisdom.[57] The two books discussed are *Crises and Sequences in Political Development,* edited by Leonard Binder et al., and *Crisis, Choice, and Change: Historical Studies in Political Development,* edited by Almond, Flanagan, and Mundt. The former, which was published in 1971 as the seventh book in the Princeton "Studies in Political Development" series, lists as coeditors no fewer than five of the ten members of that year's committee on comparative politics of the Social Science Research Council, including the chairman, Lucien Pye.

The senior editor of *Crisis, Choice, and Change*—which was published two years later—is one of the doyens of American behavioralism, a long-time member of the Committee on Comparative Politics, and a regular recipient of foundation support. Throughout these two volumes, and particularly noticeable in the Binder work, is a perspective that "is incontrovertibly that of a governing elite." Sandbrook notes that some of the developmental strategies which the political elites have utilized and those which several of the book's authors advocate "have authoritarian implications." He concludes by noting that "the interest in order of those at the top is given logical precedence over the interest in social justice and those below."

Although the social scientists concerned with developmental theory during this period were clearly recognizable by their specialities, the hard and fast disciplinary lines that often characterized other parts of the American university tended to be less rigid in the case of development studies. Perhaps this resulted from the coming together of social scientists within the framework of area-studies programs, perhaps from the fact that development was simply too large a concept to be encompassed within the confines of one discipline. Whatever the case might be, it was not unusual to find the political scientists and political sociologists dealing with the vagaries of economic growth and indicating that this was the main requisite of the political democracy that they were advocating for the developing nations. A good illustration of this tendency to cross disciplinary lines was in the related fields of economics, education, and political theory, and here James S. Coleman's *Education and Political Development*, published in 1965 as part of the "Studies in Political Development" series, set the standard.

The contributions of the political scientists and political sociologists to a coherent development theory was augmented, and perhaps exceeded, by the work of the economists, particularly those of the human-capital persuasion. This human-capital or manpower-planning approach to Third-World development first received wide currency when the Carnegie Corporation sponsored the much-heralded Ashby Commission study of educational needs in Nigeria, which was published in 1960.[58] An important part of that report was a manpower projection forecast for the period 1960–80, the work of Princeton University economist Frederick Harbison. His estimates of the high-level manpower requirements for Nigeria during the period were followed by estimates of the kinds and quantity of schools necessary to fulfill these needs. This work represented an internationalization of the efforts of Schultz and his followers at Chicago at the same time. It very quickly was accepted as the norm in the field and was viewed as a prerequisite for orderly growth and development abroad. The evident success of the manpower-planning scheme in the Ashby report led this human-resources theory of development to win numerous adherents during the next few years.[59]

To encourage this end, the Ford Foundation joined with the Carnegie Corporation to institutionalize the approach and to spread the gospel among the unconverted. On the heels of the completion of the Ashby report the two foundations convened a major conference at Princeton in 1960, out of which came a commitment to underwrite research and publication of a series of books dealing with the efficacy of human-resources theory as a prerequisite for orderly growth and development in the nations of the Third World. The publication in 1964 of Harbison and Charles Myers' *Education, Manpower, and Economic Growth* in the McGraw-Hill "Series in International Development" marked the initial effort to legitimate the manpower-planning approach as an integral component of developmental theory abroad.[60] One of the five members of the advisory editorial board for this series, John Weir, was at the time a Rockefeller Foundation officer who played an important role in the foundation's University Development Program in Africa, Asia, and Latin America.

This commitment to the Princeton gathering was not an isolated attempt by the foundations to further the particular ideology embodied in human-resource theory. In 1963, for example, a conference on the theme of Education and the Development of Nations was convened at Syracuse University with foundation support. The resulting volume, Hobart Burns's book of the same title, provides an indication of the gist of the proceedings and the increasing acceptance of the importance of human-capital theory for Third-World development. The same year the foundations channeled money through the Committee on Economic Growth of the Social Science Research Council to support a conference at the University of Chicago on "The Role of Education in the Early Stages of Development." The proceedings, edited by Anderson and Bowman and supported by foundation funds, were published under the title *Education and Economic Development.* Despite the expression of some cautionary, and even dissenting, views, the papers collected in this volume gave further credence to the efficacy of the manpower-planning and human-capital approaches to Third-World development.

Mention has already been made of the basically conservative nature of human-capital theory at home and the manner in which it tends to reinforce the existing order. Similar conservative biases accompany the transference of the theory to developing nations. Karabel and Halsey, for example, note how the theory posits that the poverty of Third-World nations is not attributable to the structure of international economic relations, but is due to "internal characteristics—most notably their lack of human capital." Such internal deficiences, consequently, support the contention that remedy lies not in radical structural change, but rather in the improvement within developing nations of "their woefully inadequate human resources." As at home so it is abroad: "attention [is] thus deflected from structural variables onto individuals."[61]

An argument could be made that the foundations were supporting human-capital theory because it demonstrated empirically the relationship between investment in individuals and economic growth. Unfortunately for the proponents of such a viewpoint this simply is not the case, certainly not to the extent that its defenders would have us believe. Carnoy, for one, argues that the contribution of schooling to growth "is probably smaller than the early human-capital theorists and development economists thought."[62] At the same time that the foundations were subsidizing the conservative ideology of human-capital theory, empirical studies were demonstrating that investment in education will not of itself lead to higher paying jobs and/or economic development without a significant increase in the total number of good jobs in the economy.[63] Put another way: investment in human resources *might* lead to a higher rate of economic growth after the economy has reached a higher level of development than at present. To get the economy to such a stage, however, would most probably entail significant structural alterations in the society, an occurrence that the ideology supporting developmental theory wanted to avoid.

This led to the paradoxical situation whereby the foundations continued to underwrite human-resource theory despite the increasing evidence that it could not attain the goals claimed for it. One reason for this was their desire to legitimate a developmental model that was ideologically congruent with their own worldview. Once this paradigm was discredited, however, they shifted their funding to other developmental concerns, e.g., nonformal education, that offered the possibility of incremental and controlled social change in the Third World.[64]

As with the political scientists and economists, the contributions of the sociologists to general developmental theory tended to extend beyond their traditional disciplinary boundaries. The emphasis in the works of Havighurst, Shils, Eisenstadt, Lerner, Bendix, Lipset, and Levy was on the cultural and psychological factors that helped individuals achieve the characteristics of "modern" men, thereby leading to greater personal satisfaction and societal development. Their schooling in functionalist theory led these scholars by and large to take an evolutionary view of the developmental process, to argue that all good things will come in time, and that traditional societies will eventually evolve along lines characterized by rational-legal authority, as in the West. Implicit in this approach is an antipathy to radical or revolutionary change (after all, one can't rush the evolutionary stages), a failure to recognize the distorting nature of European colonialism on Third-World development (viewed as just one more stage in the evolutionary process, of no more or less importance than others), and a failure to deal with structural inequalities which frequently preclude the possibility of meaningful development.[65]

The approach of Robert Havighurst, the University of Chicago sociologist, one-time officer of the Rockefeller's General Education Board, and frequent beneficiary of foundation largesse, is indicative of the way in which mainstream sociologists exercise great selectivity in their approach to developmental problems. His work indicates as well how sponsored scholars frequently manage to obfuscate the significant structural issues involved in Third-World development, while concentrating their efforts on issues peripheral to widespread human advancement, all the time arguing that they are engaged in value-free inquiry.[66]

In his *Society and Education in Brazil* (like the political scientists and economists, the sociologists frequently looked at the role of education in the developmental process), Havighurst avoids a discussion of the class inequalities which so characterize Brazil and impede the development of all but a small sector of that nation. The book does contain, however, a section arguing that the misery of the Brazilian masses is attributable to their own shortcomings, a position that serves to exonerate the socioeconomic system from its responsibilities for the gross inequalities endemic there. After acknowledging that most of the lower classes are "morally respectable," he notes that "this class also includes the majority of the unemployable, the irresponsible, and the criminal." Their problems are of their own making, however, because their "attitude toward life is one of passive fatalism—accepting their lot without making much effort to change it."[67] No mention is made either of centuries of exploitation of the masses by the elites or of the contemporary structural inequalities that favor the few and disadvantage the many; instead, we are given a treatise to the effect that all would be well if only the masses were more like those who investigated them.

The Consensus on Third-World Development

The work of these development-oriented sociologists, like that of their fellow social scientists, was heavily subsidized by the Ford, Carnegie and Rockefeller foundations, either directly or through the Social Science Research Council. Ford's Melvin Fox recalled how the foundation was "twisting arms very, very vigorously" to get scholars to concentrate on development theory.[68] Foundation subsidization of the work of these mainstream social scientists had its desired effect. By the late 1960s, as Packenham indicates, there had evolved a clearly delineated viewpoint among mainstreams social scientists in elite American universities, as well as among Washington policy makers, regarding the most efficacious path to development for Third-World nations. This consensus held that Third-World development should be carried out

> mainly in terms of stable, nonradical, constitutional, and, if possible, peaceful and pro-American policies. . . . The scholars and policymakers supplemented economic determinism with sociological and psychological determinism. Both groups also largely assumed the converse, namely, the beneficience for socio-economic transformation of stable, constitutional political systems.[69]

The fact that such conservative ideas concerning development meshed perfectly with the goals of United States was not fortuitous. Myrdal has noted that American studies of the developing world at this time were "expected to reach opportune conclusions [by their sponsoring agencies], and to appear in a form that is regarded as advantageous, or at least not disadvantageous, to national interests as these are popularly understood."[70] The interests of the United States in the Third World, as popularly understood at the time by mainstream social scientists and policy makers, were defined in terms of gradual movement toward a form of Western democracy, continued alignment to the world capitalist system, continued access to strategic raw materials, order, and stability, and at best a policy not antagonistic to the United States— all of which were to be encouraged by the nurturing of an indigenous elite that understood the benefits that could accrue from such policies.

O'Brien notes that this developmental consensus endorsed the leadership role of "technological and bureaucratic elites." The political scientists concerned with the development shared the "bureaucrat's perspective in fearing the passion and unpredictability which may be unleashed if people escape control from above."[71] Social scientists, business leaders, foundation personnel, and those who implemented United States foreign policy agreed on the importance of order and stability for Third-World development. Packenham notes that the consensus held that "radical politics, including conflict, disorder, violence, and revolution, are unnecessary for economic and political development and therefore are always bad."[72] As early as 1949 the director of the Rockefeller Foundation's Division of Social Science commented on the role of the social sciences in helping "to serve the orderly evolution of the unindustrialized countries."[73] In short, the measured and gradual development of Third-World nations was seen to serve the interests of world stability, preclude the advance of "radical" regimes and the concomitant possibility of nationalization of foreign holdings, while simultaneously affording an international context within which the major foundations could play crucial roles in developing national polities.

The views of the social scientists, foundation personnel, and government officials toward Third-World development were mutually reinforcing. Many of the key foundation personnel concerned with the social sciences had worked in one of the Washington agencies involved with foreign policy in the immediate post-1945 period, while others had close ties to major American universities.

This period was also characterized by the frequent movement of social scientists between their university bases and policy centers in Washington, where they made available to government officials their analyses of social phenomena at home and abroad and suggested policy options for implementation. So broad was the evolving consensus concerning the ideology of corporate liberalism at home and imperial liberalism abroad that such interaction only strengthened the sense of rectitude—if not arrogance—which characterized the work of the mainstream social scientists. Halberstam's analysis of the planning and implementation of the Vietnam war largely on the basis of the "expert" and "objective" advice by intellectuals with pronounced social science backgrounds of the mainstream variety is, of course, the best documented—and most appalling—manifestation of this syndrome.[74] To these people the struggle against the communist juggernaut was beyond ideology. To intimate that their work was ideologically biased was tantamount to questioning their integrity.

This ideological commitment to America's international role meant that the theories of development elaborated by the foundation-supported academics only gained currency to the degree that they were judged to be supportive of the broader foreign-policy objectives that grew out of that ideology. Such theories restricted the possible range of development in the Third World to options that were perceived as advantageous to the United States, but not necessarily to the developing nations in question, all the rhetoric to the contrary notwithstanding. Developmental theories posited on the assumptions of gradualism, the maintenance of the existing institutional order, the legitimacy and inviolability of certain elites, the importance of sustained economic growth—to name only several—refuse to recognize that the price of such development in terms of human misery and suffering may exceed that of development brought about through revolution and different forms of economic and social arrangements. Such views are also ahistorical. The development of the West was generally accompanied by revolution and civil war, as Rhodes, for one, notes. He asks how rational people can ignore this reality when focusing on the contemporary Third World and continually stressing order and stability.[75] While Barrington Moore's views on these subjects have received a polite response from academics, the implications of his work have been largely ignored.[76] The proponents of gradualism and moderation, wedded as they are to Western-oriented institutions, elite domination, and modi operandi which do little to alleviate the plight of the masses in the underdeveloped nations while ensuring extended markets for capitalist activity, continue to see their particular viewpoint prevail.

Sharing as they did in the belief of America's imperial mission, foundation personnel allocated their funds for developmental social science work to insure that only "responsible" viewpoints (read, viewpoints that generally concurred in the tenets of imperial liberalism) would be circulated among members of the academic community and to Washington policy makers. While an occasional "radical" viewpoint (e.g., Moore's or Robert Heilbroner's) might be funded, generally through the Social Science Research Council, there was little chance that his isolated voice could be of consequence as it contested with the more numerous voices of developmental orthodoxy. Indeed, it is conceivable that occasional funding of a study contravening the established position was even advantageous for the foundations. The dissenting viewpoint could be used to counter foundation critics who charged that the organizations only subsidized researchers supportive of the foundations' preconceived positions on particular issues.[77]

The social science emphasis on evolutionary development and institutional order in the Third World should be understood in the context of the international role that the social scientists, foundation officers, and government officials deemed appropriate for the United States. The messianic quality of American foreign policy, with its rigid dichotomies between the "good guys" (the United States and its allies) and the "bad guys" (the Soviet Union and its satellites) during the cold-war hysteria of the 1950s and early 1960s, coupled with the frequent movement of American academics to and from official and advisory positions in Washington, made almost inevitable the acceptance of the shibboleths of American foreign policy by numerous academics, particularly those in positions to comment on the dangers for the developing world inherent in Soviet expansionism.[78] But an understanding of the antecedents of such views in no way lessens the ideology supporting them.

The Outcomes and Implications of Sponsored Developmental Theory

The foundations' support of the "objective" research of a group of recognized social scientists helped to legitimate an ideological approach to developmental problems that took place within foundation-supported area-studies programs. The views that these social scientists articulated became, after a modicum of debate, the accepted dogma on problems of Third-World development. Their pronouncements were held to represent the only worthwhile approaches to Third-World development problems. These intellectuals acted, in Gramsci's phrase, as the "experts in legitimation."[79]

Bodenheimer's examination of the application of this developmental consensus in Latin America led her to discover its origins in "the concrete realities of U.S.-Latin American relations." She notes also "how it is deeply rooted in the political economy of mid-20th century America." This scholarly consensus, which she terms the "paradigm-surrogate," cannot be divorced from the "dominant interests within the American social order—interests which also play a decisive role in shaping United States policy toward Latin America."[80]

The Latin American-based developmental studies by United States researchers have distorted the reality of the region because of the intellectual assumptions inherent in the dominant theory. The methodological approaches utilized have led to the collection of only a limited range of data, which in turn have contributed to this skewed image. These data, which are generally supportive of existing Latin American-U.S. relations, are then used to "prove" that the presuppositions about the nature of Latin America were valid. The ideologically grounded and unidimensional theories of development that dominate United States research on Latin America tend, at the same time, to preclude the formulation of alternative development theories that might better serve the interests of greater numbers of Latin Americans. Bodenheimer notes that one salient aspects of the dominant theory "leaves room neither for the alternative routes or objectives of development, nor for the possibility that the current route may lead to a dead end or to economic stagnation."[81]

The ideology of the dominant developmental theory stands in clear relief in Latin America. Bodenheimer writes how the theory devalues the importance of class differences, thereby practically eliminating the problem of stratified power relationships. An analysis of the problems of Latin America that ignores the importance and implications of widening social-class differences is, to put it generously, myopic. But because the theory is dedicated to the concepts of order and stability, and because class conflicts invariably threaten these, the dominant theory is ill-equipped to raise the possibility that only a radical reorganization of existing social relations can lead to meaningful development. Instead, the theory "projects a pious hope that development can be achieved without paying the high cost of removing the social and economic obstacles, that the impoverished masses can somehow be upgraded without infringing on the interests of the established elites."[82] Such an attempt is consistent with the foundations' sincere efforts to alleviate the misery of the masses through gradual, ameliorative reform, while at the same time leaving society's direction—at home and abroad—in the hands of a carefully nurtured elite.

DiBona's study of the impact of Western development theory in India reaches similar conclusions.[83] He notes the influence on Indian educational planning of the American economists of the human resource school, particularly Schultz, Harbison, Myers, Denison, Anderson, and Bowman. Their emphasis on the training of high-level manpower for developmental purposes has influenced Indian economists to argue in favor of generous funding for institutions of higher learning. Because of the scarcity of resources available in the Indian economy, however, this emphasis on higher education has led to reduced levels of support for primary education, particularly in rural areas. The vast majority of

Indians, of course, are village dwellers. The increasing proportion of educational expenditures on higher education—which is generally available exclusively in urban areas—only widens the gap between the urban elites and the rural peasantry.

An increasing number of commentators have raised questions about the direction of conventional developmental theory, its efficacy, and its impact on traditional societies. Ford Foundation vice-president Francis Sutton has noted the inability of this theory and of existing Western social science to address the problems faced by most developing countries, particularly the establishment of "governments that have extensive control over their economies and are broadly socialist in character."[84] Former Secretary of State Kissinger, in discussing the overthrow of the regime of the Shah of Iran, recently alluded to a problem of conventional development theory. "The enlightened view," he said, "was that there was a sort of automatic stabilising factor in economic development. That has turned out to be clearly wrong."[85]

Others have elaborated on these assessments. F. J. Method, for one, notes how most assistance to Third-World nations "has tended to foster development also conventional lines, strengthening the modern sector . . . but doing little to support local change and to assist people with problems of living outside the modern sector."[86] John A. Smyth feels that a major shortcoming of the efforts of the Western developmental agencies has been the preoccupation with an "economically efficient educational investment" at the expense of a concern for equity.[87] This emphasis on "efficiency" derives from the need to obtain quantifiable results that demonstrate movement and "gain." The relationships linking these concepts to capitalism and Western social science are patent.

Wolf notes the disruptive impact on traditional societies of "the world-wide spread and diffusion of a particular cultural system, that of North Atlantic capitalism."[88] The distinctive economic structure of this cultural system "was profoundly alien to many of the areas which it engulfed." At the same time, such an economic structure formed the basis for the developmental theories designed for implementation in these same societies. To put the matter another way: Western capitalism was an integral part of the dominant developmental theory that emerged after 1945; this theory was dependent for its implementation on Third-World elites who accepted the organizational and social patterns inherent in a society with a capitalist orientation (whether of the laissez-faire or welfare-state variety); both these elites and the theory that they embodied were antithetical to traditional values. The newly introduced capitalist order, incorporated as it was into the conventional developmental plan, "cut through the integument of custom, severing people from their accustomed social matrix in order to transform them into economic actors, independent of prior social commitments to kin and neighbors." It is the disruptive nature of the Western developmental theory that leads observers like Mazrui to ask "whether modernization can be decolonized without being destroyed."[89]

Weisskopf doubts that this is possible. He cites especially the "dominance of the foreign-oriented [indigenous] elites . . . of educational institutions, communications media, and cultural resources," and notes how these "tend to amplify the threat to indigenous cultural development."[90] Mazrui expands on this, noting how the African universities turn out graduates who not only have come to dominate their respective societies, but who are at the same time "the most deeply westernized" and "the most culturally dependent."[91] This is no less true for graduates from those Latin American and Asian universities supported by the foundations for their African counterparts.

The increased awareness by foundation representatives and by Third-World nationals that conventional developmental theory has not fulfilled its promise has not, however, led to a reformulation of the theory's main tenets. There are several reasons for this. One of these, according to Miller, is that the emphasis on sustained economic growth has not diminished.[92]

This leads to the second reason. The developmental plans of most Third-World nations today are in the hands of indigenous policy makers. These leaders have been educated in, or at least greatly influenced by, orthodox developmental theory. This means, to borrow from Fagen, that "the majority of elites speaking in the name of the South [the developing nations in the southern hemisphere] have from the outset been spokesmen for, and in some cases even the direct creation of, national and international class interests quite satisfied with the existing world economic system if not with their share of the pie." Some of these elites are certainly interested in altering the inequitable system favoring the developed nations at the expense of their own. They are, however, powerless to alter the existing situation as long as their polities remain dependent upon the centers of world capitalism. According to Fagen: "only profound changes in the developmental strategies currently in use (not just the elites in power) can significantly alter this situation. Whether alterations this profound can be other than socialist *and* revolutionary remains to be demonstrated historically."[93]

It is doubtful if the American foundations, which have played such a crucial role in the evolution of the developmental theory that has led to this situation *and* which are dedicated to the furtherance of the capitalist system from which they sprang, will agree to support studies that lead to the significant reformulation of the existing strategies that is required to make development more than a chimera for the majority of Third-World peoples.[94] A significant alteration in the developmental strategies currently in vogue means a concomitant restructuring of international economic and political relationships. There is no evidence to date to indicate that the foundations would agree to such a drastic measure. A tangible result of the failure of the foundations and other national and multinational aid agencies to help reformulate existing developmental strategies, however, may be more mass-based revolutionary movements similar to those in Nicaragua and El Salvador.

5

Foundation Influence on Intermediate Organizations, International Forums, and Research

The Carnegie, Ford, and Rockefeller foundations regularly supported outside organizations that implemented their programs. At the same time, they funded international conferences convened to discuss particular issues. They also made grants to enable ostensibly independent researchers to examine predetermined topics. This chapter examines foundation support in each of these areas and indicates how these funding patterns have helped to legitimate the foundations' ideology, while simultaneously furthering United States foreign-policy interests.

The foundations delegate many tasks to outside agencies or individuals to avoid any semblance of involvement in particular programs or findings, and to minimize as well the charge that their financial support is tantamount to undue influence, if not to control. While they eschew any involvement in the direction of the affairs of these outside agencies, for example, they unfailingly exercise the greatest care when selecting personnel to run these agencies created through or supported by their funding. The leverage that the foundations have over these agencies is no less real for being indirect. The distance that they place between themselves and the organizations that carry out their programs is an important element in the extension of the foundations' hegemony because this arrangement gives the funded agencies the *appearance* of independence.

Caution is further exercised when the foundations determine which organization or individual should be chosen to undertake a particular study. This procedure helps to insure that the study's conclusions fall within margins of acceptability to the foundation sponsor, and at the same time serves to legitimate previous foundation thinking on the issue. The foundations deflect the criticism that their support leads to conclusions generally supportive of their earlier positions by claiming that the criteria used in the selection of scholars for their commissioned studies are limited to objectivity, independence, and professional detachment. These works frequently set the tone for public discussions of particular issues, while that same public remains unaware that the foundations' imprimatur is indelibly embossed on them.

The chapter's next section examines the pattern of foundation support for several organizations that implemented programs determined by foundation personnel. Carnegie, Ford, and Rockefeller officers recognized that their institutions' extensive concerns could only be furthered by outside agencies, whose focus was more narrowly defined than their own. If the foundations could not identify an appropriate outside agency to oversee important programs, they simply created one. Ford's F. C. Ward spoke to this point when, in 1956, he circulated a memorandum concerning the foundation's continuing support for the Institute of International Education. After noting that the institute "has been the principal 'exchange of persons' service agency for the Foundation since 1951," and indicating the annual subsidy that flowed from the foundation to the institute, Ward repeated the opinion "that if IIE did not exist the Foundation would have to create it for these purposes."[1]

An organization like the Institute for International Education was only one among several kinds that enjoyed foundation support. There were those that coordinated American educational resources for developmental aid, e.g., the Africa Liaison Committee and Education and World Affairs. The International Council for Educational Development and the Overseas Development Council were, and remain, heavily involved in field-based projects supported by the foundations. The foundations also supported agencies whose main purpose was the dissemination of propaganda designed to discourage flirtation with any variant of socialism. The Congress for Cultural Freedom warrants a few words in this context.

Foundation support for these organizations frequently was coupled with funding from an agency of the United States government, one of the multinational aid agencies, or a major corporation. Although the foundation contribution to a particular organization might be a small dollar amount, the foundation's influence was nonetheless significant in determining the organization's direction. Ford's John Howard commented on the degree of control exercised by the parent foundation several years after he establish, with Ford money, a semiautonomous agency. He noted that although his organization, the International Legal Center, had "my own board of trustees and we all have our own terms of reference, . . . we still could not survive without Ford support."[2] The degree of dependence is very real.

Among the other means used by the foundations to further their objectives was the convening of conferences, often international in nature and highly selective in their participants. The proceedings of these gatherings were sometimes published in monograph or book form. Because of their foundation sponsorship and list of respected contributors, these works frequently helped to establish the parameters within which particular issues were subsequently discussed. Several of these foundation-initiated conferences, particularly those that focused on developmental aid, will be discussed in this chapter.

There is some overlap in the following discussion of foundation support for outside organizations, international conferences, and independent research. These clearly are not mutually exclusive categories. They are presented as such, however, in an attempt to clarify the range of foundation involvement in the shaping of intellectual and cultural perspectives on certain issues and in the creation of developmental modalities.

Foundation Support for Outside Organizations

Exchange of Persons Agencies: The Institute of International Education

The Institute of International Education (IIE) was established in 1919 with a grant from Carnegie Endowment for International Peace. Until 1946 it remained a small organization administering exchange fellowships. Most of its funding during this quarter century came from grants from the Carnegie Corporation, the Laura Spelman Rockefeller Memorial (which was absorbed into the Rockefeller Foundation in 1929), and member universities affiliated with the American Council on Education.[3]

The passage in 1946 of the Fulbright Act for foreign-student exchange marked a watershed in the institute's fortunes. A late-1940s report on student exchanges recommended that a governmental agency, the Board of Foreign Scholarships, be responsible for the selection of foreign students to study in the United States and that the institute's role be limited to supervisory, counseling, and guidance functions. Despite the reservations expressed by IIE president Laurence Duggan about the dangers of using fellowships "to influence foreign students in the United States in favor of particular policies and programs,"[4] the increasing cold-war climate of the late 1940s and 1950s made just such an outcome almost inevitable. Duggan's successor, Kenneth Holland, accepted the institute's administrative role and at the same time searched for other ways to expand its service functions. As a result, the institute soon began administering student and professional exchange programs for U.S. corporations with overseas operations, the U.S. Army, and the major foundations.

The Ford Foundation initiated its overseas training programs in the early 1950s and quickly turned for assistance to IIE. As the foundation's international concerns expanded, so did its reliance on the institute's administrative apparatus. Ford's F. C. Ward placed the services rendered by IIE for the foundation into several categories: (1) logistical and administrative services for students; (2) arrangements for programs for overseas visitors; (3) a variety of supportive services for both American advisors working overseas and foreign nationals sent to the United States or a third country in connection with Ford projects; (4) procurement of overseas projects; and (5) fiscal agent.[5] The scope of the supportive services provided by the institute is suggested by Halpern's comment that "by 1966–67 the Institute was providing operational support for 95 Ford Foundation projects in approximately 40 countries."[6] In a similar vein, Ford's Melvin Fox estimated in 1965 that "there appear to be at least twenty distinct types of projects for which the Foundation uses IIE, each requiring somewhat different service responsibility and skills."[7]

Ford was not alone among the major foundations in its use of the institute to administer its programs, although its considerable expenditures frequently eclipsed the comparable activities of the Carnegie and Rockefeller foundations. In 1950, for example, the Carnegie Corporation decided to send several groups of American social scientists to Africa to ascertain the possibilities there for corporation programs. The IIE was asked to make the administrative arrangements for the project.[8]

This foundation reliance on the administrative apparatus of the institute led the foundations to become heavily involved in the institute's finances. This fiscal involvement took two forms: (1) the Carnegie, Ford, and Rockefeller foundations often granted lump sums to the institute for general support, and (2) the foundations and other institutions contracting for IIE's services paid set fees.[9] The significant level of their financial support meant that the major foundations could exert leverage on the institute to carry out internal reforms deemed necessary for more efficient operation. Such a situation occurred in the early 1950s, when the institute's functions were greatly enlarged because of its responsibility for administering the exchange programs growing out of the Smith-Mundt legislation in 1948. Representatives of three foundations met with institute president Kenneth Holland and informed him that the institute could expect significant foundation grants for general support if his organization's administrative structure were overhauled.[10]

There is a certain irony in the concern expressed by institute president Duggan in the late 1940s about the United States government using foreign fellowships as instruments of its foreign policy and his subsequent attempts, and those of his successor, to increase institute services for the major foundations, partially in hopes of lessening the institute's dependence on the government. By turning increasingly to the foundations as a source of support, the institute was only lessening its formal dependence on an official agency of the United States government, while at the same time becoming increasingly dependent on organizations whose overseas programs were designed to play integral roles in the furtherance of that government's foreign policy objectives.

Exchange of Persons Agencies: The African-American Institute

Another organization that administered some of the foundations' programs was the African-American Institute (AAI), but there was never any pretence on the part of AAI's officers that its role was other than the furtherance of United States foreign-policy interests. Nor was there any on the part of the foundations.

The AAI was founded in Washington, D.C., in 1953 and soon became an important nongovernmental organization concerned with African-American relations.[11] Its private character was a major consideration when government officials began searching for an organization to administer the growing African scholarship programs in the mid-1950s, in response to impending independence for several West African countries. The Bureau of Educational and Cultural Affairs and the International Cooperation Administrtion, which jointly were responsible for these programs, were not the only governmental agencies negotiating with the AAI at this time. The Central Intelligence Agency was centrally involved in the institute's affairs and remained so for nearly a decade. The chairman of the institute's board of trustees during the 1950s admitted that "the largest proportion of the more than $1 million which AAI spent in the 1950s came from the CIA."[12] Nor did he find this particularly noteworthy, since he felt that "AAI's scholarship programs, as well as its other activities, served the interests of African students, the countries from which the students came, and the interests of the United States."[13]

Officers of the Carnegie, Ford, and Rockefeller foundations were distressed, however, when rumors about the CIA's support for the institute began to circulate more widely in the early 1960s. Two major concerns apparently account for this discomfiture on the part of foundation officials. First, they feared that the public disclosure that such ostensibly independent organizations as AAI were in fact part of the

American foreign-policy nexus would destroy whatever credibility they had developed for their own overseas projects, as well as their fellowship programs.[14] The increasingly vocal Third-World claims regarding the omnipresence of the CIA, which was intent on insuring the continuance of indigenous regimes aligned with American interests, gained credibility as documentation of covert CIA activities affecting foreign nationals was revealed. Second, the Carnegie, Ford, and Rockefeller foundations were closely identified with the AAI through board memberships and program subsidies, associations that seemed certain to raise questions about their claims of disinterested concern for Third-World development.[15]

Several years before the 1967 disclosure about CIA funding for the institute, representatives of the foundations gathered and decided that deliberate action was necessary to place funding of the institute on a more respectable footing. Without undue delay, consequently, officers of the three foundations—joined by the Rockefeller Brothers Fund, whose president also served as chairman of AAI's board of trustees—agreed to underwrite the budget of the institute.[16] Part of this effort to legitimate the institute's standing involved the recruitment of a new president. Ford Foundation officer Waldemar Nielsen agreed to accept the position, with the proviso that CIA funding ceased. Nielsen and institute trustee Harold Hochschild met with McGeorge Bundy, then President Kennedy's special assistant for national-security affairs and subsequently Ford Foundation president, who assured them that the CIA funds would be replaced by comparable funding from the Agency for International Development (formerly the International Cooperation Administration). After this meeting the level of Ford Foundation grants to the institute increased significantly.[17]

Throughout the 1950s and 1960s the ostensibly independent and nongovernmental AAI undertook numerous tasks for the United States government, as indeed did the major foundations. The question of student exchanges became increasingly a concern after 1955 for both government officers and foundation executives. There was general dissatisfaction over the manner in which the exchange programs were administered. This led to a 1959 meeting called by the assistant secretary of state and attended by representatives of the International Cooperation Administration, the Office of Education, and the Carnegie, Ford, and Rockefeller foundations, at which it was agreed that periodic consultations and better coordination of resources was required. Everyone concerned viewed the student-exchange programs as an important foreign-policy consideration. The next year Ford's Melvin Fox wrote to a colleague that "the aggressive presence of the Communist world . . . has become a real factor in Africa in the past few years largely by means of increasing student and leader education exchange programs."

The United States could not sit by idly while the Communists indoctrinate Africa's future leaders in Iron Curtain universities, Fox argued. Rather, "educational exchange between Africa and the United States is an immediate problem of such potentially critical national and international importance that it merits Foundation attention."[18]

Later that month James P. Grant, assistant administrator of the International Cooperation Administration and later a Rockefeller Foundation trustee, wrote to Ford's John Howard regarding the intermediate role to be played by the African-American Institute in furthering these student exchanges and encouraging Ford to help out. The ICA agreed to allocate most of the money to facilitate these exchanges, but, according to Grant, aid officials "believe it extremely important that this program [of African scholarships] retain its private character both in the United States and, even more importantly, abroad. This would not be possible if the Government were to fund the administration as well as the maintenance part of the program." It would help to insure the program's credibility, he continued, if the Ford Foundation established "an effective non-governmental selection board in each African country." Then it would be "possible to screen candidates on the basis of academic qualifications without any taint of political intervention. This is extremely important in terms of the acceptability of the whole program in the African country which ultimately has to reabsorb the student into its society."[19]

The Ford Foundation decined to participate in the particular undertaking, but this did not lessen its influence at ICA. Nor did this refusal appreciably affect the foundation's relationship to AAI, whose level of government support increased significantly after 1960.[20] Ford's continuing role in AAI's affairs is suggested by the fact that Waldemar Nielsen was succeeded as institute president in 1970 by yet another former Ford official, William Cotter, who had worked for the foundation in Latin America during the 1960s. The Carnegie Corporation continued its interest in institute affairs throughout the 1960s as well. Corporation president Alan Pifer remained an AAI trustee, and in 1967 Carnegie began providing support for the institute's new school service division, which disseminated information on Africa to American schools.[21]

Agencies to Coordinate American Universities' International Activities

Africa Liaison Committee

By the late 1950s several foundation representatives had expressed concern about the haphazard nature of U.S. government and foundation developmental aid to Africa, particularly in the field of higher education.[22] This lack of a coordinated effort to address Africa's educational needs was considered particularly serious in view of the impending independence for several former colonies and the perceived Communist offensive designed to align the newly independent nations to the Soviet bloc. Carnegie's Alan Pifer led the search for a mechanism to remedy this situation and to create a clearinghouse for American universities interested in furthering African educational development.

The corporation had long-standing contacts with officials of the British colonial and foreign offices because of its work in Britain's African colonies during the interwar period. Limited by charter to ventures in British colonies and dominions, the Carnegie Corporation provided support for a number of British-affiliated universities in Africa and Asia and for others in Canada, Australia, New Zealand, and the West Indies. Additionally, the corporation had been a regular contributor to the Inter-University Council for Higher Education in the Colonies (IUC), a London-based coordinating body that oversaw colonial university development.

These contacts enabled Pifer to persuade influential members of the IUC and the Colonial Office to attend a 1958 Carnegie-sponsored conference at a West Virginia spa to discuss African educational needs with American government, foundation, and corporate officials. A number of meetings with representatives of the IUC and the Carnegie, Ford, and Rockefeller foundations took place during the following months. Participants agreed that African education would benefit if an American corrdinative body with functions similar to those of the IUC came into existence. This led to the creation, with Carnegie funding, of the Africa Liaison Committee, designed to serve as the agency through which American universities would channel proposals for work in African higher education.[23]

The Africa Liaison Committee (ALC) was formerlly established in 1959 and, after some initial squabbling over organizational matters and jurisdiction, was attached to the American Council on Education, the quasi-official lobby agency for American education. The committee received most of its early funding from Carnegie Corporation, whose officers were enthusiastic about the establishment of an organization that would keep a watchful eye on African higher education and look for American points of entry.[24]

The committee's charter members were influential members of the American higher education establishment and all had close ties to the foundations and the federal government. The committee's first chairman, J. L. Morrill, was at the time president of the University of Minnesota and subsequently became a consultant to the Ford Foundation and special assistant to the foundation's president. Morrill evinced no doubts as to the role that the foundations should play in the furtherance of American foreign-policy objectives, commenting that he and other Ford representatives regularly consulted with government agencies about the foundation's overseas work and that the foundation and the United States government "had, of course, very similar objectives" in their international programs.[25] Another charter member of the ALC was Clifford Hardin, who subsequently became secretary of agriculture in the Nixon Administration and a trustee of the Rockefeller Foundation.[26]

Organizations like the ALC were important not only for the coordinative and consultative functions that they performed, but also because their presence minimized the foundations' direct involvement in particular endeavors without in any way lessening their influence. One example involving the ALC will illustrate how Carnegie Corporation objectives were furthered by this surrogate.

ALC member Arthur Adams (who doubled as president of the American Council on Education) wrote to Carnegie's Alan Pifer on 2 May 1960 regarding the convening of the international conference later that year on the issue of "the development of higher education in Kenya, Uganda, and Tanganyika."[27] This coincided with the corporation's increased interest in African educational development. A memorandum recommending Carnegie support for Adam's proposal was circulated around the corporation's offices three days later by Pifer.[28] Even the vaguest familiarity with the norms of bureaucratic procedures suggests the impossibility of the corporation's officers having arrived at their decision to support this proposal without the most detailed consideration before submission of a formal request. The ALC request was agreed to, the funds appropriated, and the administrative details initiated to convene the large conference.

The Conference on Education in East Africa, sponsored by the Africa Liaison Committee and funded by Carnegie, was held during the first week of December 1960 in Princeton, New Jersey. The meeting was attended by representatives of the Carnegie, Ford, and Rockefeller foundations, the Department of State, the International Cooperation Administration, the African-American Institute, the Institute of International Education, the British Colonial Office, several major American universities, and the three East African territories of Kenya, Uganda, and Tanganyika.[29] The conferees noted especially the dearth of qualified secondary-school teachers available to the East African territories at a time when it was hoped that school enrolments would increase significantly. It was agreed that the foundations and the International Cooperation Administration should pool their resources, identify a significant American teacher-training institution, and support that institution's efforts to train a large number of American teachers to work in the rapidly expanding secondary-school network in East Africa.

Thus was created the Teachers for East Africa project.[30] Participants from this project staffed many East African secondary schools over the next several years.

The institution selected to administer the program was Columbia University's Teachers College, and the individual most responsible for insuring this choice was Karl W. Bigelow, who had already launched his own Carnegie-funded project in African teacher-education and who had worked with both Ford Foundation and ICA officials as well.[31] By this time Teachers College had received significant grants from ICA for educational activities around the world. These were soon augmented by additional grants for Peace Corps training programs in New York. In fact, Teachers College soon became an important center for the training of Peace Corps volunteers who would work in Africa, Asia, and Latin America.

The continuing flow of outside funding, which became an important component of the college budget as well as a source of prestige within the academic community, can perhaps be attributable to the fact that the Teachers College approach to Third-World educational development was identical to that of the funding agencies themselves, i.e., gradual, moderate, and predictable. Alternatively, an argument could be made that Teachers College received so many of these grants because of the general recognition that the college's programs and overarching ideology were supportive of the thrust of the evolving developmental theory of the time.

Education and World Affairs

Another organization created by the foundations to carry out their American university-based programs was Education and World Affairs (EWA). EWA grew out of a 1959 meeting held at the State Department and attended by the president of the Carnegie, Ford, and Rockefeller foundations and representatives of the Bureau of Educational and Cultural Affairs. Although the ALC was about to come into existence, the principals at this meeting felt that the committee's focus on African higher education necessitated the establishment of an agency concerned with the role of American universities in solving world problems and furthering American understanding of international affairs.[32] At the suggestion of Secretary of State Herter, Ford Foundation president Henry Heald commissioned a study group to recommend what action might be appropriate to focus attention of American universities on international affairs and world problems. The study group was chaired by J. L. Morrill and included the presidents of the three foundations and Senator J. William Fulbright, who had long been associated with university exchange programs. The group's recommendations were delineated in a 1961 study, *The University and World Affairs*. Later that year Ford appropriated $2 million and the Carnegie Corporation $500,000 to found Education and World Affairs. Carnegie officer William Marvel was selected EWA's president.

The main purposes of EWA were (1) the facilitation of communication "with agencies of government, business, foundations in the United States, and with institutions of other nations," for the "educational planning, the development and employment of educational competence in world affairs, and the systematic cumulation and appraisal of growing educational experience in world affairs,"[33] and (2) the initiation of "research conferences, publications, and other activities, all designed to strengthen the international dimensions of American universities."[34] Personnel at EWA saw their organization as a "neutral intermediary" or "honest broker" among the various groups involved in international education. They claimed that "the organization would provide a source of independent and authoritative advice on matters such as the development of educational institutions abroad, educational exchanges, and . . . support of American university programs for developing American competence."[35] They proclaimed their independence and neutrality while simultaneously accepting an increasing number of contracts from the Agency for International Development for specific projects and regularly consulting with Washington officials.[36]

Foundation support for EWA increased throughout the 1960s (the Ford Foundation appropriated another $2 million in 1963 and $3 million in 1966, while the Carnegie Corporation granted an additional $500,000 in 1967), but it soon became obvious that EWA had provided few vital services for the foundations. These latter, consequently, had no reason to sustain the organization, with the result that at the expiration of its foundation grants in 1971 Education and World Affairs was absorbed into yet another foundation-created organization, the International Council for Educational Development, whose key officers were former Carnegie vice-president James Perkins and former Ford officer Philip Coombs.

Agencies to Coordinate the Foundations' Developmental Strategies

International Council for Educational Development

The council focuses primarily on problems of rural development in the Third World. Council publications have paid special attention to the role of nonformal education in regenerating the rural sector. Philip Coombs has played the major role in articulating the importance of nonformal education as a means to close the gap between the relatively affluent and "modern" urban sectors and the generally poorer and traditional rural areas of many developing nations.

Coombs joined the staff of the Ford-created Fund for the Advancement of Education in the early 1950s. Several years later he was the guiding force behind the fund's air-borne educational television project. Utilizing a converted air-force plane, this project sought to provide televised instruction for school districts in several Midwestern states, which at the time were thought to be suffering from teacher shortages or a dearth of appropriate curriculum materials. As noted in Chapter 1, from 1961 to 1965 Coombs was assistant secretary of state for educational and cultural affairs and author of a book detailing the role of educational and cultural affairs in foreign-policy formulation. In the mid-1960s Coombs left the State Department to become head of the Paris-based International Institute of Educational Planning, a multinational organization supported by funds from UNESCO, the major American foundations, and member governments.

Foundation officers and other aid personnel recognized by the early 1970s that the developmental paradigms that they had supported were not significantly bettering the plight of the masses in the Third World. Poverty and stagnation, disease and illiteracy were as endemic then as when the foundations had conceptualized their initial development strategies two decades earlier. The foundations, consequently, took the lead in gathering the major donor agencies to discuss the future of their programs in light of a decade's depressing evidence. Several of these meetings took place at the Rockefeller Foundation's villa in northern Italy. One of the works emerging from these meetings appeared in 1974 and bore the suggestive title *Education and Development Reconsidered.*

What becomes clear from an examination of these gatherings was the concern among aid agencies that they develop new strategies for alleviating the problems of underdevelopment, even if they could not devise a new paradigm.[37] The search for a more viable developmental strategy led the aid agencies to a renewed interest in the potential contribution that nonformal education could make to rural development. The concept was not new; Coombs and his associates at the International Institute of Educational Planning in Paris had studied it in the 1960s. The developmental realities of the 1970s, however, gave the concept new life. By the mid-1970s the foundations, the World Bank, UNICEF, and the Agency for International Development were all championing nonformal education as the latest panacea for the problems of Third-World underdevelopment.

A significant part of the foundations' direct support for nonformal education was channeled through the International Council for Educational Development, which produced must of the seminal work detailing not only the efficacy of the concept, but elaborating as well specific strategies to be utilized.[38] The foundations' funding was frequently coupled with that from the World Bank, which supported its own research and field projects in nonformal education as well.

An analysis of the council's work on nonformal education reveals that this approach rested on a worldview remarkably like that of its foundation sponsors. This view held that change in the Third World was indeed desirable, but that it should be orderly, incremental, nonthreatening to the existing order, and controlled by indigenous elites. Coombs's work argues that nonformal education must be closely integrated with overall national-development policy and planning. Occasionally, he notes, client groups should be consulted to ascertain their views on the programs. But they should be consulted by the leaders of the society, those who decide upon and them implement nonformal education programs. Here we have echoed a staple of foundation developmental strategy, and the new vintage hardly differs from the old. Major decisions regarding developmental objectives and programs are made by society's leaders; those for whom the programs are intended are infrequently consulted, if at all. The involvement of the masses in decisions and programs affecting their lives is minimal.

Nonformal education programs that escape the control of society's leaders are no less a threat to the existing order than is a locally controlled formal educational program. Coombs's repeated contention that nonformal education programs should be run through existing bureaucratic channels in the interest of efficiency is a clear manifestation of a technocratic mentality grounded in a functionalist worldview. This is to be expected, however, given the support that nonformal education has had, in Paulston's words, "under United States and Western European foundation, government, and international organization sponsorship."[39]

Innovative approaches to Third-World development, such as those encompassed in nonformal education, receive foundation support as long as they are domesticated and monitored by those elites who dominate society. The domestication of nonformal-education projects helps to reproduce existing structural inequalities, whereby society's benefits flow disproportionately to the elite and only infrequently reach the dispossessed masses. Nonformal education efforts that have escaped the domestication process and have the possibility of giving the masses a modicum of control over their lives, such as Freire's consciousness-raising programs in Brazil and Chile, are not included among the foundations' funding priorities.

Overseas Development Council

The work of the Washington-based Overseas Development Council provides another example of the way in which the foundations and major corporations attempt to domesticate and control the pace of change in the Third World. The council's activities demonstrate as well how the foundations sometimes work through affiliated agencies to support radical research that, unintentionally or otherwise, generates information unavailable to official agencies and more conservative scholars. Such support is not without contradictions for the foundations, however.

The Overseas Development Council was organized in 1969 and received half of its operating budget from the Ford and Rockefeller foundations.[40] The council's board of directors included numerous individuals associated with the Carnegie, Ford, and Rockefeller foundations. Council president James P. Grant was soon to become a trustee of the Rockefeller Foundation, where he joined fellow council directors Theodore M. Hesburgh and Clifton Wharton. Ford Foundation representatives on the council board in the early 1970s included David Bell, then Ford vice-president and former head of the Agency for International Development; Eugene Black, Ford trustee, former president of the World Bank and vice-president of the Rockefellers' Chase Manhattan Bank, and at the time head of the American Express Company; and Arjay Miller, Ford trustee and dean of Stanford University's School of Business. James Perkins, head of the International Council for Educational Development, former Carnegie Corporation vice-president, and Chase Manhattan Bank director, was another prominent member of the council's board of directors. The corporate sector was represented most directly and prominently by David Rockefeller, Emilio Collado, vice-president of Standard Oil Company of New Jersey; and Robert Anderson, chairman of the board of the Atlantic-Richfield Company. A number of these men from the corporate sector also had close ties to the foundations.

The main purpose of the Overseas Development Council was to build support for developmental assistance provided by multilateral aid agencies and by multinational corporations.[41] This need arose because of the failure of the traditional bilateral aid arrangements, such as those epitomized in the work of the Agency for International Development, to further Third-World development in a manner that insured regional stability. Council president James P. Grant spoke to this point in a statement justifying the organization's role. "If we are to develop a firm deterrent to anarchy and subversion in two-thirds of the world seized by the revolution of rising expectations," he wrote in 1971, "something more fundamental than AID is required."[42] Multilateral agencies such as the one he headed were not, he felt, perceived as aligned with a donor nation's foreign policy by potential client states, as were national aid agencies, e.g., the Agency for International Development. Such an advantage meant that these multinational organizations had, according to Grant, "greater potential for intervention directly into the affairs of a developing country."[43]

The council today receives financial support from American corporations with large investments in Africa, Asia, and Latin America. It is not surprising, consequently, that through its overseas programs the council endeavors to create a climate conducive to the continued operations of its corporate members, for example, the Bechtel Overseas Corporation, the Chase Manhattan Bank, the Mobile Oil Corporation, the Standard Oil Company of New Jersey. A particularly important council activity designed to achieve this objective includes its support for research on topics affecting Third-World development and the publication of these findings. Recent council publications have examined the role of women in development, international commodity arrangements, the mounting external debt problems of Third-World nations, and, more generally, alternatives to the orthodox developmental models that evolved after 1945.[44]

The council and similar organizations, like the International Council for Educational Development, determine the research to be undertaken as well as the researchers selected to conduct it. Council staff do not hestitate to commission radical researchers to investigate particular problems and prepare reports.[45] This willingness by the council to support researchers who politics are to the left of the sponsoring agency represents a significant departure from earlier practice. It is difficult to imagine the African-American Institute or the Congress for Cultural Freedom (discussed in the next section) sponsoring, during the 1950s and 1960s, the work of researchers whose politics were decidedly leftish.

The foundations, sponsored agencies like the Overseas Development Council, and some multinational corporations represent, as has been noted above, the progressive wing of late-20th-century state capitalism. While they clearly seek to create a better world for all and ostensibly are less concerned about ideological issues than other institutions involved in foreign-policy formulation, their location within the system of state capitalism leads them to attempt to reshape the world within a framework congenial to their interests. They recognize that Third-World development may be advanced by numerous strategies; consequently, they seek to investigate these and to support some while devaluing others. An indispensable part of this effort involves the collection of information about the societies in question. It is in just this area, the collection and dissemination of information, that the major foundations and their affiliated organizations excel. The source of the data and the politics of the researcher are of less importance to the sponsors than the information generated.

What have been the results of this support for radical researchers? Several seemingly contradictory and irreconcilable outcomes can be identified. First, the council and the institutions supporting it have played important, perhaps catalytic, roles in identifying new developmental modalities that have the potential to benefit more Third-World peoples than the strategies that previously characterized their developmental assistance. This support for radical research has clearly helped to challenge some of the theoretical assumptions upon which earlier developmental aid rested. It also suggests that pressure is being exerted by officers within international aid organizations, such as the major foundations, to explore developmental modalities that might apear heretical to their more conservative colleagues. These internal differences within the foundations, if indeed they are such, clearly have implications for the maintenance of the foundations' hegemony. Internal dissent holds the possibility that some within the organizations will become detached from institutional orthodoxy.

Second, the council and institutions funding it can point to their support of radical research as a demonstration of their interest in exploring the whole range of developmental possibilities, including those that are implemented in revolutionary societies. This is important to substantiate the claims of objectivity by council and foundation officers, particularly since the goals of the revolutionary societies studied do not always appear to be congruent with the interests of the United States.

In these situations the foundations and their surrogate, the Overseas Development Council, clearly hold all the cards. They counter criticism of their restrictive approach to development by sponsoring the work of scholars with impeccable radical credentials. The data that they collect are duly published and disseminated, thereby enabling the sponsoring agencies to demonstrate their dedication to the unfettered search for developmental modalities designed to benefit the greatest numbers. These data, however, are also available to United States agencies that have the potential to utilize the information against the society where it was collected. The recommendations flowing from the research become the object of academic debate and are frequently ignored by the aid agencies—except insofar as they can be domesticated and actually implemented in a manner that does not seriously challenge the existing order. The moral dilemma in which this places radical researchers should not be minimized. This issue has not received the attention that its importance warrants, although it was roundly debated during the Vietnam war.

The Overseas Development Council is only one of several agencies that serves to legitimate the activities of the foundations and multilateral organizations like the World Bank. Another is the London-based Overseas Development Institute, funded mainly by the Ford Foundation and the World Bank.[46] The operations of the council and the institute are sophisticated, low-keyed, and generally unknown. In this they resemble another foundation surrogate, which for a time at least managed to have its true objectives masked from the general public. The Congress for Cultural Freedom was more concerned with propaganda than development per se, but it too began to view the problems of Third-World development with great interest in the 1960s.

Support for Propaganda Organizations

Congress for Cultural Freedom

The Congress for Cultural Freedom was established in the late 1940s as a clearinghouse for the propagation of anticommunist dogma and, at the same time, the dissemination of favorable pronouncements about Western liberal democracy. The congress and the Ford Foundation were closely associated through both program subsidies and high-ranking personnel; in the mid-1960s Ford director of international programs Shepard Stone became president of the congress.

The congress, based in Paris, focused its programs on Europe in the immediate postwar period, a decision growing out of the domination of so much of that continent by the Soviet Union. It soon became apparent, however, that the communist-dominated governments of Eastern Europe could not be overthrown, a realization that was coupled with growing concern in Washington about Soviet expansionism. If the Soviets could not be unseated in Eastern Europe, at least their efforts to make gains in certain Western European nations had to be resisted. At the same time, the USSR's efforts to dominate the nations of Africa, Asia, and Latin America were of growing concern. Congress personnel accordingly shifted much of their attention to the Third World after 1955 and, with support from the Ford and Rockefeller foundations and the CIA, set out to win the hearts and minds of Third-World peoples.

The congress, the foundations, and the CIA were determined to persuade the peoples of Africa, Asia, and Latin America through a variety of means that their interests would only be served through alignment with the United States and her allies. Epstein summarized this new thrust in the following way: by the 1960s "the major problem was not with the national will, but in the hearts and minds . . . of Asians and Africans who must be saved from Communism and thus not lose their chance to shop or live in the great emporium which America was building for the world—though how they were to afford the bargain was hard to understand."[47] The anticommunist and pro-capitalist ideology sustaining these attempts was patent, although denied as such by the congress, the foundations, and the sponsored intellectuals.[48] The Ford Foundation, working through the congress, sought to mold intellectual perspectives in ways designed to serve United States foreign-policy objectives, while at the same time denying any partisan interests. A 1957 Ford-funded and congress-administered conference concerned with Third-World economic development illustrates how the foundation's unacknowledged ideology determined the limits of discourse on this important topic and legitimated the outcome.

Included with the initial grant application to the Ford Foundation on behalf of the Congress for Cultural Freedom was a letter of support naming W. Arthur Lewis, winner of the 1979 Nobel Prize in economics, as chairman of the proposed conference. This appeal for Ford support was couched in familiar cold-war terms:

> The success of the Soviet Union in increasing output per head rapidly has raised the challenging question whether appropriate rates of growth are attainable in underdeveloped countries within a democratic framework . . . [Consequently] the major purpose of the [proposed] seminar is to consider the dangers to freedom inherent in some plans to achieve rapid growth and [to suggest] alternative measures which achieve growth while preserving and strengthening freedom.[49]

Ford support for these objectives was unequivocal, as indicated by the material prepared by foundation staff for the trustees' approval. The staff's written grant request noted that "it is vital to the interests of the free world that economic growth in the underdeveloped countries should take place in a democratic framework. The various means which provide for such a framework continue to need to be supported and strengthened, that authoritarian methods which might seem to promise quicker solutions to economic development will not gain acceptance."

Ford personnel were certain that this conference would fulfill their expectations because they were well acquainted with the true purpose of the congress from long and close contacts. The internal foundation document discussing the qualifications of the congress to receive the grant for the Tokyo conference noted that "the Congress for Cultural Freedom, whose major objectives have been to combat tyranny and to advance freedom in Europe and Asia, has become the rallying ground [sic] for anti-Communist forces." Later in the same document the Ford officer noted that "support for the seminar has been recommended by high United States government officials," and "by prominent persons in this country and in Europe," and that the "Rockefeller Foundation has made four separate grants. . . . . to the Congress during the past three years."

Ford personnel were explicit in their hopes for the Tokyo conference. These clearly indicate how foundation officials and their like-minded academic fellows hoped to use the incremental approach to development, with its emphasis on economic growth, for their own well-defined ideological purposes. In recommending support for the grant application a Ford official reasoned that "the seminar in Tokyo will help to strengthen the democratic approach to economic growth and to have these by-products: (1) It will be widely publicized in Tokyo and have considerable importance in Japanese academic life *where the need is large for anti-Marxist thinking*; and (2) it will contribute . . . to the strengthening of communication between Western and Eastern scholars."[50]

Foundation Support for International Conferences and Studies

The foundations sponsored conferences focusing on international issues that they considered in the national interest regularly after 1950, just when their international programs expanded. These conferences were often multipurposed, but central to each was the attempt to educate influential individuals about particular global issues and to forge a consensus around the appropriate means of dealing with these by representatives of the government, the business community, and other interested parties. The next section will examine several of these conferences initiated by the Carnegie Corporation; this will be followed by a comparable discussion dealing with the Ford and Rockefeller foundations. Both sections will examine as well how the developmental aid decisions emanating from these gatherings were disseminated.

How Carnegie Corporation Brought Africa into America's Consciousness

The decade of the 1950s witnessed a rekindled interest in Africa by the Carnegie Corporation.[51] Staffing changes in the corporation's British Dominions and Colonies section, from which the African work was funded, set the stage for Carnegie's focus on (1) higher education in Africa, and (2) an educational program to bring Africa to the active consciousness of the American commercial, political, and academic communities. Alan Pifer joined the staff in 1953 and began stressing the importance of American-supported education for the orderly development of independent African nations.[52] Pifer and his colleague Stephen Stackpole immediately took the lead in focusing American attention on the African continent.

Several years later Pifer and Stackpole advocated corporation funding for the annual meeting of the American Assembly, a Columbia University-affiliated organization that periodically sponsored conferences and research seminars. The assembly's officers, with a little urging from Pifer and Stackpole, agreed that the topic for the 1958 conference would be the relationships between the United States and Africa. The materials prepared by Pifer and Stackpole supporting the proposed grant specified the corporation's objectives for this conference. "It is to be hoped that the background papers and Assembly discussion will help to define the limitations and opportunities of this [United States] policy [toward Africa] and point to some guiding principles for it." They felt that the potential for determining this policy was high because, in their words: "The nature of the attendance at Assembly meetings, including representatives at policymaking levels from industry, government, labor and the professions, and the wide publicity given to its proceedings and conclusions make it a unique agency for influencing public attitudes and actions."[53]

Pifer worked closely with assembly officers in determining the agenda for the four-day conference and in selecting participants whose views on the importance of Africa for the United States paralleled his and those of his Carnegie colleagues. His background paper provided a framework within which much of the conference discussion took place. He argued that "the three central questions that will confront the United States as it looks at Africa from now onward [sic], and which the Assembly will want to discuss, are economic development, political development, and race relations." While none of these was new, they took on added significance in view of Asian and African independence, political realities that make these peoples "important in the struggle between Communism and democracy."[54]

Carnegie influence on the conference conclusions was patent, as a perusal of the published report reveals.[55] This document noted that "for the development of Africa in every field, literacy and schooling are critical. . . . American aid should give priority to strengthening Africa technical and higher education and the training of African teachers." Additionally, conference participants recognized not only "the need for education of Africans, but also for education of Americans about Africa."[56] Later that year Carnegie's trustees approved a grant that would send influential American business and political leaders on study tours of Africa.[57]

Pifer and Stackpole were planning an equally influential conference dealing with the corporation's involvement in Africa even before the convening of the American Assembly gathering. Toward the end of May 1958, within three weeks of the conclusion of the assembly conference, Carnegie officials brought together at the Greenbrier Hotel in White

Sulfur Springs, West Virginia, twenty-three individuals who, according to one observer, "represented the most relevant American foundations, the key U.S. Goverment aid agencies, and important business and individual interests, as well as a number of Britons concerned with Africa."[58] This conference evolved from discussions that included Pifer, Stackpole, Carnegie vice-president James Perkins, John Howard and Melvin Fox of the Ford Foundation, Sir Andrew Cohen, Britain's representative to the United Nations' Trusteeship Council, and several university professors. The conference organizer was political scientist Vernon McKay, who subsequently became a valued policy advisor to both the Carnegie Corporation and the Ford Foundation. Among the invited participants were the director of the International Cooperation Administration, an economist from the World Bank, an official of the Rockefeller Brothers Fund, several representatives from the British Colonial Office, and executives from British and American corporations with investments in Africa (e.g., Unilever, American Metal Climax).

Heyman notes that the primary purpose of the gathering was to devise programs which "themselves were to be based on the common interests of the African states and the free world nations, which interests the Greenbrier participants saw as new African states with political and economic viability, and friendship, or dependency, on the west." Carnegie personnel viewed their organization as the impartial sponsor, "free from motives other than a desire to serve the best interests of the Africans."[59] There is difficulty reconciling this expression of disinterested altruism with Pifer's claim in his background paper for the American Assembly conference earlier the same month that "the basis for our concern with Africa in the future is going to be self-interest."[60]

Andrew Cohen, whose role in insuring the success of this conference and numerous future Anglo-American undertakings in African education was pivotal, shared Pifer's opinion regarding the furtherance of Western interests in Africa. The month before the Greenbrier conference he gave a lecture at Northwestern University, which was reprinted and distributed to Greenbrier participants. In his address he identified three reasons for increased Anglo-American aid to Africa. These included (1) moral and humanitarian interests; (2) economic interests, specifically the need to assure continued access to sources of African raw materials and to insure that African markets remained open to capitalist penetration; and (3) political interests, so that African nations would remain stable and friendly to the Western alliance. Cooperative Anglo-American and Western aid programs would reduce conditions in which communism flourishes, Cohen claimed, while at the same time furthering African development.[61]

The Greenbrier participants shared the concern of Cohen and Pifer that increased American (and other Western) aid to Africa was vital if African development was to proceed smoothly. The conference, and those smaller meetings that followed over the next several years, were important in insuring that the foundations would play central roles in the determination of the nature of Western developmental aid to Africa for the foreseeable future.[62]

One of the topics discussed at Greenbrier was the feasibility of launching a study of Nigeria's postsecondary educational requirements. This was not the first time that the issue had been raised; Pifer and Stackpole had been lobbying for just such a study since 1954.[63] By the time of the Greenbrier conference, however, Carnegie officials were in a stronger position to have their plans implemented. The main stumbling blocks before 1959 had been the Colonial Office and the Inter-University Council, which feared the incursion of American influence into their educational work. The same officials who had previously resisted the study had been won over to the idea by the realities of impending independence for Nigeria and their country's inability to provide the required assistance. The rapid and seemingly chatoic school-expansion efforts in eastern and western Nigeria, which caused concern on both sides of the Atlantic, were certainly factors encouraging some officials to change their minds.[64] The cordiality and atmosphere of cooperation that permeated the Greenbrier conference removed any lingering doubts that they still held. While all the parties concerned now agreed on the need for the study, the principal difficulty appeared to be, according to Pifer, "who would initiate it." Carnegie Corporation took the lead, and within several months the trustees appropriated $100,000 for the work of the study commission, whose personnel included three Britons, three Nigerians, and three Americans.

The study commenced in 1959 and the final report was issued the following year.[65] The impact of the report on the planning of Nigerian education was immense, particularly that section prepared by Princeton University economist Frederick Harbison on Nigeria's manpower requirements for the period 1960–80 and the educational infrastructure necessary to attain these projections. The Nigerians were led to believe, particularly by Pifer and corporation president John Gardner, that the study had really been their idea from its inception. In reality, the entire undertaking was planned in conversations between Carnegie representatives and individuals from the IUC and Colonial Office and presented to the Nigerians as a fait accompli, to accept or reject.[66] The subsidization of the Commission and its report by the Carnegie Corporation insured a future role for American pedagogical concepts and notions of "human capital" in African education, which had been important objectives of corporation officials from the first. One observer has described the influence of this report in the following manner: "[t]he Ashby Commission's procedures served as a model for educational planning in other African territories. No longer would planning commissions be exclusively British or even African-British. Americans were almost obligatory after Ashby."[67]

The Bellagio Conferences on Third-World Development

The foundations' decision during the 1950s and 1960s to provide strategic developmental aid to selected African, Asian, and Latin American nations, and to act as catalysts for complementary aid from national and multinational donor agencies, was posited on the assumption that these countries would quickly move along the appropriate road to modernization once an institutional infrastructure was in place and individuals were trained to manage their independent societies. The halcyon days of the 1960s soon gave way to the more sober realization that the road to modernization was strewn with many pitfalls, not all of which could be avoided. The days were past when all that was required to assure the evolutionary development of the Third-World nations, was, as a Rockefeller Foundation officer had put it some years earlier, an acquaintance "with the accumulated lore of 'Western' social science."[68] The foundations reluctantly accepted the developmental reality of the 1970s and decided that a reconceptualization of their earlier ideas regarding aid might be in order. Or if a reconceptualization was too drastic a step, at least they should get together to discuss future strategy.

Representatives of the major donor agencies gathered at the Rockefeller Foundation's villa at Bellagio on Italy's Lake Como in 1974 to reevaluate their approach to developmental aid. Participation in the conference was by invitation, a factor helping to insure that only those viewpoints supportive of developmental orthodoxy were represented. Rockefeller Foundation personnel compiled the invitation list, after consultation with Ford colleagues.[69] The proceedings of the conference appeared later the same year, edited by Ford's F. Champion Ward, and suggest that the foundations had decided to adhere to the broad outlines of their former approaches to Third-World development, although some of the presentations did argue for variations on the earlier models.[70]

Discussions at this conference, couple with a January 1974 report by the foundation-created International Council for Educational Development, led to the decision to undertake a major study of the role of education, particularly universities, in the developmental process. The study's conclusions served to legitimate the previous work of the foundations in university development in Africa, Asia, and Latin America, and to suggest the importance of the foundation-sponsored approach for subsequent undertakings. An examination of the origins and sponsorship of this study, as well as its major contributors and their conclusions, indicates how foundation support for ostensibly independent research leads to conclusions supportive of the foundations' ideology.

The first of the two-volume study, entitled *Higher Education and Social Change: Promising Experiments in Developing Countries,* appeared in 1976. The senior editor and project director was Kenneth W. Thompson, former vice-president of the Rockefeller Foundation. Thompson had been primarily responsible for the foundation's University Development Program during its first decade. In his introduction to the study Thompson noted that "an audit and review by outsiders" of the direction of developmental aid "was long overdue."[71] He indicated that the work was published in cooperation with the International Council for Educational Development and that among the criteria for the study was the selection of three regional directors "with authority to select their own team members and the institutions to be studied." This "represented a sharp departure from the established practice of calling on Western educators for this function." The coordination of the study by Third-World educators insured that it fulfilled "its mandate to listen to developing countries' voices."[72] Many of these Third-World educators, however, advocated approaches remarkably like those previously propounded by the foundations, the World Bank, and the Agency for International Development. This is not surprising since most of these individuals has been closely associated with the major foundations for years before the study was initiated.

The director of the Asian regional team was Puey Ungphakorn, at the time rector of Thammasat University, Bangkok, and a member of the Thai National Assembly. The uninitiated observer would have had difficulty knowing that the Rockefeller Foundation had supported Thammasat University since the 1955 foundation decision to commit $25 million over a five-year period to a number of African, Asian, and Latin American universities. In all fairness, the first volume of the study does mention in passing the foundation's long-standing interest in Thammasat; however, only the most careful reader could glean the degree of the foundation's involvement or the methods whereby the foundation helped to shape the university's curriculum and administrative structure and to train its staff.

The deputy director of the Asian regional team was Suppanondha Ketudat, acting deuty secretary-general of Thailand's National Education Commission and, like Ungphakorn, a member of the Thai National Assembly. He was equally well known to Rockefeller Foundation personnel from years of professional acquaintance. Among the consultants to the Asian team was Soedjatmoko, then with Indonesia's National Development Planning agency. He had long-standing contacts with foundation officials and with influential American foreign-policy and corporate personnel. Soedjatmoko played an important role in his nation's developmental planning after the overthrow, with active American support, of the Sukarno government in the mid-1960s. He was also a trustee of the Ford Foundation.[73]

The relationships linking the members of the Latin American regional team to the major foundations were similar to those characterizing the Asian study group. The Rockefeller Foundation's major university development program in Latin America after 1955 was at the University of Valle in Colombia. By the early 1970s the work there was considered successful enough to allow Foundation personnel to designate it a regional university center, to facilitate the development of universities in contiguous areas.[74]

Gabriel Valazquez had been one of the foundation's principal contacts in Colombia during the building of the University of Valle center. In the early 1970s he moved to another foundation-supported university, Bahia in northeastern Brazil, to fulfill the same function as in Colombia. Valazquez, not surprisingly, was a member of the Latin American regional team, as as the current Rockefeller representative in Cali, home of the University of Valle, Farzun Arbab. The deputy director of the Latin American team was Rene Corradine of the University of Valle, and the director was Alfonso Ocampo Londono, a long-time Rockefeller Foundation associate and at the time president of the Fundación para el Desarollo Industriel in Cali.

These individuals chosen to study the university's role in national development generally shared the foundations' views on the appropriate path to achieve this goal. Thompson's rhetoric about the independence of these investigators and the importance of selecting Third-World nationals to coordinate the study's major components must be weighed against the possibility that these individuals were selected because their intellectual and political dispositions predisposed them to reach conclusions supportive of the foundations' approach to development.

The conclusions of the Asian regional team present in clear relief the conservative ideological underpinnings of the foundation approach to development. Thompson recapitulates these in the following words:

> The conclusion set forth by the Asian team is that unemployment performs a vital social and economic function. The Philippine case, in particular, and the Thai, Malaysian, and Indonesian studies, to some extent, are predicated on the existence of a free market economy with the natural forces of supply and demand and income disparity working themselves out in practice. The Asians, therefore, are less concerned about mass education and temporarily high levels of unemployment because they look forward to natural adjustments within the economy.[75]

Such viewpoints divert attention from the inequitable distribution of wealth in these countries and the ways in which this situation helps the urban and land owning class to continue its domination over the majority. These perspectives also lead to the conclusion, as expressed again by the Asian team, that "the highest payoff in the aid programs has been in training people."[76] Again, we have echoed a staple of foundation policy: the importance of training, particularly overseas, of indigenous elites who will run national polities in ways designed to insure stability, gradualism, and controlled development while remaining linked to the world capitalist economy.

The list of those associated with this study, either as members of the task force or as corresponding members, reads like a Who's Who of the post-1945 developmental-aid fraternity. Without exception, they have been associated with programs of the Carnegie, Ford, and Rockefeller foundations, either directly or through one of the foundation-supported outside agencies.[77] The foundations' selection of individuals, whether Americans or foreign nationals whose views coincide with their own, represents an important way to insure, as was noted by a dissenting voice at the 1974 foundation conference on developmental aid at Bellagio, that "nothing radically different from the 'free enterprise' view of development is apparent," or even likely to be forthcoming.[78]

Foundation Sponsorship of "Independent" Research

An important way in which the foundations legitimate their ideology is by providing support for individuals unconnected to the foundations, but whose views lead them to conclusions not dissimilar from those held by the foundation officers who commission the research. We have seen how the foundations accomplished this in one area in the examination in Chapter 4 of the institutionalization of social science and developmental theory in the United States. The provisions of research funds for individuals outside their organizations to undertake studies they deem important enables foundation officers to claim that the conclusions reached have been arrived at by independent scholars, who were selected on the basic of their reputations as disinterested researchers. This procedure also enables foundation personnel to deflect potential criticism that their organizations fund only that research which will arrive at predetermined conclusions shared by the foundations themselves. In reality, the foundations exercise the greatest care in the selection both of the topics to be investigated and the researchers to be supported. The detailed administrative aspects of this procedure generally fall to a handful of major universities, but occasionally the foundations rely on nonuniversity agencies to carry out research they desire. The Brookings Institution, the Institute of Defense Analysis, and the Council on Foreign Relations have been among the favored organizations since 1945. The foundations' ties to the Council on Foreign Relations are long-standing, as was indicated in Chapters 1 and 2. The council's status as an independent organization competent to undertake studies on the determination of United States foreign policy was enhanced during the cold-war period, at least in part because of the close association between many foreign-policy architects and the council during the period. The recognition of the council's important role led Carnegie officers to consider again the corporation's support for these activities in 1953.[79]

The manner in which the council facilitated Carnegie programs was summarized in a 1959 corporation document that proposed an additional $500,000 for the council's research programs in international relations and American foreign policy. This draft memorandum noted that over the years "the Council has contributed to the advancement of knowledge on many particular problems and areas within the field of foreign relations which have been of quite specific interest to Carnegie Corporation." Examples include "Kissinger's book on *Nuclear Weapons and Foreign Policy*, William Hance's on *African Economic Development*, and the discussion group recently organized on Problems of Government and Newly Independent Countries." The relationship between Carnegie Corporation and the council was summarized in the following words: "The importance of our support of the Council lies in the unique role which that institution occupies in keeping a relatively limited but strategically situated group of business, professional and educational leaders informed about important foreign policy matters." The council's "highly significant if indirect support of wiser foreign policies for the United States" is deserving of a higher level of support.[80]

The Ford Foundation's links to and support of the Council on Foreign Relations' research endeavors were also significant during this period. In 1954, for example, the foundation made a grant of $1.5 million to the council for research projects; this was followed by many others in subsequent years.

Shortly after its programs began in earnest in the early 1950s, Ford officers decided that the foundation should play a role in determining the defense needs of the United States.[81] To this end, the foundation granted $214,800 to Harvard University in 1955 for "a three-year experimental program [in] studies in national defense policy." The ultimate objective of this undertaking was "the establishment of an educational center where independent civilian and military thought and analysis can be brought to bear on the problems and effects of defense policy."

The next year Ford joined the Carnegie Corportion, the Rockefeller Foundation, and the Department of Defense in funding the Institute of Defense Analysis, which, according to Ford consultant William Green-leaf, was "an association of five . . . [universities] organized at the suggestion of the Secretary of Defense." The institute's main purpose was the conduct of studies "for strengthening the national security through increasing the use of scientific and technological resources in the development of defense policy." Through support for the institute and kindred organizations, the foundations could play important, if covert, roles in the furtherance of United States foreign policy.[82]

Interest in Africa on the part of Washington policy makers and United States business concerns increased significantly after 1960—at least partly because of the efforts of the Carnegie Corporation to make Americans more aware of the importance of Africa—and led to several major studies of U.S.-African relations. Several of these were funded directly by the foundations, as was the case with the Ford- and Rock-efeller Brothers Fund-financed book entitled *Southern Africa and the United States*, which appeared in 1968.[83] Others grew out of Council on Foreign Relations' study groups, and the authors of these invariably had close links to one of the major foundations. Such was the case, for example, with Waldemar Nielsen's *African Battleline*, which appeared in 1965, and his *The Great Powers and Africa*, published in 1969. While no consensus emerged from these several studies—especially on the intractable issue of United States relations to the white-ruled nations of southern Africa—they did serve to establish the parameters within which the "responsible" debate over United States interests in and strategy toward southern Africa would take place.

Nielsen had left Ford to become president of the African-American Institute a few years before the public disclosures in the mid-1960s that the institute worked closely with and was subsidized by the CIA. In both *African Battleline* and *The Great Powers and Africa*, Nielsen argued that it would be a mistake for the United States to ignore the growing nationalist movements in southern Africa. Prudent policy, he claimed, should seek to broaden United States contacts with these movements while simultaneously loosening somewhat U.S. ties with the white regimes of Angola, Mozambique, Rhodesia, and South Africa. To do otherwise would only insure a violent confrontation between black and white in southern Africa and provide an area of instability ripe for Soviet and Chinese intervention.

In the first book Nielsen argued for an increased level of aid for cultural and educational work in southern Africa, while lamenting that to date these "programs have been conducted on a small scale and without benefit of a clear framework of political consideration."[84] Four years later he acknowledged the increased African scholarship programs and relief supplies for southern African refugees made available under Presidents Kennedy and Johnson, but also warned that this aid "has been insignificant in checking the drift of the national movements into bitterness, extremism, and growing dependence on Communist support."[85] What was required was a more vigorous prosecution of the cultural cold war to wean the African nationalists away from their dependence on the Communists.

These concerns, which were shared by other American observers in both official and unofficial positions, were taken seriously in Washington, where State Department officials decided that increased contact with the nationalist movements had become a matter of some urgency. The African-American Institute, which Nielsen headed, was designated by the State Department to administer the expanded fellowship program for members of the southern African nationalist movements. Rich notes that this Southern African Student Program (SASP) "provided more than five hundred students from the still dependent areas of southern Africa with an opportunity to secure technical and college training in the U.S."[86] She also identifies the institutional network involved in this program as follows:

> The SASP partnership consisted of the Bureau of Educational and Cultural Affairs (CU) of the Department of State, the Africa Centers at Lincoln University (Pennsylvania) and the University of Rochester, U.S. colleges and universities, the African-American Institute, and liberation movements in southern Africa. . . . The Bureau of Educational and Cultural Affairs took the lead in the recruitment and selection of SASP students. In that process political criteria tended to overshadow academic factors. Both AAI and the liberation movements cooperated in identifying students for SASP. CU/Washington made the final selection on the recommendation of CU's staff in Africa.[87]

In all of this the influence of the foundations is hardly discernible, that is, until one probes the sources of support and identifies the personalities involved. The foundations were making available grants to enable the Council on Foreign Relations to undertake studies related to United States foreign-policy concerns during the early 1960s. Such studies were undertaken by individuals linked to one of the foundations. In the case of Waldemar Nielsen these links extended to a foundation-funded intermediate organization as well. These studies made certain recommendations, which in turn were translated into foreign-policy choices. The implementation of a recommended program was then undertaken by a government agency—in this case the Bureau of Educational and Cultural Affairs—in cooperation with a foundation-funded organization, the African-American Institute.

One final example will suffice to illustrate how the foundations fund those researchers who will produce studies supportive of the foundations' work. In 1973 Carnegie Corporation president Alan Pifer approached

E. Jefferson Murphy and requested that he undertake a study of the corporation's African work since 1953. Murphy accepted the charge 'with keen interest, since I had spent virtually my entire career close to African educational development, and during that career . . . . interacted frequently with Carnegie Corporation and many of its partners in Africa."[88] Many of these contacts had been made when Murphy served as executive vice-president of the African-American Institute in New York and earlier as a guiding force in the establishment of the Kurasini International Education Center for southern African refugees in Tanganyika in the early 1960s.

The book that resulted from Murphy's research, *Creative Philanthropy: Carnegie Corporation and Africa, 1953–1973*, was published in 1976 by Teachers College Press, which had published numerous studies on African education with Carnegie support.[89] Murphy himself acknowledged the book's limitations, noting that "the book . . . is not a rigorous evaluation or a comprehensive scholarly analysis. It is a fairly detailed historical account. . . . To a large extent . . . I have tried to present a descriptive account."[90]

Murphy's decision to emphasize the descriptive materials and minimize the analytical was self-imposed. Indeed, it was probably an important consideration in his selection by Carnegie officials.[91] Such self-censorship also is important in minimizing that descriptive material which might prove embarassing to the foundations or their sponsored organizations. How else can we account for the fact that Murphy fails to mention the background to the Carnegie, Ford and Rockefeller Brothers Fund decision early in 1960 to reorganize the financial base of the African-American Institute? The foundation decision to increase the level of support for the Institute preceded by a few years published reports about covert CIA support. Murphy need not have gleaned this from Carnegie's archives; he was vice-president of the African-American Institute in Washington at the time when foundation funding was replacing that of the CIA.[92]

For many scholars and lay readers, *Creative Philanthropy* will remain the authoritative source on the work of the Carnegie Corporation in Africa between 1953 and 1973. It is informative, published by a reputable university press, and seemingly objective. Many readers will doubtlessly applaud the good works of the corportion, as indeed Murphy does. To be sure, much of that work is deserving of such applause. However, we must examine at the same time the implications of studies such as this one, which maximize the foundations' positive work while minimizing or ignoring altogether the less laudatory aspects. The dangers of such sponsored research in obscuring the historical record are obvious, yet the foundations have consistently been among the primary funding sources for such sponsored and "objective" research.[93]

The Extension of the Foundations' Hegemony

This chapter has indicated how the foundations use intermediate organizations to implement programs that they determine and to conduct research of their choosing. These programs and research projects are frequently conceptualized in conversations between foundation personnel and individuals from a government agency, e.g., the International Cooperation Administration, the Agency for International Development, or a multilateral organization, e.g., the World Bank.

Washington bureaucrats are anxious to have the foundations assume responsibility for a particular project because this arrangement gives the undertaking a private, nongovernmental character. This arrangement also helps to reduce somewhat the tensions caused by the contradictory roles that the capitalist state is increasingly called upon to perform, those of accumulation and legitimation.[94] Recent analyses have documented the state's accumulation function when examining the support provided by the state for the expansion of capitalism and the privatization of profit.

Fagen, for example, argues that "an important part of the history of contemporary capitalism could be organized around a description of the way in which the various classes, groups, and economic interests attempt to use state power to give themselves advantages in a world in which the 'free market' is even less operative than it was a few decades ago."[95] It has become, as he notes, "increasingly difficult in today's world to 'do business,' nationally or internationally, without the active cooperation and participation of the state."[96] Castells's observations are along similar lines, if indeed not more directly to the point. He notes, among other things, how "the state subsidizes private capital directly and indirectly, particularly the hegemonic fractions of monopoly capital," how "the state assumes more and more of the social costs of private capital," and how "the state contributes to the continuous expansion of outlets in order to counteract monopolistic overaccumulation and prevent a crisis of overproduction."[97] The state has become, to put his argument succinctly, "the center of the process of accumulation and realization in advanced capitalism."[98]

This accumulation function is difficult to reconcile with the state's need to legitimate its activities, if indeed not its very existence. This may be one reason, then, why Washington bureaucrats are pleased that nonstate agencies, e.g., the foundations, assume a role in the legitimation process. Foundation personnel, in turn, delegate many of the program responsibilities to an organization that they control, if indeed they have not actually created it. The direct involvement of the foundation decreases accordingly, thereby giving the appearance that the organization executing the program operates independently. There is in reality little independence for these intermediate organizations, linked as they are to the foundations. These linkages take numerous forms, but among the most common are direct financial subsidies and movement of personnel between the funded organizations and the foundations.

An important aspect of the hegemonic process is the ability to convince people that certain perspectives are right, that particular ways of viewing the world are correct. One way that the foundations have helped to do this is by supporting intermediate organizations that prepare reports and make recommendations on particular issues. The findings of such groups are then widely disseminated and, failing a strong challenge from a rival perspective, tend to shape discussion among specialists and laymen alike. An organization like the International Council for Educational Development, which pioneered in the field of nonformal education, is one example of this. The Congress for Cultural Freedom is another. Both organizations appear to be independent. Both are also closely aligned with the major foundations, an important consideration for anyone attempting to ascertain the "objectivity" and reliability of the organizations' recommendations. The links between these organizations and the foundations are neither generally known nor widely publicized, however.

The foundations on occasion convene conferences such as that at Greenbrier in the late 1950s and those at Bellagio in the 1970s to discuss particular issues. Those invited are generally well known to foundation personnel and are recognized experts in their fields. Individuals possessing comparable expertise but views incompatible with those held by the foundations are not invited, although there are important exceptions here. The proceedings of these conferences are duly distributed and, because of their prestigious sponsorship and list of recognized contributors, help to establish the parameters for subsequent discussions of the issue under consideration.

An outsider looking at this procedure would probably conclude that the conference participants arrived at their findings independently, with no coercion or pressure applied. This conclusion would be correct. There was no pressure or coercion. None was necessary. The participants were chosen largely because the conferences' foundation sponsor(s) understood that the participants would say nothing that fell outside the margins of acceptability to foundation officers. In this way the conclusions that help to shape future research and program agendas appear to have been reached independently, a crucial consideration in the furtherance of the foundations' hegemony.

The foundations are not, however, monolithic institutions whose officers agree on all particulars. Their differences may account, for example, for the fact that a few participants at foundation-sponsored conferences challenge the conventional wisdom.[99] This does not mean, however, that conference participants detached from orthodoxy will see their views prevail. This is so because, even when individuals with unconventional views are invited, they form a distinct minority among the conference membership.

Foundation personnel sometimes support those with whom they disagree. They may do so because, as previously noted, some within the organizations are bothered by their liberal consciences or because some feel that a radical approach may be the only way to seek solutions to seemingly intractable problems. The support provided by the foundations for radical research on new developmental modalities is one example of this tendency. Such support should not be understood to signify universal agreement among foundation officers for the views expressed, however; rather, it should be seen as an indication of the contradictions within liberal ideologies.

Having said this, we need to note also that foundation personnel, of liberal persuasion or otherwise, demonstrate no reluctance to incorporate some of the findings of radical researchers into their conventional programs. These findings may eventually serve the interests of one of the groups that the foundations support. At the same time, utilization of the results of radical research has the potential to deflect criticism concerning the foundations' unwillingness to consider radical solutions to problems susceptible to no other approach. It also helps to domesticate the findings, to lessen their potential ability to effect radical systemic and structural change as part of a larger developmental effort. By incorporating only certain elements of a radical approach into their own programs, the foundations can demonstrate that change nonthreatening to the existing order can be effected through conventional means. Such a tactic helps to lessen the influence of those advocating more far-reaching reforms.

6

Technocracy, Cultural Capital, and Foundation Programs

Foundation officers believed that many Third-World developmental problems were susceptible to a combination of sustained economic growth, detailed planning and program evaluation, and the application of the appropriate technologies. The attack on these problems was to be led by indigenous leaders, whose education at home and abroad was designed to help them reach conclusions about the approaches to development that were congruent with the broad outlines of foundation-sponsored developmental theory.

The developmental strategies championed by the Carnegie, Ford, and Rockefeller foundations were sincerely held and implemented with great seriousness of purpose. The emphasis on economic growth, planning and evaluation, and technology was a manifestation of a rationalist-technocratic approach to problem solving and Third-World development. This approach was, and remains, a salient characteristic of the foundations' operational methods and of their staffs. It was neither politically neutral nor value-free, however, as foundation representatives frequently claimed. Rather, this rationalist-technocratic approach was rooted in certain assumptions of the culture from which it sprang.

The foundations' approach to Third-World development assumed that the problems could be analyzed dispassionately, appropriate strategies determined and implemented, adjustments made in the original plans, and the pace and scale of the developmental process managed accordingly. Their belief in the principle of incremental reform precluded the possibility of considering rapid and widespread change managed by people not beholden to foreign-aid donors. Foundation personnel perceived "radical" change uncontrolled by identifiable elites as threatening to existing Third-World stability, regional order, and the continued activity in these areas of their institutions, the United States government, and American-dominated multinational corporations.

161

This chapter examines the foundation addiction to the creation of a technocratic order presided over by educated elites and discusses the political implications of the attempts to create this. Third-World nations, particularly in the 1960s, were frequently laboratories for the application of novel educational techniques imported from the United States and subsidized by the foundations, the Agency for International Development, and the World Bank. These experiments epitomized one aspect of the technocratic mindset and were sometimes modeled after similar efforts at home; frequently they were not.

Foundation personnel have long felt that careful monitoring of their projects, coupled with rigorous evaluation of their effectiveness, could provide clues as to the more sophisticated (and efficacious) design of future projects, which would benefit even greater numbers of Third-World peoples. These objectives are laudable. Viewed in isolation, however, they serve to obscure some significant problems in the apparently rational and logical decision-making processes that foundation personnel claim are characteristic of their approach to problem-solving and development. An examination in this chapter of their dedication to technologically based solutions and insistence on rigorous evaluations reveals not only contradictions between their pronouncements and their actions, but significant political and economic overtones as well.

The Carnegie, Ford, and Rockefeller foundations have long been concerned to reproduce abroad educational and cultural institutions that complement those in the United States. These institutions were designed to train indigenous leaders who would guide their societies along lines generally supportive of, or minimally not antagonistic to, the interests of the United States as defined by the foundation elites. The individuals selected to run the foundations are chosen largely because they too subscribe to the broad outlines of the American economic and political order, and because they have demonstrated their ability to carry out their tasks in a logical, methodical, technocratic, and seemingly neutral fashion. The chapter's third section discusses the foundations' attempts to reproduce abroad a form of cultural capital resembling that which they have produced at home.

The Carnegie, Ford, and Rockefeller foundations are, in the final analysis, class institutions that attempt to create a world order supportive of the interests of the class that they represent. The chapter's fourth section discusses the profound impact of these class interests on the foundations' overseas activities, if indeed these interests do not make the foundations' activities inevitable. This section also raises some questions about the implications for a democratic society when self-perpetuating institutions that are answerable to no public body have the wherewithal to determine the cultural and educational agendas for this and other societies.

Technocracy as a Developmental Panacea

The foundations' belief in the ability of technology and managerial rationality to solve a host of problems is a reflection of American society's similar faith. This belief has frequently led, at home as well as abroad, to the neglect of social and political factors, whose investigation might have revealed that not all problems are susceptible to technical solutions. The American attempt to win the Vietnam War through the application of sophisticated (and lethal) technology, and the concomitant neglect of the political and social realities of Vietnamese society, is an example of this tendency.

The foundations' efforts to nurture at home a technocratically inclined elite to run the complex machinery of this society grows logically from their belief in the power of technocracy.[1] The attempts to accomplish similar ends in Africa, Asia, and Latin America are based on the hope that Third-World development will be along lines similar to those that characterize American society. Foundation and other aid officials feel that technocratically directed development will minimize the appeal of ideology. The deemphasis of ideology is important because, as the American developmental consensus has it, attachments to ideological positions invariably lead to political polarization. Such political divisiveness, in turn, has the potential for creating societal discord, which threatens order and stability and the possibility of sustained economic growth, the trinity of American-derived developmental theory. Development that has at its core the acceptance of the efficacy of technocracy is, according to the consensus, nonideological, a factor that enables the developmental process to continue apace.

Third-World development carried out along scientific-technical lines requires, in Schroyer's phrase, "an ideology of scientific politics."[2] Such an ideology requires its ideologues, who will be able to respond "rationally" to crises and to maintain their developing societies on stable courses. This emphasis on rationality means that moral or philosophical issues raised by policy choices are avoided and are instead defined in purely technical terms. Once the issues are transformed into technical problems—generally couched in social science jargon and thereby authorized by that impartial arbiter, science—the appropriate technique can be produced to resolve the issue at hand.

Schroyer has termed as the "technocratic strategy" the perspective which views the drift of development "as an increasing utilization of state support for a permanent revolution of scientific and technological innovation to serve the specific purpose of mediating conflict and controlling social change."[3] This "technocratic strategy" has characterized the foundations', as well as the state's, support for Third-World educational development and is considered to be the only "rational" approach to seemingly intractable problems. Alternative approaches or development schemes that vary markedly from this "technocratic strategy" have minimal currency among the major donor institutions and agencies concerned with development.

Ford Foundation officer Melvin Fox commented that people at the foundation believed that they could transfer to developing nations the technology and the concepts about modernization that they had helped to popularize. They assumed that the transference of the concepts and techniques necessary for modernization would quickly result in full-blown development. Indeed, once the transference was accomplished, "modernization, it was felt, would flow like water over a dam automatically." There was a genuinely held belief at Ford during the 1960s, Fox continued, that by "transferring some of our know-how, we would enable [those] countries to, if not take off in the sense in which that term was used by Walter Rostow some years ago, at least begin the climb toward modernization."[4] The foundation's faith in the ability of certain concepts and techniques to solve myriad problems abroad is perhaps more understandable when considering that throughout the 1950s and well into the 1960s the foundation's domestic programs were based on similar assumptions.[5] Problems were solvable if the best minds could be applied to them and the requisite technique and technology made available. Ford had access to all of these in sufficient quantities.

Several commentators have noted the implications of the attempts to transfer Western techniques, concepts, and technology to Third-World countries. Farrell, for one, considered it unfortunate that so many attempts were made "to use the poor nations as laboratories for testing out theoretically interesting educational novelties which . . . [the Western nations] had been unable to sell completely in their own societies (two good examples being manpower planning and rate-of-return analysis)."[6]

Another educational novelty that the foundations and other donor agencies have vigorously championed in Third-World settings is, as noted in chapter 5, the so-called nonformal approach to educational development. Di Bona notes how in an Indian setting this nonformal education was supposed "to be integrated with the life of the country." It was "to result in the development of community resources, be linked to development projects and make education a life-long, life-wide process so as to create a learning society."[7] The outcomes from this and similar projects have not fulfilled the high expectations of their sponsors, however. What they have done is to provide some rural sectors in Third-World nations with a low-cost education that does little to alter the rural population's disadvantaged position within the larger society. The Indian case is not unusual. La Belle and Verhine, in a study of the impact of nonformal education in Latin America, concluded that this pedagogical fare did "little more than prepare non-elites to be more productive workers while relegating them to relatively inferior status positions."[8]

At times the foundations attempted to transfer to the Third World educational concepts that had been implemented—or at least had been researched—in the United States. Early in 1961, for example, Ford Foundation officers recommended board of trustees approval of a $110,500 grant to support a conference to examine the possibility of adapting to a number of African school systems the work of the Physical Science Study Committee at the Massachusetts Institute of Technology.[9] The work of this committee was part of the United States national response to the Soviet Union's launching of an orbiting space satellite in 1957.[10]

The grantee and conference organizer was Educational Services, Incorporated, a corporation affiliated with MIT. This corporation had close links to the Ford Foundation through board memberships both at MIT and at the foundation itself. Indeed, Educational Services, Inc., was a favored agency chosen by the foundation to implement its programs, and over the years it received many sizable grants from the foundation.[11] Ford officers wrote in the grant prospectus of their belief in the "need for special pedagogy and curricula" to help "Africans from village backgrounds and remote cultures . . . to be brought to grasp the knowledge and habits of thinking of the modern world."[12] An adaptation of the work of the Physical Science Study Committee was viewed as a vehicle to accomplish this.

Such forms of "intellectual colonialism," as Farrell calls them, are all too commonplace in developmental aid. He feels that "it is time that . . . [the agencies and institutions involved in development work] got out of the business of peddling untried nostrums once and for all."[13] The Carnegie, Ford, and Rockefeller foundations can certainly be numbered among the peddlers of these nostrums. It is doubtful that they will cease this activity, however, because of their collective addiction to treating developmental problems by administering more varied solutions. By focusing on technical solutions and managerial reorganization—staples of the technocratic approach—the structural and systemic problems that impede Third-World development can remain unaddressed, as does the search for solutions antithetical to orthodox developmental theory.

The foundations' post-1945 developmental strategies have consistently ignored the arguments of the dependency theorists, who argue that meaningful Third-World development can occur only after a reformulation of the existing economic relationships between the industrialized and the nonindustrialized nations.[14] Such a restructuring would attempt to alter the historically exploitative relationships between the developed and underdeveloped nations, to lessen the gap between the developed nations that form the metropolitan center and the developing nations of the periphery. The foundations are products of the world capitalist order that, according to dependency theory, largely accounts for the current state of underdevelopment and dependency among Third-World nations. Consequently, it is naive to assume that the foundations will forsake their heritage and support approaches that might call for developmental strategies that remove Third-World nations from the world capitalist economy from which they benefit.

Program Evaluation and the Technocratic Strategy

The rationality and logical decision-making processes that are characteristic of foundation procedures are paralleled by the belief that flaws in their projects can be corrected through the application of more technique. It is felt that shortcomings can be discovered through detailed project evaluations, carried out by disinterested specialists. This too is characteristic of the "technocratic strategy."

The politics of educational evaluation have recently become a topic of concern for numerous scholars.[15] Some have sought to strip away the mask of impartiality and the mantle of "objective" science with which practitioners wrap themselves. The ideological nature of some of this evaluation effort has, consequently, become clearer. This is the case when the evaluation efforts of the Carnegie, Ford, and Rockefeller foundations are examined. To be sure, the foundations have had many of their programs evaluated, both at home and abroad. With few exceptions, however, these evaluations are conducted by people who either worked for one of the foundations formerly or who currently serve as staff members.[16] Such evaluations are designed to make their projects more efficient. At the same time, foundation sponsorship of these efforts helps to insure that these evaluations fall within margins determined by the foundations themselves. This procedure is important in legitimating their activities.

Evaluations of the Ford Foundation-sponsored National School of Law and Administration in the Congo illustrate how this is accomplished.[17] In the mid-1960s an evaluation of the National School was commissioned by Ford. Two consultants were hired for this undertaking. One was James T. Harris, the first secretary general of the National School. Harris was a Ford officer stationed in the foundation's New York headquarters at the time the evaluation was commissioned.[18] The consultants submitted their findings in 1966 and, not surprisingly, the tone was generally supportive of the endeavor. The report recommended continued foundation involvement and concluded by noting that "the end of such a relationship [between the foundation and the National School] would also . . . mean a loss for the Foundation."[19]

A decade later an article discussing the National School's history and accomplishments appeared in a scholarly journal edited at Cambridge University. The author, Gaston V. Rimlinger, had a long association with the Ford Foundation. Rimlinger's generally positive assessment of the project was augmented by a discussion designed to illustrate that the foundation's involvement in the National School had been catalytic rather than directive. To this end, the author presented data indicating the total full- and part-time "man years" given to the National School between 1961 and 1971 by the most important contributing aid agencies. The Ford Foundation headed the list with 128 full-time man years, followed by French technical-assistance agencies with 97, the Congolese-Zairean government with 50, Belgian technical-assistance with 31, and the United Nations with 11. These figures lead Rimlinger to claim that "the highly varied international composition" of the National School was an important factor in its success.[20]

There is a clear attempt here to minimize the role played by Ford in the fortunes of the school, despite the data indicating a preponderance of foundation appointees on the staff and the fact that overall direction during the institution's formative period was determined by the foundation-appointed secretary general. Rimlinger appears to want to convince his readers that the National School was a truly international endeavor rather than one sponsored by the Ford Foundation, which recruited staff from several nations. This is intended to minimize the foundation's role, thereby deflecting any potential criticism regarding the direction that Ford gave to the National School.

Several years later Ford vice-president Francis Sutton argued along similar lines in discussing the foundation's overseas activities. He wrote that the foundation has "over the years deliberately sought non-American staff and [has] made great efforts to be both international and eclectic in our programs."[21] There is little with which to disagree in this statement. However, an internationalization of staff is no guarantee that the role of a donor agency—in this case, Ford—in project direction is minimized, although it might be useful in helping to legitimate the activities by giving the impression that a particular project grew from a consensus among several organizations, rather than being fostered by only one.

The strategies utilized by the foundations to evaluate their projects— when they are evaluated at all—are clearly grounded, as Paulston puts it, "in the liberal world view or ideological paradigm."[22] Liberal evaluation strategies seek to foster, again in Paulston's words, "efficient change using technological rationality and such measures as cost-benefit or cost effectiveness analysis." They focus on analyzing technical and/

or administrative aspects of a problem and are accepting of the institutional and political framework within which it operates. Liberal evaluation stresses the "scientific" and nonideological nature of its methodology, values quantitative measures, tends to be ahistorical, and abjures any semblance of politicization by its practitioners.

Far from being nonideological and value-free, however, the liberal evaluation strategy supports the existing political and economic system and refuses to allow that incremental reform may be incapable of alleviating identified problems. The perspective of liberal evaluation is congruent with the liberal ideology of the foundations. It stresses incremental and adaptive change and takes an evolutionary view of the change process; it supports institution building, using Western models and technical assistance; and it features "innovative" approaches to problem solving and development, e.g., educational television, nonformal education. This ideological congruity helps to explain liberal evaluation's general acceptance among foundation personnel and their refusal to employ evaluation strategies grounded in a critical or conflict mode.

There is some question regarding the ability of the foundation-supported technocratic approach to further meaningful Third-World development, except for a few. A recent study argues that adherence to an educational plan based on a rationalist-technocratic strategy may be a significant factor in its failure.[23] A major stumbling block inherent in this strategy, the authors contend, is the attempt to minimize ideology while searching for consensus, and the concomitant refusal by funding agencies to accept the political realities required to implement even incremental educational reform. Such an approach tends to ignore "the crucial role of human actors pursuing personal and collective goals. It assumes shared goals and ideologies where in fact there is conflict, and it expects change to result automatically on presentation of a technically excellent proposal." This is consistent with the thrust of foundation-supported developmental theory and also those of the Agency for International Development, the Inter-American Development Bank, and the World Bank.

McGinn and others note how the majority of technical assistance personnel sent to developing nations by international and national aid agencies carry the technocratic-rationalist perspective. Furthermore, the Third-World nationals that "they train either in-country or abroad reproduce this conception of decision-making." Not all of the projects that derive from this perspective fail, however. The important foundation-supported university-development programs in Africa, Asia, and Latin America are products of this technocratic-rationalist approach. They have been successful in achieving at least one of their major objectives—the education of an indigenous elite capable of manning the leadership positions within their societies.

These universities supported by the foundations have, by and large, remained attached to the norms of the technocratic order, at least to date. Perhaps this is because they serve such a limited clientele. Many of these institutions are in the process of being politicized by events peculiar to their respective societies. It remains to be seen if they will continue to adhere to the broad goals inherent in the foundations' developmental strategy, or whether they will in future lead the demands for a more rapid and structural reorganization of their societies.[24] If they follow the latter course, the United States foreign-policy establishment will lose valuable, but generally unrecognized, allies in strategic geopolitical locales.

Foundations and the Reproduction and Control of Cultural Capital

The Carnegie, Ford, and Rockefeller foundations have played central roles in the production and dissemination of certain kinds of knowledge. Their grants have facilitated the development of agricultural and veterinary science, as well as the natural and biomedical sciences. They have encouraged experimentation in the fields of teacher education, instructional technology, and nontraditional modes of education. This country's major international and area-studies programs exist largely because of foundation encouragement and support, as do the most important centers of developmental planning. Contemporary American social science assumed its current aspect at least in part because of the foundations' interest in moving it in a certain direction.

The knowledge that becomes acceptable within a particular society forms an important part of that society's cultural capital. It also determines the society's intellectual norms. The choices made by national leaders concerning a society's direction are frequently based on these norms, whether consciously recognized as such or not. An increasing number of commentators have examined not only the mechanisms that facilitate the production of this cultural capital, but also the vehicles for its transmission both intranationally and internationally. They have analyzed as well the impact on a dependent society's cultural autonomy when the production and dissemination of this cultural capital is controlled by forces outside the dependent society.[25]

A dependent nation's store of cultural capital and its resultant cultural autonomy—of its lack—cannot be separated from the realities of the world economic system. Marx and Engels spoke about the symbiotic relationship between economics and ideas 125 years ago. They noted then that "the class which has the means of material production at its disposal, has control at the same time over the means of mental production, so that thereby, generally speaking, the ideas of those who lack the means of mental production are subject to it." To put this another way: "the ideas of the ruling class are in every epoch the ruling ideas; i.e., the class which is the ruling material force in society is at the same time its ruling intellectual force."[26] It is here that the activities of the major foundations become so crucial because of their roles in the production and dissemination of cultural capital *and* because of their roles at the center of the world capitalist system.

Economic dependence and cultural dependence are synonomous for most Third-World nations. The economic relationships between the peripheral or dependent nations and the metropolitan centers are replicated in the cultural and intellectual interactions between the periphery and the center. The university in Third-World nations is the most visible and important source of a developing nation's intellectual and cultural life.[27] These Third-World universities are at the same time part of an international stratification system. Their autonomy is limited by their attempts to become more like the universities in the West, attempts that lead them to duplicate the structure, organizational and recruiting patterns, and functions of the metropolitan university. The nurturing of these Third-World universities has been the centerpiece of the foundations' developmental strategy. The success of this strategy helps to account for the current state of cultural and intellectual dependency that characterizes those universities that the foundations have assiduously cultivated.[28]

Mazrui likens the impact of the university in Africa to that of the multinational corporation and indicates the mutually reinforcing role of each.[29] As multinational corporations expanded their operations in newly independent African nations, they turned to the local universities to supply indigenous, Westernized manpower capable of managing the economic enterprise more cheaply than it could be run by expatriates. The universities responded to the requisites of the multinationals for skilled manpower, but by doing so they deepened their nation's economic dependence on the centers of world capitalism.

The growing importance of the peripheral African economies for the health of the world capitalist system led the multinationals in search of expanded markets for consumer goods. The growth of these markets depended on the spread of Western values. The universities helped to spread these. According to Mazrui: "As a European life-style became part of the measure of social prestige, the market for Western consumer goods widened, with the more educated Africans setting the pace."[30] These educated Africans were frequently graduates of universities supported by the Carnegie, Ford, and Rockefeller foundations. They had been socialized into the value of a consumer culture at least partially in the imported university setting supported by these institutions.

The structure of Third-World universities, their curriculum, and their recruiting patterns reinforce their cultural dependence on the world economic and intellectual centers. Mazrui remarks that universities in Africa "have been virtually defined as institutions for the promotion of Western civilization."[31] This civilization has long been defined in both cultural and economic terms.[32] These purposes were clearly delineated by the colonial powers that founded many of these universities.[33] They were also important considerations for the donor agencies that appeared after World War II.

Most Third-World universities utilize recruiting criteria for faculty appointments similar to those that characterize metropolitan universities. Again, this is testimony to the efficacy of the professional socialization patterns encouraged by the foundations, patterns that dictate the possession of a doctoral degree as a minimal qualification for a university appointment. Many of the Third-World nationals possessing these degrees have been educated in North American universities influenced by foundation perspectives. Others have been educated in Third-World universities equally influenced by foundation norms. In both instances the foundations have helped to define the university structure within a dependent nation by educating the scholars who staff Third-World institutions. In this way the foundations have played important roles in helping to define dependent nations' cultural capital.

Silva comments on how the university in a peripheral nation helps to legitimate the perspective of those at the center. The dependent universities "create a higher education paralleling and reproducing the center's organizational form and curriculum rather than establish[ing] a higher learning more nearly realizing their society's potential for cultural autonomy." At the same time, this reliance on metropolitan university forms and intellectual substance results in a paucity of acceptable indigenous ideas and perspectives. This in turn means that dependent universities "disseminate as best they can the center's established ideologies, complete with more recent elaborations, for their students and local literati."[34] The fact that there is no viable alternative to metropolitan intellectual perspectives invariably leads to the dominance of those ideas. At the same time, the claim is made that these ideas dominate only because of their inherent intellectual superiority, thereby helping to legitimate their status.

The diffusion of knowledge and ideas from a metropolitan center to the university in a Third-World nation occurs almost exclusively in a European language. Altbach notes how the use of a European language for intellectual exchange "blocks access to knowledge for large portions of the populations of many multi-lingual Third-World nations. Language becomes a mechanism of social stratification."[35] Those who command a European language also command an important form of cultural capital. They comprise a very small elite in Third-World nations, although the linguistic barrier per se is not as marked a factor in Latin America as it is in Africa and Asia. It is the indigenous elite in possession of this linguistic ability with whom foundation personnel regularly deal. Support for this elite is consistent with the foundations' belief that the developmental effort can best be forwarded by well-educated and carefully nurtured national elites, and that these groups represent the voice of meaningful opinion in their respective societies.

These elites' alliance with foundation and other aid personnel has not furthered the cultural autonomy of Third-World nations, however. To the contrary, Mazrui notes, the elites' influence has strengthened their nations' cultural and economic dependency on the metropolitan centers. This is so in Africa because there the university graduates "were the most deeply Westernized Africans, the most culturally dependent. They have neither been among the major cultural revivalists nor have they shown respect for indigenous belief systems, linguistic heritage, modes of entertainment, or aesthetic experience."[36] The African example finds its parallel particularly in Asia.

Third-World universities not only import information and ideas that originate in metropolitan universities, thereby perpetuating the developing nations' cultural dependence. These same universities also transfer knowledge to the metropolitan centers in a manner that parallels the exportation of material resources from the developing to the industrialized world. This intellectual exchange, like its economic counterpart, is between unequal partners, with the metropolitan centers benefiting more from the exchange than the dependent nations. Eisemon, Rabkin, and Rathgeber point out that important scientific information produced by researchers at the University of Ibadan and the University of Nairobi is incorporated into the intellectual network of the industrialized, northern nations, while this information generally remains unknown in the country where the research was conducted.[37]

This situation is attributable, in part, to the metropolitan dominance of the mechanisms of publishing, particularly of scholarly works. Altbach notes that branches of metropolitan publishing houses continue to play a determining role in Third-World intellectual life, much as they did during the colonial era. His data indicate, for example, that thirty-four industrialized countries with only 30 percent of the population produce some 81 percent of the world's book titles. Also, some 62 percent of the journals in the social sciences are published in three countries— the United States, Britain, and France. These are, needless to say, published in English or French. At the same time, Altbach continues, "copyright agreements, commercial publishing practices, etc., are dominated by the industrialized nations and reflect their interests." Although scholarly journals do exist in nations such as India, there are "relatively few advanced-level scholarly, intellectual, and professional journals in most Third-World countries, and virtually none that are published in the Third World have an international circulation."[38] There is at present no indication that this imbalance is altering in favor of the Third-World nations.

This domination of the sources of scholarly publication by a few industrialized centers means that Third-World scholars desirous of having their views widely disseminated—a major source of professional accomplishment—must send the results of their research to periodicals which publish in languages foreign to the majority of their countrymen and whose circulation within Third-World nations is severely limited. Their research, however, does find its way into the metropolitan intellectual networks, although it is doubtful if more than a few of the researcher's Third-World colleagues know of its existence because of their lack of access to the scholarly journals where the information appears. Nor is there any assurance that the results of this research will be utilized within the dependent nation where it was collected for the benefit of that nation's people.

Arnove notes the foundations' role in educating Third-World nationals whose research serves the metropolitan centers more than it helps to loosen their nations' cultural and economy dependency.[39] In an analysis of Ford's activities in Latin America, he documents how the foundation developed the research competencies of talented Latin American nationals, primarily in a number of leading North American universities. These researchers then conduct investigations in Latin American settings that would be difficult for foreigners to conduct because of local political conditions. The results of these investigations appear in scholarly journals published in Europe or North America, and the data collected in Third-World settings are incorporated into the intellectual and policy-making networks of the metropolitan centers.

By the mid-1970s many of these Latin American researchers—and their African and Asian counterparts—were affiliated with a foundation-supported research center located in Latin America. These centers sometimes were attached to a foundation-supported university; at other times they formed part of a private research organization receiving foundation support, e.g., the Carlos Chagas Foundation in São Paulo. They served the same important function, whatever their organizational arrangements, of enabling research to be conducted in Third-World countries on socially and/or politically sensitive topics that United States policy makers considered important. The information generated from this research flows back to North American or European academic communities and to governmental agencies. Arnove writes how these "regional networks [of researchers] supported by the foundation contribute to facilitating the movement of ideas . . . between the metropolitan center and the periphery."[40]

These networks serve to encourage the production and dissemination of ideas and data deemed important by universities and agencies in the metropolitan centers. At the same time, this arrangement helps to deflect Third-World researchers from concerns that these same agencies are less anxious to have investigated. This is a conscious foundation policy. As Arnove notes: "[F]oundation support prevents Third-World activists from coping with their domestic problems in their own terms and addressing them with a level of resources consonant with their level of development. Foundation-induced reform efforts, then, tend to divert Third-World nations from more realistic, and perhaps revolutionary, efforts at social change."[41] The foundations are as effective in limiting the production of certain kinds of knowledge as they are in disseminating ideas that they consider important.

An important factor in the extension of one group's hegemony is its ability to encourage intellectuals to investigate certain problems, those which are "important," while ignoring or devaluing others. Once the selection process assumes an autonomy of its own, the direct presence of the dominant group—the foundations in this instance—decreases while its hegemony increases accordingly.

The Foundations as Class Institutions

The overseas activities of the Carnegie, Ford, and Rockefeller foundations since 1945 have afforded benefits to a number of Third-World people in such divergent fields as agriculture and education. These beneficial aspects of the foundations' programs must be applauded by those desirous of seeing a world in which mass suffering and exploitation are decreased. At the same time, however, we should understand that these benefits are not merely tangible results of the foundations' altruism.

Many foundation officers certainly want to better the lot of the world's underprivileged; however, the evidence presented in this study indicates that most want to accomplish this while simultaneously strengthening the position of the United States in the international community. It could hardly be otherwise, however, given the foundations' origins and personnel, as well as their ideology regarding the nature of the world.

The foundations' links to the world capitalist system mean, predictably, that their programs do nothing to threaten the system responsible for their existence. At the same time, their programs do what they can to strengthen that system. To assume otherwise would be naive. The foundations' definition of the best interests of the capitalist system and of the United States cannot be divorced from the individuals who shape foundation policies. These people are closely aligned to the upper echelons of the American corporate and financial structure. Theirs is unequivocally a capitalist worldview, as indeed is that of the federal government that so many of these men serve from time to time.

The Carnegie, Ford, and Rockefeller foundations are class institutions. They seek to better the lot of the world's poor and dispossessed, while simultaneously attempting to make the world more secure for the world capitalist system in which they are rooted and from which their personnel benefit. Their class natures make them wary of far-reaching structural change, since this poses a potential threat to their privileged positions. Rather, their class natures make them proponents of a worldview that emphasizes order, stability, rationality, and efficiency. The foundations' large expenditures for educational programs, particularly university development in the Third World, are designed to train educated elites who will implement programs of gradual change and reform.

The foundations finance conferences, research studies, and projects that generally reach conclusions similar to their own. While there is not complete unanimity among the numerous sponsored findings, an examination of these since 1945 indicates a clearly identifiable direction and thrust. These findings, the products of elite planning, frequently set the tone for subsequent discussions on particular issues. By supporting studies that help to establish future agendas, the foundations assure that certain topics will be discussed and others ignored. Current foundation funding for the Council on Foreign Relations' 1980's Project suggests the continuity of their support for the concept of elite planning, particularly if it promises to be supportive of their worldview.

In 1975 the Council on Foreign Relations agreed to sponsor a series of studies to examine the nature of the world community in the next decade.[42] Much of the funding for this 1980's Project came from the Ford and Rockefeller foundations. An important purpose of this undertaking, as in the council's earlier War-Peace Studies Project and numerous foundation studies over the years, was to outline a world order congenial to American interests, while at the same time convincing the public of the appropriateness of the design.

An examination of several works sponsored by the 1980's Project indicates that Third-World nations are to remain subordinated to the interests of the major capitalist centers: the United States, western Europe, and Japan. There is significant overlap between the work of the 1980's Project and that of the Trilateral Commission, an international group including members from these same geographical areas. While Third-World concerns are to be secondary to the needs of the major capitalist centers, planners continue to recognize the developing nations' importance both in terms of material resources and as markets for overseas economic expansion.[43]

The conclusions set forth by the 1980's Project and the reports of the Trilateral Commission do not differ markedly from the assumptions undergirding much of United States foreign policy since 1945. There is a consistent pattern from that time to the present of a few individuals developing blueprints for a world order. This world order remains one congenial to the interests of the United States and her allies. This is explainable at least in part by the fact that the major foundations have played central roles in selecting the architects who draw up the blueprints.

The class nature of American philanthropy has resulted in an approach to Third-World development supportive of the centers of world capitalism, particularly the United States. The foundations' conservatism has effectively precluded the search for models that *might* benefit more people than do existing schemes, but that are perceived as threatening to the world capitalist system. This has meant that the potential value of developmental models directed by Third-World masses has been minimized by the foundations. Elite-directed planning has formed a stable of foundation activity from the beginning. This reflects the foundations' belief that societies are better led by the few than the many, more especially when those few receive the foundations' imprimatur.

This approach raises a fundamental question: Who benefits from this arrangement, whereby the few determine what is in the best interests of the many? There is scant evidence that more than a handful of Third-World nationals have benefited from the foundations' extensive endeavors, a conclusion that foundation personnel themselves have acknowledged.[44] There is, at the same time, evidence that the interests of the United States have been furthered, particularly those corporations and financial institutions that are active in areas where the foundations have programs. The American corporate and financial structure is inextricably intertwined with the major foundations; to argue otherwise is to gingerbread the obvious.[45]

The foundations are clearly part of the American ruling class. Their vast wealth enables them to articulate programs, set certain agendas, and shape the world order in a manner consonant with the interests of the few associated with them. Much of their work is carried out by carefully chosen and subsidized intellectuals, who elaborate ideologies supportive of the existing social, economic, and political order, in which the foundations play key, but generally unrecognized, roles. Viewpoints that do not support those of the foundations are ignored or dismissed as "irresponsible" or "radical."

The unwillingness of this self-appointed and nonaccountable foundation elite to listen to arguments counter to its preconceived notion concerning the appropriate organization and institutional structure for this and other societies is redolent of noblesse oblige. Such a situation makes a mockery of the democratic ethos that foundation representatives claim to champion. It also raises many crucial questions concerning the foundations' role in a society dedicated to the principle that those who govern are in the final analysis accountable for their actions.

On the Contradictions of Liberal Philanthropy

The Carnegie, Ford, and Rockefeller foundations are liberal institutions, whose programs sometimes succeed and, like those of other major institutions, sometimes fail. Their role in the liberal capitalist state differs from that of, say, the multinational corporation, whose primary function of surplus accumulation links it in a particular way to the state. The foundations, through their numerous activities, play major roles in legitimating the existing world economic and political order, which in the final analysis is a capitalist order.

The foundations also play important roles in the extension of capitalist hegemony. This hegemony is more than just abstract ideology. It is, rather, a way of viewing the world that influences a society's norms, its morality, its perspectives, its political principles. Hegemony, to be successfully incorporated into a society, cannot be imposed on unwilling subjects. It must appear to have developed autonomously and independently, and to represent as well a consensus within the society.

The foundations have helped to further capitalist hegemony by determining which projects should be supported and by identifying potential collaborators to undertake these. This has been the case at home and abroad. An argument could be made that in some, or many, instances their support merely furthered tendencies already initiated. For example, some might argue that social science and developmental theory would have turned out much as they did even without foundation support. Even if we accept this view, that the foundations' involvement in the growth of American social science and developmental theory was supplemental rather than catalytic, one point seems indisputable: the *thrust* of foundation funding has been to encourage and support perspectives that were both nonrevolutionary and procapitalist. This is perhaps understandable, given the foundations' location in the capitalist state and the cultural cold war that the state felt compelled to wage after 1945. But, once again, we must recall that the foundations' own pronouncements repeatedly denied any role in the furtherance of particular interests.

Liberal institutions within the capitalist state are not monolithic; they do allow differing points of view to be expressed, although these may never or only infrequently form the basis for policy. These differing viewpoints within the foundations may account for the occasional support for an individual whose perspectives are anticapitalist. Several of these have been noted throughout this study. These differences are of potential political significance because there exists the possibility that (1) they will cause some of the decision makers within the foundations to become detached from political and economic orthodoxy, and (2) the anticapitalist viewpoints supported by the foundations will be disseminated to greater numbers. As more people learn about and internalize these unorthodox views, they may challenge, overtly or otherwise, the hegemony that has been incorporated into the larger society, which helps people to determine the "correct" way of approaching the world. At the same time, the other major institutions of this society, which, like the foundations, play important roles in the determination of a worldview, may be subjected to critical scrutiny revealing some distance between their public expressions of disinterested humanitarianism and their long-standing links to state and other interests. The resulting contradictions between the rhetoric and reality present the possibility for challenging the very legitimacy of the foundations themselves and the material base upon which they rest.

Similar contradictory outcomes are evident in the foundations' international programs. There is no guarantee that a program with a capitalist intent, e.g., foundation support for Third-World universities, will result in a capitalist outcome. Put another way: there is evidence that some few Third-World students subsidized by the foundations and educated in foundation-supported universities in the developing nations and/or in the United States are challenging the developmental orthodoxy championed by the foundations and are advocating developmental models that might weaken their nations' dependence on the world capitalist system.[46] Should the foundations' efforts for Third-World development be repeatedly questioned by those for whom these were ostensibly designed (and this is not to suggest that such will be the case), the influence of these institutions could be seriously challenged.

The reproduction of a particular kind of cultural capital has historically been the primary activity of the Carnegie, Ford, and Rockefeller foundations. There now exists the ironic possibility that some recipients of that cultural capital will utilize part of their capital (in the form of their education and training) to examine in greater detail the foundations' programs. Such investigations might reveal contradictions between the foundations' public rhetoric and their institutional activities, thereby presenting a challenge to their continuing cultural hegemony. The foundations' liberalism, as well as their hopes for continued legitimacy, effectively preclude them from trying to prevent this examination through overt censorship, although they can of course place numerous obstacles in the paths of would-be investigators. It is to state the obvious to say that the Carnegie, Ford, and Rockefeller foundations are powerful institutions. At the same time, we need to understand that they are not omnipotent, nor is their continuing influence as purveyors of capitalist hegemony assured or unassailable.

Notes

Introduction

1. David Horowitz and David Kolodney, "The Foundations: Charity Begins at Home," *Ramparts*, 7 (April 1968); David Horowitz, "Billion Dollar Brains," *Ramparts*, 7 (May 1968); David Horowitz, "Sinews of Empire," *Ramparts*, 7 (October 1968); Jay Schulman, Carol Brown, and Roger Kahn, "Report on the Russell Sage Foundation," *The Insurgent Sociologist*, II (Summer 1972); Waldemar Nielsen, *The Big Foundations* (New York and London: Columbia University Press, 1972).

2. As reported in Philip H. Coombs, *The Fourth Dimension of Foreign Policy: Education and Cultural Affairs* (New York and Evanston: Harper and Row, 1964), p. 70.

3. *Ford Foundation Annual Report, 1968*, p. xvii.

4. Philip Green, "Necessity and Choice in Foreign Policy," in *A Dissenter's Guide to Foreign Policy*, ed. Irving Howe (New York: Praeger Publishers, 1966), p. 138.

5. Robert A. Packenham, *Liberal America and the Third World: Political Development Ideas and Social Science* (Princeton, N.J.: Princeton University Press, 1973).

6. Manfred Stanley, "Literacy: The Crisis of Conventional Wisdom," *School Review*, 80 (May 1972). See also his *The Technological Conscience* (New York: Free Press, 1978).

Chapter 1. Foundations and the Extension of American Hegemony

1. The book was published for the Council on Foreign Affairs by Harper and Row in 1964.

2. *Ford Foundation Annual Report, 1968*, p. xvii.

3. For more on this point, see the discussion pp. 00–00. For a contemporary manifestation of the attempt to promote elite governance, see Holly Sklar, ed., *Trilateralism: The Trilateral Commission and Elite Planning for World Management* (Boston: South End Press, 1980).

4. Lewis Coser, *Men of Ideas* (New York: Free Press, 1965), pp. 339, 344.

5. Antonio Gramsci, *Selections from the Prison Notebooks*, ed. and trans. Quintin Hoare and Geoffrey Nowell Smith (New York: International Publishers, 1971).

6. Thomas R. Bates, "Gramsci and the Theory of Hegemony," *Journal of the History of Ideas*, 36 (Apr.–July 1975), p. 353.

7. Ralph A. Miliband, *The State in Capitalist Society* (New York: Basic Books, 1969), p. 183.

8. This foundation-sponsored development theory is the subject of Chapter 4.

9. The evolving United States conventional wisdom regarding Third-World development is the subject of Robert A. Packenham's *Liberal America and the Third World: Political Development Ideas in Foreign Aid and Social Science* (Princeton, N.J.: Princeton University Press, 1973).

10. Christopher Lasch, "The Cultural Cold War: A Short History of the Congress for Cultural Freedom," in *Towards a New Past: Dissenting Essays in American History*, ed. Barton Bernstein (New York: Pantheon Books, 1968). The respected China scholar John K. Fairbank spoke to this need when assessing the Chinese communist triumph in a 1950 article: "Our key problem is, therefore, to find and support those Asian leaders who have the youthful vision and the dynamic idealism to seek a genuine reconstruction of the life of the peasant masses on a non-totalitarian basis." John K. Fairbank, "The Problem of Revolutionary Asia," *Foreign Affairs*, 29 (Oct. 1950), p. 103. Such an approach would characterize foundation programs not only in Asia, about which Fairbank was writing, but in Africa and Latin America as well.

11. United States Advisory Commission on International Education and Cultural Affairs, *A Beacon of Hope—The Exchange of Persons Program* (Washington, D.C.: Government Printing Office, 1963), p. 4. My emphasis.

12. On earlier American philanthropy, see Merle Curti, *American Philanthropy Abroad: A History* (New Brunswick, N.J.: Rutgers University Press, 1963).

13. Details of the Rockefeller Foundation involvement in the field of Chinese medicine can be gleaned from E. Richard Brown, "Public Health in Imperialism: Early Rockefeller Programs at Home and Abroad," *American Journal of Public Health*, 66 (Sept. 1976); and his "Rockefeller Medicine in China: Professionalism and Imperialism," in *Philanthropy and Cultural Imperialism: The Foundations at Home and Abroad*, ed. Robert F. Arnove (Boston: G. K. Hall, 1980).

14. Among the most important revisionist studies of the Progressive Era are Robert Wiebe, *The Search for Order, 1877–1920* (New York: Hill & Wang, 1967); Gabriel Kolko, *The Triumph of Conservativism: A Reinterpretation of American History* (New York: Free Press, 1967); James Weinstein, *The Corporate Ideal in the Liberal State, 1900–1918* (Boston: Beacon Press, 1968).

15. For an insightful discussion of attempts to rationalize production in the new corporate structure, see Harry Braverman, *Labor and Monopoly Capital* (New York and London: Monthly Review Press, 1974).

16. Gates's role in Rockefeller's philanthropic plans is discussed in E. Richard Brown, *Rockefeller Medicine Men: Medicine and Capitalism in America* (Berkeley and Los Angeles: University of California Press, 1979), *passim*, but especially chapter 2.

17. Barry Karl, "Philanthropy, Policy Planning, and the Bureaucratization of the Democratic Ideal," *Daedalus*, 105 (Fall 1976), p. 146.

18. Brown, *Rockefeller Medicine Men*, p. 51.

19. The standard study of education during this period is Lawrence A. Cremin, *The Transformation of the School: Progressivism in American Education, 1876-1957* (New York: Vintage Books, 1961).

20. Barry Karl and Stanley N. Katz, "Donors, Trustees, Staffs: An Historical View, 1890-1930," *Proceedings of the Third Rockefeller Archives Center Conference*, Oct. 14, 1977, p. 6.

21. These comments on the early programs of the Carnegie Institute and the Russell Sage Foundation are drawn from Sheila Slaughter and Edward T. Silva, "Looking Backwards: How Foundations Formulated Ideology in the Progressive Period," in Arnove, *Philanthropy and Cultural Imperialism.* Quotations are from the same source.

22. Unless otherwise noted, these comments and the accompanying quotations dealing with the early work of the General Education Board are drawn from James D. Anderson, "Philanthropic Control over Private Black Higher Education," in Arnove, *Philanthropy and Cultural Imperialism.*

23. Brown, *Rockefeller Medicine Men*, presents some interesting material on the General Education Board's concern with public-health programs in the American South. See especially pp. 43-49.

24. On the Capon Springs conferences and the rise of the "Tuskegee philosophy," see Henry A. Bullock, *A History of Negro Education in the South from 1619 to the Present* (Cambridge, Mass.: Harvard University Press, 1967); and Louis R. Harlan, *Separate and Unequal: Public School Campaigns and Racism in the Southern Seaboard States, 1900-1915* (New York: Atheneum, 1968).

25. Details on the work and ideology of the Phelps-Stokes Fund can be found in Edward H. Berman, "Education in Africa and America: A History of the Phelps-Stokes Fund, 1911-1945," Ed. D. diss., Columbia University, 1969; and Kenneth J. King, *Pan-Africanism and Education: A Study of Race Philanthropy and Education in the Southern States of America and East Africa* (Oxford: Clarendon Press, 1971).

26. This discussion and that in the next several paragraphs is drawn from Edward H. Berman, "American Influence on African Education: The Role of the Phelps-Stokes Fund's Education Commissions," *Comparative Education Review*, 15 (June 1971); and his "Tuskegee-in-Africa," *Journal of Negro Education*, Spring 1972.

27. On the role of the Carnegie Corporation during this period, see Richard D. Heyman, "The Role of Carnegie Corporation in African Education, 1925-1960," Ed. D. diss., Columbia University, 1970.

28. Brown, "Public Health in Imperialism," p. 899.

29. Brown, *Rockefeller Medicine Men*, pp. 43-49.

30. For a critical study of the role of the Rockefeller Foundtion in the "Green Revolution," see Henry McBeath Cleaver, Jr., "The Origins of the Green Revolution," Ph.D. diss., Stanford University, 1974.

31. Brown, "Rockefeller Medicine in China," in Arnove, *Philanthropy and Cultural Imperialism.* See also Mary Brown Bullock, *An American Transplant:*

The *Rockefeller Foundation and Peking Union Medical School* (Berkeley and Los Angeles: University of California Press, 1980).

32. Ibid., p. 136. Cf. Mazrui's assessment in Africa, discussed at pp. 000-00 of the text.

33. Frederick T. Gates, John D. Rockefeller's chief lieutenant, was particularly outspoken on this point. For example, he wrote to Mr. Rockefeller as follows in 1905: "[O]ur imports are balanced by our exports to these same countries of American manufactures. Our export trade is growing by leaps and bounds. Such growth would have been utterly impossible but for the commerical conquest of foreign lands under the lead of missionary endeavor. What a boon to home industry and manufacture!" Gates to Rockefeller, 31 Jan. 1905, Rockefeller Family Archives: Letterbook no. 350, Record Group 1, as quoted in Brown, "Public Health in Imperialism," p. 899.

34. Quoted in Brown, "Rockefeller Medicine in China," p. 132.

35. This argument accepts the major tenets of Cold War revisionist historiography. See, for example, David Horowitz, *The Free World Colossus: A Critique of American Foreign Policy in the Cold War* (New York: Hill & Wang, 1965).

36. Peter Bachrach, *The Theory of Democratic Elitism* (Boston: Little-Brown, 1967), p. 93.

37. The Carnegie, Ford, and Rockefeller foundations regularly made grants to organizations or other foundations, which in turn elaborated the theory of democratic elitism. Details on the level of Ford Foundation support for this theory can be found in Peter J. Seybold, "The Development of American Political Sociology—A Case Study of the Ford Foundation's Role in the Production of Knowledge," Ph.D. diss., State University of New York at Stony Brook, 1976. In 1955, according to Seybold, pp. 318-19, the Ford Foundation transferred to the Russell Sage Foundation the sum of $750,000 for a series of awards to young researchers working on the theory of democratic elitism and pluralism.

38. J. Franklin Jameson to James R. Angell, 15 April 1921. Carnegie Corporation Archives: file, Negro Life and History.

39. For the influence of the Cold War on American educational policy and intimations of the foundations' roles, see Joel Spring, *The Sorting Machine: National Education Policy since 1945* (New York: David McKay, 1976).

40. These arguments are elaborated in Chapters 2, 3, and 4.

41. Michael W. Apple, *Ideology and Curriculum* (London: Routledge & Kegan Paul, 1979), p. 123.

42. Karl Marx and Friedrich Engels, *The German Ideology, Parts I and II* (New York: International Publishers, 1947), p. 39.

43. Raymond Williams, "Base and Superstructure in Marxist Cultural Theory," *New Left Review*, 82 (Nov.-Dec. 1973), pp. 8-9.

44. David L. Sallah, "Class Domination and Ideological Hegemony," *The Sociological Quarterly*, 15 (Winter 1974), p. 41.

45. For an explication of the ideology that permeates history textbooks in the United States, see Jean Anyon, "Ideology and United States History Textbooks," *Harvard Educational Review*, 49 (Aug. 1979); and Frances Fitzgerald, *America Revised* (Boston: Little-Brown, 1979). Apple, *Ideology and Curriculum*, discusses the manner in which the teacher and the curriculum disseminate a

selective version of reality. For the influence of the upper class on the mass media, see G. William Domhoff, *Who Rules America?* (Englewood Cliffs: Prentice-Hall, 1967); and Todd Gitlin, *The Whole World Is Watching: Mass Media in the Making and Unmaking of the New Left* (Berkeley and Los Angeles: University of California Press, 1980). For a case study of how the upper class in Australia determines what information reaches newspaper readers, see R. W. Connell, *Ruling Class, Ruling Culture: Studies in Conflict, Power and Hegemony in Australian Life* (Cambridge: Cambridge University Press, 1977), especially pp. 190-204.

46. Williams, "Base and Superstructure in Marxist Cultural Theory," p. 9.

47. Robert A. Dahl, "The Behavioralist Approach in American Political Science: Epitaph for a Movement to a Successful Protest," *American Political Science Review*, 55 (Dec. 1961). In this same article, p. 765, Dahl also commented on the relationship between the foundations and foundation-supported academics. "Perhaps the simplest accurate statement is that the relationship is to a very high degree reciprocal: the staffs of the foundations are very sensitive to the views of distinguished scholars, on whom they rely for advice, and at the same time [since] even foundation resources are scarce, the policies of foundation staff and trustees must inevitably encourage or facilitate some lines of research more than others."

48. David W. Eakins, "The Development of Corporate Liberal Policy Research in the United States, 1865-1965," Ph.D. diss., University of Wisconsin, 1966, p. 525.

49. Seybold, "Development of American Political Sociology." pp. 413-14.

50. This quotation is contained in a letter from Joseph McDaniel to Milton Katz, both ranking Ford Foundation officials, 21 Nov. 1951, and appears in Seybold, pp. 413-14.

51. Gwyn A. Williams, "The Concept of 'Egemonia' in the Thought of Antonio Gramsci: Some Notes on Interpretation," *Journal of the History of Ideas*, 21 (Oct.-Dec. 1960), p. 587.

52. James Joll, *Antonio Gramsci* (Harmondsworth: Penguin Books, 1978), p. 130.

53. Ford Foundation, John J. McCloy, Oral History Transcript, p. 18.

54. Ben Whitaker, *The Philanthropoids: Foundations and Society* (New York: William Morrow, 1974), p. 88.

55. Ibid., p. 90.

56. William H. Whyte, Jr., "What Are the Foundations Up To?" *Fortune*, 52 (Oct. 1955), p. 260. Eduard C. Lindeman, *Wealth and Culture* (New York: Harcourt, Brace, 1936), p. 12. Cf. the recent conclusions contained in David E. Weischadle, "Carnegie: A Case Study in How Foundations Make Decisions," *Phi Delta Kappan*, Oct. 1977, p. 108, viz., "Until recently, when a black, several women (from the professions), and a union official were added, the Carnegie board of trustees was predominantly male, well over 40 in average age, white, Protestant, and involved in business, law, banking, or the operation of other foundations. The members lived in the northeast, and with only a few exceptions were graduates of Harvard and Yale—in some cases both."

57. Francis X. Sutton, "American Foundations and U.S. Public Diplomacy," an address delivered before the Symposium on the Future of U.S. Public

Diplomacy, Subcommittee on International Organizations and Movements, House Committee on Foreign Affairs, 22 July 1968, p. 9.

58. McCloy, Oral History Transcript, pp. 16, 18.

59. Ibid., pp. 16–17.

60. Ibid, pp. 17–18.

61. Figures drawn from the *Rockefeller Foundation Annual Report, 1955*, p. 217 and *passim*. The Foundation's international work during this year was concentrated in two programs areas: Biological and Medical Research, which was budgeted at $2,601,860, and Agriculture, which was allocated $3,400,950 of the total budget of $19,152,353. The Social Science division received $3,332,155 of the total.

62. *Carnegie Corporation of New York Annual Report, 1956*, pp. 63–73. Carnegie appropriations are divided into two broad categories: programs in the United States, and programs in the British Dominions and Colonies. The amount appropriated by the trustees for the latter category in 1956 was $1,070,700. This amount was augmented by approximately another $500,000 from the appropriations for U.S. programs, but in reality earmarked for international endeavors.

63. *The Ford Foundation Annual Report, 1956*, pp. 163–90. Almost three-fifths of the year's total appropriation was designated for programs that fell within the Ford category of education in the United States. Of this amount, $210 million went for general support of American colleges and universities, while $50 million was designated for large block grants to be given to select colleges and universities. Grants to hospitals claimed $195 million of the year's budget. The monies specifically designated for international activities were broken down as follows: $16,355,161 under the category entitled International Understanding (this included grants to, among others, the Institute of International Education, the Council on Foreign Relations, the Congress for Cultural Freedom, and the Royal Institute of International Affairs in London). A total of $7,465,670 was appropriated under the heading of Overseas Development. Most of this went to particular Third-World universities and governments for educational activities. Other grants for international activities are interspersed throughout the budget.

64. *Rockefeller Foundation Annual Report, 1960*, p. 7 and *passim*.

65. *Carnegie Corporation of New York Annual Report, 1960*, pp. 66–79. The trustees' appropriation to the British Dominions and Colonies program, from which the corporation's overseas activities were funded, totaled only $649,500. But this figure tells only part of the story. In this same budget, the following amounts for international training and education were appropriated from the almost $9 million budget established under the heading of United States Programs: $225,000 to fund the Afro-Anglo-American Program in Teacher Education (about which more in Chapter 3), $350,000 to the University of Chicago for a research and training program on new nations, $85,000 to the University of California, Berkeley, for a study of leaders in selected middle African states, $121,000 to Berkeley for a study of the leaders in the Federation of the West Indies.

66. *The Ford Foundation Annual Report, 1960*, pp. 125–73. Of the total budget, $24 million was voted for the International Training and Research

program, $6 million for the International Affairs program, and $30.5 million for the Overseas Development program. These formal categories do not tell the whole story of appropriations for international work, however. For example, $11.3 million was voted to fund the program in Economic Development and Administration. Included in this amount was almost $4 million worth of grants to American universities to study developmental problems in selected Third-World nations.

67. *Rockefeller Foundation Annual Report, 1966*, p. 188 and *passim*.

68. *Carnegie Corporation of New York Annual Report, 1966*, pp. 74–89.

69. *The Ford Foundation Annual Report, 1966*, pp. 68–117.

70. See, particularly, G. William Domhoff, *Who Rules America?* and his *The Higher Circles* (New York: Random House, 1970). For a detailed listing of the interlocks among the foundations, policy formulation groups, and the decision-making processes that derive from these connections, see Mary Anna Culleton Colwell, "The Foundation Connection: Links among Foundations and Recipient Organizations," in Arnove, *Philanthropy and Cultural Imperialism*.

71. Domhoff, *Higher Circles*, p. 115. Perusal of relevant materials in the archives of the Carnegie, Ford, and Rockefeller foundations suggests that the proportion reported by Domhoff may in fact be low. Additional information detailing foundation support for council activities can be found in Laurence H. Shoup and William Minter, *Imperial Brain Trust: The Council on Foreign Relations and United States Foreign Policy* (New York and London: Monthly Review Press, 1977), especially pp. 92–96.

72. See particularly Shoup and Minter, *Imperial Brain Trust*. Their recent study only elaborates on earlier arguments along this line. Cf. Joseph Kraft, "School for Statesmen," *Harper's*, July 1958; and Lester W. Milbrath, "Interest Groups and Foreign Policy," in *Domestic Sources of Foreign Policy*, ed. James N. Rosenau, (New York: Free Press 1967).

73. See, respectively, "Pursuing Justice in an Unjust Society: The Centre for Applied Legal Studies in South Africa," *Carnegie Quarterly*, 29 (Winter/Spring 1981); and Jeffrey M. Puryear, "Higher Education, Development Assistance, and Repressive Regimes," *Studies in Comparative International Development*, 17 (Summer 1982).

74. In 1969 the United States Congress passed legislation that limited somewhat the manner in which the foundations dispense their grants. Details on this legislation and the reasons prompting it are discussed in Whitaker, *The Philanthropids*. No convincing case has yet been made that these restrictions appreciably affected the abilities of the major foundations to function much as they had before 1969.

75. Samuel Bowles and Herbert Gintis, *Schooling in Capitalist America: Educational Reform and the Contradictions of Economic Life* (New York: Basic Books, 1976); and Jay Schulman, Carol Brown, and Roger Kahn, "Report on the Russell Sage Foundation," *The Insurgent Sociologist*, 2 (Summer 1972).

76. The foundations' lack of support for "controversial" or "radical" activities or research has been noted by several commentators. The prestigious Peterson Commission report [Commission on Foundations and Private Philanthropy, *Foundations, Private Giving, and Public Policy: Report and Recommendations* (Chicago: University of Chicago Press, 1972] found, p. 84, that only 0.1 percent

of the foundation grants awarded in the 1966–68 period could be considered "controversial," while some 3 percent during the same period were classified as "innovative." Whitaker, *The Philanthropoids*, reports, p. 106, that up to 1952 "out of 28,753 grants made by the Rockefeller Foundation, only twenty-three had gone to people, and two to organizations, which were on the comprehensive lists of the House Un-American Activities Committee." Finally, Waldemar A. Nielsen, *The Big Foundations* (New York and London: Columbia University Press, 1972) reports, p. 414, that less than 8 percent of the grants made by the Ford Foundation up to 1969 could be considered either innovative or radical.

Chapter 2. United States Foreign Policy and the Evolution of the Foundations' Overseas Programs, 1945–1960

1. This victory came only after a prolonged struggle with those advocating a very different approach toward the Soviet Union. The struggle is well documented in Daniel Yergin, *Shattered Peace: The Origins of the National Security State* (Boston: Houghton Mifflin, 1977).

2. Godfrey Hodgson, *In Our Time: America from World War II to Nixon* (London: Macmillan, 1976), pp. 73, 72.

3. Irving Kristol, "American Intellectuals and Foreign Policy," *Foreign Affairs*, 45 (July 1967), p. 609.

4. Joan Nelson, *Aid, Influence and Foreign Policy* (New York: Macmillan, 1968), p. 11.

5. Yergin, *Shattered Peace*, p. 84.

6. This discussion relies heavily on William Appleman Williams. *The Tragedy of American Diplomacy* (New York: Delta Books, 1959); Lloyd G. Gardner, "The New Deal, New Frontiers, and the Cold War: A Reassessment of American Expansion, 1933–1945," in *Corporations and the Cold War*, ed. David Horowitz (New York and London: Monthly Review Press, 1969); Gardner's *Economic Aspects of New Deal Diplomacy* (Boston: Beacon Press, 1964); and David W. Eakins, "Business Planners and America's Postwar Expansion," in *Corporations and the Cold War*.

7. Details on the War-Peace Studies Project are drawn from Laurence H. Shoup and William Minter, *Imperial Brain Trust: The Council on Foreign Relations and United States Foreign Policy* (New York and London: Monthly Review Press, 1977). This quotation can be found on p. 128.

8. Ibid., pp. 135–36.

9. David A. Baldwin, *Economic Development and American Foreign Policy, 1943–62* (Chicago and London: University of Chicago Press, 1966), p. 14.

10. Ibid.

11. Eakins, "Business Planners and America's Postwar Expansion," p. 163. Michael Harrington, in his *The Twilight of Capitalism* (New York: Simon & Schuster, 1976), pp. 242–48, notes how attempts to combat communist "aggression" during this period invariably took the form of policies beneficial to the giants of American corporate capitalism. He tells how from 1949 to 1951 the Department of State enacted policies that provided a multibillion-dollar tax

subsidy to the oil industry, which "was justified in the name of anti-communism." After noting the degree to which private interests benefited from policies that at best could be judged marginal in their professed political designs, Harrington concludes: "[T]he oil companies were not using the government as an instrumentality, which is the conspiratorial interpretation of the events that are documented here. Rather, industry and government were honest and sincere participants in a process in which both articulated a policy that was logically based on the very structure of the American economy. Under such circumstances, the notion of giving away billions of federal dollars to private interests could and did come from the federal bureaucracy itself, with no hint of corruption involved." It is significant in the context of the present study that one of the oil cartel's most trusted lawyers for over two decades was John J. McCloy.

12. The most important statement calling into question the necessity of establishing formal political control over territories to extend the favorable trading patterns of imperial powers remains John Gallagher and Ronald Robinson, "The Imperialism of Free Trade," *Economic History Review*, 2d ser., 45 (August 1953), pp. 1–15. William Roger Lewis, *Imperialism at Bay: The United States and the Decolonization of the British Empire, 1941–1945* (New York: Oxford University Press, 1978), examines the American position on this question in the period after World War II.

13. For an assessment of the links between the Committee on Economic Development and the major foundations, see Mary Anna Culleton Colwell, "The Foundation Connection: Links among Foundations and Recipient Organizations," in *Philanthropy and Cultural Imperialism: The Foundations at Home and Abroad* ed. Robert F. Arnove (Boston: G. K. Hall, 1980). Cf. the assessment of the influence of the Committee on Economic Development in Leonard Silk and Mark Silk, *The American Establishment* (New York: Basic Books, 1980).

14. Eakins, "Business Planners and America's Postwar Expansion," p. 164.

15. Quoted in Gabriel Kolko, *The Roots of American Foreign Policy: An Analysis of Power and Purpose* (Boston: Beacon Press, 1969), p. 65.

16. Quoted by R. B. Sutcliffe in the Introduction to Paul A. Baran's *The Political Economy of Growth* (Harmondsworth: Penguin Books, 1973), p. 81.

17. Alfred E. Eckes, Jr., *The United States and the Global Struggle for Minerals* (Austin and London: University of Texas Press, 1979), documents this concern from the 1920s to the present.

18. Shoup and Minter, *Imperial Brain Trust*, p. 136.

19. Ibid., p. 141.

20. Eckes, *The United States and the Global Struggle for Minerals*, p. 120.

21. *Resources for Freedom*, 5 vols. (Washington, D.C.: Government Printing Office, 1952), 1:60.

22. John Kerry King, *Southeast Asia in Perspective* (New York: Macmillan, 1956), p. 9.

23. Percy W. Bidwell, "Raw Materials and National Policy," *Foreign Affairs*, 37 (Oct. 1958), p. 153.

24. Quoted in Kolko, *The Roots of American Foreign Policy*, p. 50.

25. Robert A. Packenham, *Liberal America and the Third World: Political Development Ideas in Foreign Aid and Social Science* (Princeton, N.J.: Princeton University Press, 1973), p. 132 and *passim*.

26. Harry Magdoff, *The Age of Imperialism: The Economics of American Foreign Policy* (New York and London: Monthly Review Press, 1969), p. 182. Baran, *The Political Economy of Growth*, p. 379, indicates the substantially larger earnings realized from United States overseas investment compared to domestic investment. More recent data to support Magdoff's and Baran's contention can be found in Manuel Castells, *The Economic Crisis and American Society* (Princeton, N.J.: Princeton University Press, 1980), especially pp. 107-14.

27. Richard A. Humphrey, "The Plane of Government-Academic Dialogue: An Introduction," in *Universities . . . and Development Assistance Abroad*, ed Richard A. Humphrey (Washington, D.C.: American Council on Education, 1967), pp. 1, 3.

28. Waldemar Nielsen, *The Big Foundations* (New York and London: Columbia University Press, 1972), p. 409.

29. Quoted in Williams, *Tragedy of American Diplomacy*, p. 270. For an analysis of the institutional mechanisms utilized by the United States government to encourage private investment and enterprise in developing nations, see Robert E. Wood, "Foreign Aid and the Capitalist State in Underdeveloped Countries," *Politics and Society*, 10 (1980), no. 1. This emphasis on private investment and initiative, and the concomitant discouragement of state-sponsored development in the Third World continues to form a staple of United States foreign policy. See, for example, the 21 Sept. 1981 speech to the United Nations General Assembly by Secretary of State Alexander Haig, as reported in the *New York Times*, 22 Sept. 1981. This speech was consistent with the Reagan administration's evolving policy toward developmental aid. Earlier in the year a position paper developed by the State and Treasury departments outlined the main themes of the administration's approach. According to a report in the *New York Times*, 19 Feb. 1982, p. 34, the paper argued that "the Administration wants to channel development aid toward countries that encourage free markets, emphasize private sector development with minimal government involvement and take economic steps to help themselves." Cf. the assessment in David Kinley, Arnold Levinson, and Francis Moore Lappe, "The Myth of 'Humanitarian' Foreign Aid," *The Nation*, 11-18 July 1981.

30. Articles in the *New York Times*, 21-22 Oct. 1981, present the main points of Reagan's approach.

31. Ralph A. Miliband, *The State in Capitalist Society* (New York: Basic Books, 1969), pp. 85-86.

32. Shoup and Minter, *Imperial Brain Trust*, p. 166.

33. For an analysis of the bank's role in this regard, see Wood, "Foreign Aid and the Capitalist State in Underdeveloped Countries." For a case study of the role of the International Monetary Fund in aligning the economies of the developing nations with the world capitalist system, see James Phillips, "Renovation of the International Economic Order: Trilateralism, the IMF, and Jamaica," in *Trilateralism: The Trilateral Commission and Elite Planning for World Management*, ed. Holly Sklar (Boston: South End Press, 1980).

34. Baldwin, *Economic Development and American Foreign Policy, 1943-1962*, p. 32.

35. Ibid., pp. 19-21. Cf. Wood, "Foreign Aid and the Capitalist State in Underdeveloped Countries."

36. Ibid., p. 67.

37. Quoted in ibid., p. 41.

38. Sutcliffe, in Introduction to *Political Economy of Growth*, p. 81. The fact that foreign aid was supposed to encourage private investment and lending while simultaneously *discouraging* Third-World statist development has been noted by numerous commentators. Wood, "Foreign Aid and the Capitalist State in Underdeveloped Countries," comments as follows (pp. 3, 4, 6, 11, 12): "The history of foreign aid, therefore, can be seen as a history of efforts to transfer resources to governments without encouraging statist development—without encouraging, in particular, state investment in direct industrial or agricultural production . . . [There is] a logic that regulates both the relationship of aid to private lending and investment and the relationship among different types of aid. This logic systematically undercuts the possibility of state-controlled development and fosters the structural dependence of the state on the process of private accumulation. It encourages a form of integration into the capitalist world economy that prepares the way for penetration by international capital . . . From its beginning in the early postwar period, foreign aid from the U.S. and multilateral organizations, and later from other DAC members, has been explicitly administered so as *not* to compete with private investment or lending . . . [T]his policy of avoiding competition with the private sector is written into the statues of American aid agencies and the World Bank."

39. Report to the President of the United States from the Commission to Strengthen the Security of the Free World [the Clay Commission], entitled *The Scope and Distribution of United States Military and Economic Assistance Programs* (Washington, D.C.: Government Printing Office, 1963), p. 3.

40. Kolko, *Roots of American Foreign Policy*, p. 69.

41. Quoted in ibid., p. 70.

42. Eugene Black, "The Domestic Dividends of Foreign Aid," *Columbia Journal of World Business*, 1 (Fall 1965), p. 23.

43. *Report to the President on Foreign Economic Policies* (Washington, D.C., Government Printing Office, 1950), pp. 8–9. The chairman of this commission, Gordon Gray, had a long involvement with national security affairs, serving as Secretary of the Army, Director of the Office of Defense Mobilization, Assistant Secretary of Defense for International Security Affairs, and for three years as Special Assistant to the President for National Security Affairs.

44. Quoted in Baldwin, *Economic Development and American Foreign Policy*, p. 109.

45. Quoted from the *New York Times*, 12 Jan. 1956, and reported in ibid., p. 119.

46. *Scope and Distribution of United States Military and Economic Assistance Programs*, p. 5.

47. Ibid., pp. 12–13.

48. These are elucidated in Teresa Hayter, *Aid as Imperialism* (Harmondsworth: Penguin Books, 1971), p. 47. See also n. 38.

49. For insights into the activities of this latter gentleman, Edward S. Mason, see Steve Weissman, "Foreign Aid: Who Needs It?" in *The Trojan Horse* ed. Steve Weissman (San Francisco: Ramparts Press, 1974). Mason's views on the role of American foreign assistance are succinctly summarized in his *Foreign*

Aid and Foreign Policy (New York: Harper & Row, 1964), which was an expanded version of a talk given to the Council on Foreign Relations.

50. Interoffice memorandum to Rockefeller Foundation staff from Bryce Wood, 18 Mar. 1948. Rockefeller Foundation Archives, New York City (hereafter RFNYC): folder 900, Program and Policies, Underdeveloped Areas.

51. Interoffice memorandum to Rockefeller Foundation staff from Philip E. Mosely, 3 Feb. 1949. RFNYC: folder 900, Program and Policies, Underdeveloped Areas.

52. Carl Spaeth, "Program for Asia and the Near East," pp. 1–4, 10–11. Ford Foundation International Training and Research Papers, Administration, Board of Overseas Training and Research, 1952.

53. Ibid., pp. 2–3.

54. Ford Foundation, John B. Howard, Oral History Transcript, pp. 4–5.

55. Cleon O. Swayzee to John Dickey, 15 June 1953. Ford Foundtion International Training and Research Papers, Administration, Board of Overseas Training and Research, Minutes of Meetings and Other Reports, 1953/4.

56. Ford Foundation International Training and Research Papers, Administration, Board of Overseas Training and Research, Meeting, 15 Sept. 1953.

57. Alan Pifer, background paper, 14 May 1957. Carnegie Corporation Archives (hereafter CCA): file, Columbia University—American Assembly Conference on "The United States and Africa."

58. Draft proposal from Arthur Adams to John Gardner, 25 Mar. 1959. CCA: file, American Council on Education—Committee on Educational Liaison with African Countries.

59. John D. Rockefeller III to Dean Rusk, 7 Dec. 1954. RFNYC: folder 900, Program and Policies, Underdeveloped Areas.

60. Pifer, background paper, 14 May 1957.

61. Donald K. Price to Rowan Gaither, 12 June 1956. Ford Foundation International Training and Research Papers, Administration, Training and Research, Africa.

62. Donald K. Price to J. W. Gardner, 24 Mar. 1954. Ford Foundation International Training and Research Papers, Administration, Board of Overseas Training and Research, Meeting, 31 Mar. 1954.

63. *Rockefeller Foundation Annual Report, 1956*, pp. 6–7.

64. Charles B. Fahs to J. George Harrar, "Comments on United States Overseas Aid Program," 5 Jan. 1961. RFNYC: folder 900, Program and Policies, Underdeveloped Areas, 1961–63.

65. A critical appraisal of the Rockefeller Foundation's involvement in the revolution can be found in Harry McBeath Cleaver, Jr., "The Origins of the Green Revolution," Ph.D. diss., Stanford University, 1974. Cf. the positive assessments in, for example, Elvin Charles Stakman, Richard Bradfield, and Paul C. Mangelsdorf, *Campaign against Hunger* (Cambridge, Mass.: Belknap Press, 1967); and Clifton Wharton, ed., *Subsistence Agriculture and Economic Development* (Chicago: Aldine, 1969).

66. Humphrey, "Plane of Government-Academic Dialogue," p. 3.

67. L. C. DeVinney, "Rough Draft Notes on Backward Areas Discussion," 5 April 1949. RFNYC: folder 900, Program and Policies, Underdeveloped Areas.

68. Dean Rusk, "Background for Proposal of Increased Program in Non-Western Underdeveloped Areas, Memorandum to the Trustees," 29 Nov. 1955. RFNYC: folder 900, Pro-Unar, 6, filed with 900, Program and Policies, Underdeveloped Areas.

69. *Rockefeller Foundation Annual Report, 1956*, p. 7.

70. Francis X. Sutton, "American Foundations and United States Public Diplomacy" (p. 8), an address delivered before the Symposium on the Future of United States Public Diplomacy, Subcommittee on International Organizations and Movements, House Committee on Foreign Affairs, 22 July 1968. Available in a Ford Foundation reprint.

71. Howard, Oral History Transcript, pp. 109–10.

72. E. Jefferson Murphy, *Creative Philanthropy: Carnegie Corporation and Africa, 1953–1973* (New York: Teachers College Press, 1976), p. 28, gives a figure of $1,200,000 for these activities. The figure of $2,500,000 comes from George M. Beckmann, "The Role of the Foundations in Non-Western Studies," in *U.S. Philanthropic Foundations: Their History, Structure, Management, and Record* ed. Warren Weaver (New York: Harper & Row, 1967), p. 397, and seems to be much closer to the mark. See Chapter 4 for more on the growth of these area-studies programs.

73. Murphy, *Creative Philanthropy*, p. 29.

74. From the unpaginated copy of the "Final Report of the 13th American Assembly," 4 May 1958. CCA: file, Columbia University-American Assembly, Africa.

75. "Report to the Carnegie Corporation of New York on the Special Africa Project," n.a., n.d., but c. Oct. 1961. CCA: file, Council on Foreign Relations-Travel Groups.

76. This pattern of intervention is the subject of Richard J. Barnet's *Intervention and Revolution: America's Confrontation with Insurgent Movements around the World* (New York and Cleveland: World Publishing Company, 1968). The forces motivating this intervention are examined in John L.S. Girling, *America and the Third World: Revolution and Intervention* (London: Routledge & Kegan Paul, 1980).

77. The conventional wisdom regarding Third-World development is examined in Packenham, *Liberal America and the Third World*. These themes are developed in Chapter 4 of the present book.

78. A notable exception to this pattern is the support provided by the Ford Foundation for educational programs in socialist Tanzania. While the Tanzanian commitment to the construction of a socialist society is unequivocal, President Julius Nyerere has been careful to retain independence from the socialist nations dominated by communist parties, a fact that makes his brand of African socialism less offensive to organizations like the Ford Foundation. At the same time, Ford support for Tanzania is viewed as a way of insuring that Nyerere continues to adhere to his unaligned brand of socialism, a more desirable outcome than alignment with the more doctrinaire socialist countries.

79. David Halberstam, *The Best and the Brightest* (New York: Fawcett-Crest, 1973), p. 377.

80. The term "imperial liberalism" comes from Hodgson, *In Our Time*. Alan Wolfe and Jerry Sanders term the dominant ideology "Cold War liberalism."

See their "Resurgent Cold War Ideology: The Case of the Committee on the Present Danger," in *Capitalism and the State in US-Latin American Relations,* ed. Richard Fagan (Stanford: Stanford University Press, 1980).

81. *Rockefeller Foundation Annual Report, 1958,* p. 128.

82. Ford Foundation International Training and Research Papers, Administration, Board of Overseas Training and Research, Meeting, 15 Sept 1953.

83. See especially Yergin, *Shattered Peace.*

84. Mary Kaldor, *The Disintegrating West* (New York: Hill & Wang, 1978), p. 152.

85. Geoffrey Barraclough, "The Struggle for the Third World," *New York Review of Books,* 25 (9 Nov 1978), p. 54. Cf. references cited in n. 26 and the viewpoint of Jonathan Power, "Bound by Hoops of Steel," *New York Times,* 2 July 1978, in which Power notes the following: "United States exports to developing countries are more important than United States exports to the E.E.C., Eastern Europe, the Soviet Union and China combined.

"Over 20 percent of United States direct investment goes to the third world. The rate of return is double that of investments in the developed countries."

Chapter 3. The Implementation of Foundation Programs in the Third World

1. In the book's preface, p. xi, Rostow gives thanks to "the Carnegie Corporation, which offered the freedom and resources of a Reflective Year Grant," enabling him to concentrate his "attention wholly on the elaboration of a single line of thought."

2. Kenneth W. Thompson, *Higher Education for National Development: One Model for Technical Assistance* (New York: International Council for Educational Development Occasional Paper No. 5, 1972), p. 3.

3. Ibid., p. 12.

4. Robert F. Arnove, "Foundations and the Transfer of Knowledge," paper presented to the Conversation in the Disciplines: Universities and the New International Order, State University of New York at Buffalo, 23-25 Mar. 1978.

5. L. C. DeVinney to social science staff, "Rough Draft Notes on Backward Areas Discussion," 5 April 1949. Rockefeller Foundation Archives, New York City (RFNYC): folder 900, Program and Policies, Underdeveloped Areas.

6. Charles B. Fahs, "Development Programs and the Rockefeller Foundation," 26 Sept. 1950. RFNYC: folder 900, Pro, Unar-3, with Program and Policies, Underdeveloped Areas.

7. Dean Rusk, "Background for Proposal of Increased Program in Non-Western Underdeveloped Areas, Memorandum to the Trustees," 29 Nov. 1955. RFNYC: folder 900,. Pro, Unar-6, filed with Program and Policies.

8. *Rockefeller Foundation Annual Report, 1956,* p. 7.

9. Norman S. Buchanan, "Notes for Office," 3 Jan. 1956. RFNYC: folder 900, Program and Policies, Underdeveloped Areas.

10. Robert S. Morison to J. G. Harrar and staff, 26 Jan. 1961. RFNYC: folder 900, Program and Policies, Underdeveloped Areas, 1961-63. These views paralleled those of foundation president Harrar, who noted in a 16 Feb. 1960

memorandum to the staff of the social sciences division that the foundation should "provide core personnel [for foreign universities] who would work with local faculty and investigators in strengthening existing programs and in the establishment and development of others of critical importance." Filed in same folder.

11. Kenneth W. Thompson to social science staff, 31 Oct. 1960. RFNYC: folder 900, Program and Policies, Underdeveloped Areas.

12. *Rockefeller Foundation Annual Report, 1960*, pp. 10-11.

13. J. George Harrar, "Proposed University Development Program," 13 Nov. 1961. RFNYC: folder 900, Pro, Unar-9, filed with 900, Program and Policies, Underdeveloped Areas.

14. Thompson, *Higher Education for National Development*, p. 7.

15. Ford Foundation Archive reports 001438 and 000583 provide details on these 1956 and 1958 trips, respectively.

16. For details on the work of the Fund for the Advancement of Education, see Dennis C. Buss, "The Ford Foundation and the Exercise of Power in American Public Education," Ed.D. diss., Rutgers University, 1972.

17. Don K. Price to Henry Heald, 7 Feb. 1958. Ford Foundation International Training and Research Papers, Administration, Board of Overseas Training and Research.

18. E. Jefferson Murphy, *Creative Philanthropy: Carnegie Corporation and Africa, 1953-1973* (New York: Teachers College Press, 1976), p. 37.

19. Alan Pifer, "Some Notes on Carnegie Corporation Grants in Africa," n.d., but c. 1954. Carnegie Corporation Archives (CCA): file, Alan Pifer.

20. Ford's Alfred C. Wolf wrote to his colleague Frank Sutton on 23 July 1958 of a meeting earlier that day with Carnegie's Alan Pifer, in which Pifer had observed that "Carnegie proposed to concentrate largely on Nigeria over the next few years and that anything we did in Central and in East Africa would be to the good." Ford Foundation General Correspondence file, Carnegie Corporation, 1958. In 1961 Rockefeller vice-president Kenneth Thompson wrote of his discussions with Ford Foundation officials regarding Ford and Rockefeller support for the University of Ibadan at a time when "regional" universities were also seeking foundation funding. It is clear from this memorandum that Rockefeller officials, and most probably Ford officers as well, wanted to build up the University of Ibadan in hopes that it would subsequently provide assistance to the "regionals." Two years later Thompson and Ford's F. Champion Ward discussed the need to draw up a statement delineating the responsibilities of the two foundations at Ibadan to avoid duplication and conflict. This is contained in an interoffice memorandum of a phone conversation between Kenneth W. Thompson and F. Champion Ward, 16 April 1963. Rockefeller Archives Center, Pocantico Hills (hereafter RAC): folder 497, University College Ibadan, 1962.

21. Melvin J. Fox, "Education Goals and Achievements, Future Prospects," paper prepared for the Ford Foundation Staff Conference, 9-11 June 1970, pp. 1-10 of Appendix. Ford Foundation Archives report 002387.

22. "Rockefeller Foundation University Development Program, University Development Centers, Expenditures, Allocations, and Appropriations, 1963-72."

RFNYC: folder 900, Pro, Unar-14, filed with Programs and Policies, Under-developed Areas.

23. The quotation appears in a memorandum entitled "Comments on U.S. Overseas Aid Programs," 5 Jan. 1961, from Charles B. Fahs to J. George Harrar. RFNYC: folder 900, Programs and Policies, Underdeveloped Areas, 1961-63. See p. 000 of the present volume for the way in which Rockefeller Foundation grants helped to shape one department at Ibadan.

24. These figures come from Murphy, *Creative Philanthropy*, pp. 245-51.

25. A 1955 grant of $25,000 provided support for a study of East African leadership by Institute staff. Murphy, *Creative Philanthropy*, p. 245.

26. *Rockefeller Foundation Annual Report, 1961*, p. 185.

27. The role of the Africa Liaison Committee and its links to the foundations are discussed in Chapter 5.

28. Some six weeks before the conference convened at the end of October 1963, representatives of the three foundations, the Agency for International Development, the World Bank, and the Africa Liaison Committee, met in Washington to discuss their approach at the forthcoming conference. Details of this meeting and the individuals involved can be found in a 6 Sept. 1963 memorandum from Stephen H. Stackpole to Alan Pifer and Frederick Mosher. CCA: file, University of East Africa, 1.

29. On 8 May 1963 de Kiewiet had written to Sir Donald MacGillivray, chairman of the University of East Africa's Provisional Council, to make this clear: "[I]t is of the very first importance that the effort should be resolutely continued to develop a common planning mechanism and program for the University as a whole. . . . The most significant and substantial aid from American sources without any question is still to be found in the context of University development as a whole." RAC: box R100, folder 477, University of East Africa Conference, 1962-Aug. 1963.

30. *Rockefeller Foundation Annual Report, 1963*, p. 60.

31. *Rockefeller Foundation Annual Report, 1964*, p. 51.

32. John Weir to Philip Bell, 6 Nov. 1963. RAC: box R100, folder 477, University of East Africa, 1963.

33. From Ford Foundation grant file PA64-430.

34. Robert West, Associate Director of the Rockefeller Foundation's social sciences division, noted this Ford Foundation interest in a concerned memorandum of 30 Aug. 1965 to James S. Coleman. RAC: box 1010, file 4925, Makerere College, Political Science Research, 1965-67.

35. Stephen Stackpole to Alan Pifer and Frederick Mosher, 4 Nov. 1963. CCA: file, University of East Africa, 1.

36. Agenda item for Board of Trustees, 7 May 1964, by Stephen H. Stackpole, entitled "The University of East Africa." CCA: file, University of East Africa, 2.

37. Stackpole to Pifer and Mosher, 4 Nov. 1963.

38. Trent Schroyer, *The Critique of Domination* (New York: Braziller, 1973), p. 220.

39. Joseph H. Willets, "Preliminary Conclusions from the Study of Crete," 8 Mar. 1949. RFNYC: folder 900, Pro, Unar-2.

40. Interoffice memorandum to staff from Bryce Wood, 10 Mar. 1948. RFNYC: folder 900, Program and Policies, Underdeveloped Areas.

41. A discussion of government support for the social sciences in the United States can be found in Gene M. Lyons, *The Uneasy Partnership: Social Science and the Federal Government in the Twentieth Century* (New York: Russell Sage Foundation, 1969).

42. Peter Bell, "The Ford Foundation as a Transnational Actor," in *Transnational Actors and World Politics*, ed. Robert O. Keohane and Joseph S. Nye, Jr. (Cambridge, Mass.: Harvard University Press, 1972), p. 116.

43. Robert F. Arnove, "The Ford Foundation and 'Competency-Building' Overseas: Assumptions, Approaches, and Outcomes," *Studies in Comparative International Development*, 12 (Sept. 1977), p. 118.

44. Walter E. Ashley, "Philanthropy and Government: A Study of the Ford Foundation's Overseas Activities," Ph.D. diss., New York University, 1971, Chapter 4.

45. For details by a Rockefeller Foundation officer on the growth of social science in East Africa, see David Court, "The Idea of Social Science in East Africa: An Aspect of the Development of Higher Education," *Minerva*, 17 (Summer 1979).

46. In late 1963 representatives of a group of donor agencies—including the Ford, Carnegie, and Rockefeller foundations, the World Bank, the Agency for International Development, the British Ministry of Overseas Development— met with representatives of the University of East Africa at the Rockefeller Foundation villa outside Bellagio, Italy. The final report of that gathering concluded that "for the near term the University of East Africa ought to concentrate on developing a cadre of professional, executive, and technical personnel required for economic and social development by offering 'education for investment.' The group agreed that university education represents a necessary infrastructure investment to achieve economic growth." *Report of a Conference on the University of East Africa—Final Report.* RAC: box R100, folder 477, University of East Africa.

47. See Chapter 5 for details on the organization of the Ashby Commission study.

48. Materials in the archives of the Rockefeller Foundation, particularly at RAC for example, attest to the care with which these expatriates were selected by foundation officers.

49. For specifics on the placement of Rockefeller-funded students, see *The Rockefeller Foundation Directory of Fellowships and Scholarships, 1917-1970* (New York: The Rockefeller Foundation, 1970).

50. Thompson, *Higher Education for National Development*, p. 21.

51. Ibid., p. 15.

52. From "University Development, Education for Development Program Review," n.a., 14 Oct. 1975. RFNYC: folder 900, Program and Policies, Pro, Unar-16, p. 33.

53. Arnove notes that "Latin Americans selected for doctoral study are often those who have already received a master's degree in one of the U.S. universities receiving Foundation support as a 'resource base.' These resource bases in education are Stanford, Chicago, and Harvard, which over the past eight years

have been awarded close to $1 million to provide advanced training in education and social sciences to some 150 Latin American educational researchers, planners, administrators, and faculty. The Stanford Program in International Development Education, alone, has trained some 82 graduate students to the Master's level from Latin America in the concepts and methods of educational research and planning; and with Ford funding also has trained some 66 Southeast Asian educators (principally from Malaysia, Indonesia, Thailand, and the Philippines) at the Master's level." Arnove, "Foundations and the Transfer of Knowledge," p. 16.

54. This point will be explored in more detail in Chapter 4.

55. This supposedly close relationship is increasingly being questioned, however. See, for example, the review by Andrew Hacker of Charles Lindbloom and David Cohen's *Social Science and Social Problem Solving* in the *New York Times Book Review*, 29 July 1979.

56. Gunnar Myrdal, *Asian Drama: An Inquiry into the Poverty of Nations*, vol. 1 (Harmondsworth: Penguin Books, 1968), p. 12.

57. This discussion is drawn from David Ransom, "Ford Country: Building an Elite for Indonesia," in *The Trojan Horse*, ed. Steve Weissman (San Francisco: Ramparts Press, 1974).

58. Ibid., p. 99.

59. Ibid., p. 111.

60. Court, "The Idea of Social Science in East Africa," notes several examples of this at the University of East Africa. Although the evidence is as yet circumstantial, such a situation *may* have arisen in Kenya over the last few years. The University of Nairobi has long been a centerpiece of Ford and Rockefeller university development activities in Africa. The social sciences there have received particular foundation attention, as have several other departments. Faculty and students at the university, as well as other intellectuals in Kenya, have become increasingly critical of the regime of President Daniel Arap Moi in recent years. Moi's increasingly American-leaning government has not veiled its irritation over this criticism. It is perhaps instructive that the university and its personnel were treated with particular brutality in the aftermath of the failed coup attempt of 1 Aug. 1982 to topple the Moi government. For initial reactions to these events and the *possible* role of Kenyan intellectuals as catalysts, see the articles and editorial comments in *The Guardian* (Manchester and London), 2–7 Aug. 1982, and *The Observer* (London), 8 Aug. 1982.

61. Henry H. Lunau, "Interim Report on the Congolese Leaders Project," 11 Aug. 1960, p. 2. Ford Foundation grant file PA60-165.

62. Ibid. See also Ashley, "Philanthropy and Government," chapter 6.

63. Ashley, "Philanthropy and Government," pp. 94–95.

64. Ibid.

65. Ford Foundation, Melvin J. Fox, Oral History Transcript, pp. 112–113.

66. For an indication of Harris's involvement with the CIA, see Dan Schechter, Michael Ansara, and David Kolodney, "The CIA as an Equal Opportunity Employer," *Ramparts*, 7 (1969), pp. 25–33.

67. For details, see Ford Foundation grant file PA61-103.

68. David Heaps to James T. Harris, 5 Apr. 1962. Ford Foundation grant file PA61-103.

69. Ford Foundation, James L. Morrill, Oral History Transcript, p. 21. For some specifics on Morrill's work in other aspects of overseas development, see Murphy, *Creative Philanthropy*, pp. 75, 102, and *passim*.

70. Ashley, "Philanthropy and Government," p. 97.

71. David Heaps to Francis X. Sutton, 17 May 1962. Ford Foundation grant file PA61-103.

72. For a running commentary on this conflict, see the *New York Times*, 16–31 May 1978.

73. Alvin W. Gouldner, *The Dialectic of Ideology and Technology: The Origins, Grammar, and Future of Ideology* (New York: Seabury Press, 1976), p. 233. My emphasis.

74. Background information on this conference can be found in the Karl W. Bigelow papers, Teachers College Archives (hereafter TCA), box 8, folder 8/3, and box 9, folder 9/3.

75. Karl W. Bigelow, "Rough Notes of Meeting March 26, 1948." TCA: Bigelow papers, box 11, folder 11/12.

76. Stephen H. Stackpole to staff, 17 Dec. 1959. CCA: file, Columbia University Teachers College, Afro-Anglo-American Program, 1959–60.

77. Alan Pifer, docket excerpt for Board of Trustees meeting, 26 April 1960. CCA: file, Columbia University Teachers College, Afro-Anglo-American Program, 1959–60. The initial grant in 1960 was for $450,000, followed by a similar grant in 1963, and by $335,000 in 1966.

78. For documentation of these contentions and details on the corporation's work during this period, see Edward H. Berman, "Educational Colonialism in Africa: The Role of American Foundations, 1910–1945," in *Philanthropy and Cultural Imperialism: The Foundations at Home and Abroad*, ed. Robert F. Arnove (Boston: G. K. Hall, 1980); and Richard D. Heyman, "The Role of Carnegie Corporation in African Education, 1925–1960," Ed.D. diss., Columbia University, 1970.

79. In April 1959, for example, Carnegie trustees approved a grant of $110,000 to the council. Docket excerpt for trustees meeting, 24 April 1959, CCA: file, Inter-University Council, 4.

80. Murphy, *Creative Philanthropy*, provides specifics.

81. Ibid., p. 124.

82. F. X. Sutton, memorandum to the files, 10 Nov. 1958. Ford Foundation general correspondence 1958, file Africa.

83. This conference is discussed by Murphy, *Creative Philanthropy*, chapter 8.

84. Figures culled from Murphy's list of Carnegie expenditures, 1953–1973, *Creative Philanthropy*, pp. 245–51.

85. Murphy, *Creative Philanthropy*, pp. 133–36, provides details on the evolution of the Afro-Anglo-American Program in Teacher Education. Consult also TCA: Bigelow papers.

86. In a memorandum of 29 Sept. 1965 to Carnegie staff, Stephen Stackpole wrote that "it is clear that this [AAA] program has become so valuable and is so supportive to all that CC is doing with the institutes in Africa that a further grant should be recommended." CCA: file Columbia University Teachers College, Afro-Anglo-American program, 1964–65.

87. Raymond Williams, "Base and Superstructure in Marxist Cultural Theory," *New Left Review*, 82 (Nov.-Dec. 1973), p. 9.

88. "Report on the ATEA 11th Conference in Addis Ababa, 26-31 March, 1972," by K. W. Bigelow, p. 2. Typescript in TCA: Bigelow papers.

89. For specifics, see Heyman, "The Role of Carnegie Corporation in African Education"; Edward H. Berman, "Education in Africa and America: A History of the Phelps-Stokes Fund, 1911-1945," Ed.D. diss., Columbia University, 1969; Kenneth J. King, *Pan Africanism and Education: A Study of Race Philanthropy and Education in the Southern States of America and East Africa* (Oxford: Clarendon Press, 1971), and pp. 00-00 of this text.

90. Murphy, *Creative Philanthropy*, pp. 25, 48-51, provides details on these early Carnegie Corporation fellowship provisions.

91. Harry McBeath Cleaver, Jr., "The Origins of the Green Revolution," Ph.D. diss., Stanford University, 1974, p. 185.

92. Chiu-sam Tsang, "Nationalism in School Education in China," Ph.D. diss., Columbia University, 1933, p. 151. Quoted in Cleaver, "Origins of the Green Revolution," p. 189.

93. Details on the CIA's involvement with the National Student Association can be found in "A Short Account of International Student Politics and the Cold War, with Particular Reference to the NAS, CIA, etc," *Ramparts*, 5 (Mar. 1967), pp. 29-39; and "How the CIA Turns Foreign Students into Traitors," *Ramparts*, 5 (April 1967), pp. 22-24.

94. Ford Foundation grant file PA55-221.

95. "United States National Student Association Program Notes for Foreign Student Leadership Program, #1, January 1956," filed in Ford Foundation grant file PA55-221.

96. Christopher Lasch, *The Agony of the American Left* (New York: Alfred A. Knopf, 1967), p. 100.

97. *Rockefeller Foundation Annual Report, 1960*, pp. 30-33.

98. Daniel Yergin, *Shattered Peace: The Origins of the National Security State* (Boston: Houghton Mifflin, 1979), p. 401, provides a revealing commentary on the mindset of Paul Nitze, who was an important figure in the overseas activities of the Carnegie, Ford, and Rockefeller foundations. Yergin notes how "[the] paper was drafted in February and March by State and Defense Department officials, under the leadership of Paul Nitze, an investment banker who had succeeded George Kennan as head of the Policy Planning Staff. The document, which became known as NSC-68, is as important as Kennan's Long Telegram and the Truman Doctrine in postwar history. It was the first formal statement of American policy. It expressed the fully formed Cold War set of American leaders, and provided the rationalization not only for the hydrogen bomb but also for a much expanded military establishment. . . .

"But the paper then jumped to the conclusion that there was a necessary connection between domestic and foreign practice, that the Soviet goals were unlimited, that they were dictated by ideology, and that coexistence with the USSR was impossible." Nitze was head of the Committee on the Present Danger in the late 1970s and was an important foreign-policy advisor to candidate Ronald Reagan. For specifics on his role in this group, see Alan Wolfe and Jerry Sanders, "Resurgent Cold War Ideology: The Case of the Committee on the Present Danger," in *Capitalism and the State in US-Latin American Relations*, ed. Richard Fagen (Stanford: Stanford University Press, 1980).

99. Alvin W. Gouldner, *The Coming Crisis of Western Sociology* (New York: Avon Books, 1971), p. 5.

100. Arnove, "Ford Foundation and 'Competency-Building' Overseas," p. 114.

101. Francis X. Sutton, "American Foundations and U.S. Public Diplomacy," an address delivered before the Symposium on the Future of U.S. Public Diplomacy, Subcommittee on International Organizations and Movements, House Committee on Foreign Affairs, 22 July 1968, p. 9.

102. This discussion is drawn from Kenneth W. Thompson, Barbara Fogel, and Helen E. Danner, eds., *Higher Education and Social Change: Promising Experiments in Developing Countries, vol. 2, Case Studies* (New York: Praeger Publishers, 1977); pp. 258-69.

103. Ibid., p. 260.

104. Ibid., p. 265.

105. Thompson, *Higher Education for National Development*, p. 12.

106. The case study on the activities at the Federal University of Bahia notes how "in July, 1973, after an agreement was signed with the Rockefeller Foundation, UFBa created a Research and Education Program for Development (PROPED), a program to enable the University to participate in the socioeconomic development of the northeastern part of Brazil. The vice-rector and the Rockefeller Foundation representative submitted to a group of professors from different UFBa faculties and schools a proposal to create various interdisciplinary centers." Thompson, Fogel, and Danner, *Higher Education for Social Change*, p. 315.

107. Arnove, "Foundations and the Transfer of Knowledge," p. 14.

108. Ibid., p. 16.

109. For a discussion of Carnegie Corporation attempts to create "a worldwide network of research centers dedicated to the comparative study of child development," see *Carnegie Quarterly*, 27 (Fall 1979).

Chapter 4. The Foundations Define a Field: Foreign Area Studies, Social Science, and Developmental Theory

1. George Beckmann, "The Role of the Foundations in Non-Western Studies," in *U.S. Philanthropic Foundations: Their History, Structure, Management, and Record*, ed. Warren Weaver (New York: Harper & Row, 1967), notes, p. 396, that the Rockefeller Foundation granted approximately $1 million between 1934 and 1942 for the establishment of university-based programs in Slavic, East Asian, Near Eastern, and Latin American studies.

2. The growth of the field of national-security studies is the subject of Gene M. Lyons and Louis Morton, *Schools for Strategy: Education and Research in National Security Affairs* (New York: Praeger Publishers, 1965), and will not be a concern of this chapter. The current attempts by government agents and their university collaborators to define university-based programs that would serve the interests of the U.S. national security apparatus is the subject of

Andrew Kopkind's "A Dillar, a Dollar, an N.S.C. Scholar," *The Nation*, 25 June 1983.

3. Ford Foundation, Melvin J. Fox, Oral History Transcript, p. 72.

4. Don K. Price to Henry T. Heald, 7 Feb. 1958. Ford Foundation International Training and Research Papers, Administration.

5. Beckmann, "Role of the Foundations in Non-Western Studies," p. 398.

6. The figures comes from ibid., pp. 396-98.

7. Carl Spaeth, "Program for Asia and the Near East," 1952, p. 27. Ford Foundation International Training and Research Papers, Board of Overseas Training and Research: file, Establishment of Board of Overseas Training and Research, 1952.

8. The figure comes from Beckmann, "Role of the Foundations in Non-Western Studies," p. 398.

9. Excerpt from Draft Minutes of the Meeting of the Board of Overseas Training and Research, 5 May 1953. Ford Foundation International Training and Research Papers, Administration, Board of Overseas Training and Research, Minutes of Meetings and Other Reports, 1953/54.

10. Charles B. Fahs to J. George Harrar, 5 Jan. 1961. Rockefeller Foundation, New York City (RFNYC): folder 900. Program and Policies, Underdeveloped Areas, 1961-63.

11. Beckmann, "Role of the Foundations in Non-Western Studies," pp. 399-400.

12. An article in *The Chronicle of Higher Education*, 28 Sept. 1980, suggests how graduates of these few universities dominate American corporate life.

13. Philip E. Mosely, "International Affairs," in Weaver, *U.S. Philanthropic Foundations*, pp. 385-92.

14. Press Release, for release 22 June 1953, Ford Foundation International Training and Research Papers, Minutes of Meetings and Other Reports.

15. See, e.g., Minutes of Meeting of Board of Overseas Training and Research, 15 Sept. 1953, Ford Foundation International Training and Research Papers, Administration; and Don K. Price to Henry Heald, 7 Feb. 1958, Ford Foundation International Training and Research Papers, Administration. Also, Don K. Price to John W. Gardner, 24 Mar. 1954, Ford Foundation International Training and Research Papers, Administration, Board of Overseas Training and Research, Meeting, 31 Mar. 1954.

16. Beckmann, "Role of the Foundations in Non-Western Studies," p. 402, claims that "of 984 former fellows, 550 hold faculty positions in 191 colleges and universities in 38 states." He further notes that former fellows "have published 373 books and over 3000 articles and short monographs; moreover, they have edited and contributed to another 516 volumes."

17. For example, Everett C. Ladd and Seymour M. Lipset, *The Divided Academy: Professors and Politics* (New York: McGraw-Hill, 1975).

18. See pp. 000-00 of the text.

19. Samuel Bowles and Herbert Gintis, *Schooling in Capitalist America: Educational Reform and the Contradictions of Economic Life* (New York: Basic Books, 1976).

20. See pp. 000-00 of the text.

21. Rolland G. Paulston, "Ethnicity and Educational Change: A Priority for Comparative Education," *Comparative Education Review*, 20 (Oct. 1976), p. 275.

22. See p. 00 of the text for the view of Ford's John Howard on the primacy of information over source in the case of Third-World nations.

23. Robert F. Arnove, "Foundations and the Transfer of Knowledge," in *Philanthropy and Cultural Imperialism: The Foundations at Home and Abroad,* ed. Robert F. Arnove (Boston: G. K. Hall, 1980), p. 321.

24. This information on early Rockefeller support for the social sciences is drawn from Donald Fisher, "The Ideology of Rockefeller Philanthropy and the Development of a Policy for the Social Sciences, 1910 to 1940," mineo., Faculty of Education, University of British Columbia.

25. For the way in which two Rockefeller philanthropies accomplished this in Britain during the 1920s and 1930s, see Donald Fisher,"American Philanthropy and the Social Sciences: The Reproduction of a Conservative Ideology," in *Philanthropy and Cultural Imperialism.*

26. John Van Sickle, "Notes on Possible Foundation Programs in Fields of International Relations and Economic Security," 17 Dec. 1934. Rockefeller Archives Center (RAC): folder 44, 910, Program and Policy-Economic Security, 1931–38. Reported in Fisher, "Ideology of Rockefeller Philanthropy," p. 53.

27. John Van Sickle, "Recommendations for a New Program, 1935." RAC: folder 44, 910, Program and Policy-Economic Security, 1931–38. Quoted in Fisher, "Ideology of Rockefeller Philanthropy," p. 53.

28. Raymond Fosdick to S. H. Walker, 9 Nov. 1937. RAC: folder 4, 910, Program and Policy, 1937–39. Quoted in Fisher, "Ideology of Rockefeller Philanthropy," p. 30.

29. Alvin W. Gouldner, *The Coming Crisis of Western Sociology* (New York: Avon Books, 1971), pp. 188–96.

30. Stanislav Andreski, *Social Science as Sorcery* (London: Andre Deutsch, 1972), pp. 57, 146.

31. Gouldner, *Coming Crisis of Western Sociology,* p. 281.

32. Perusal of the acknowledgment sections of the major works of these mainstreams political sociologists will illustrate the degree of support they have received over the years from the foundations. For example, Reinhard Bendix's influential *Nation Building and Citizenship* (New York: Wiley, 1964) was funded by the Carnegie Corporation, and Shils, Eisenstadt, and Lipset were regular recipients of foundation grants.

33. The total revenue of the Social Science Research Council between 1956 and 1969 was approximately $39 million. Of that amount, $23.6 million came from Ford Foundation grants, $4.3 million from Carnegie Corporation grants, and $3.3 million from Rockefeller Foundation grants. The remaining $6.4 million was derived from investment income and other grants. Figures are drawn from Peter J. Seybold, "The Development of American Political Sociology—A Case Study of the Ford Foundation's Role in the Production of Knowledge," Ph.D. diss., State University of New York at Stony Brook, 1978, p. 201.

34. Cf. Robert A. Dahl, "The Behavioralist Approach in Political Science, Epitaph for a Monument to a Successful Protest," *American Political Science Review,* 55 (Dec. 1961), p. 765. Seybold's study, "Development of American Political Sociology," is an excellent discussion of the manner in which the foundations, particularly Ford, fostered the behavioralist "revolution" during the 1950s and 1960s.

35. David Horowitz, "Billion Dollar Brains," *Ramparts*, 7 (May 1969), p. 42.

36. Jerome Karabel and A. H. Halsey, *Power and Ideology in Education* (New York: Oxford University Press, 1977), p. 307. For an attempt to place the human-capital movement in perspective, see Irvin Sobel, "The Human Capital Revolution in Economic Development: Its Current History and Status," *Comparative Education Review*, 22 (June 1978), pp. 278–308.

37. For example, Schultz's influential *The Economic Value of Education* (New York: Columbia University Press, 1963) was commissioned by the Ford Foundation; Gary Becker's *Human Capital: A Theoretical and Empirical Analysis with Special Reference to Education* (New York: National Bureau of Economic Research, 1964) by the Carnegie Corporation; and the Oct. 1962 special supplement of the *Journal of Political Economy*, devoted to the topic "Investment in Human Beings" and edited by Schultz, was supported by the Carnegie Corporation.

38. Karabel and Halsey, *Power and Ideology in Education*, p. 14.

39. Samuel Bowles and Herbert Gintis, "The Problem of Human Capital Theory—A Marxian Critique," *The American Economic Review*, 65 (May 1975), p. 82.

40. Andreski, *Social Science as Sorcery*, p. 117. Cf. C. Wright Mills's views on this and related issues in his *The Sociological Imagination* (New York: Oxford University Press, 1959).

41. Gunnar Myrdal, *Asian Drama: An Inquiry into the Poverty of Nations*, vol. 1 (Harmondsworth: Penguin Books, 1968), p. 12.

42. Dean C. Tipps, "Modernization Theory and the Comparative Study of Societies: A Critical Perspective," *Comparative Studies in Society and History*, 15 (Mar. 1973), p. 210.

43. Quoted in Robert C. Packenham, *Liberal America and the Third World: Political Development Ideas in Foreign Aid and Social Science* (Princeton, N.J.: Princeton University Press, 1973), p. 61.

44. W. W. Rostow, *The Stages of Economic Growth: A Non-Communist Manifesto* (Cambridge: Cambridge University Press, 1960), pp. 142, 134.

45. Packenham, *Liberal America and the Third World, passim*.

46. Donal Cruise O'Brien, "Modernization, Order, and the Erosion of a Democratic Ideal: American Political Science, 1960–1970," *Journal of Development Studies*, 8 (1972), p. 355.

47. Irving L. Horowitz and James E. Katz, *Social Science and Public Policy in the United States* (New York: Praeger Publishers, 1975), p. 160.

48. Seybold, "Development of American Political Sociology," deals at some length with the work of the Committee on Comparative Politics.

49. The first in the series, all published by Princeton University Press, was Gabriel Almond and James Coleman, eds., *The Politics of Developing Areas* (1960). Others included Joseph La Palombara, ed., *Bureaucracy and Political Development* (1963); Robert Ward and Dankwart Rostow, *Political Modernization in Japan and Turkey* (1964); Lucien Pye and Sidney Verba, eds., *Political Culture and Political Development* (1965). O'Brien, "Modernization, Order, and the Erosion of a Democratic Ideal," comments on the ideology which informed the work of Almond and Pye, who as leading members of the Social Science Research Council played crucial roles in determining perspectives in the field

of political development theory in the Third World. Cf. the views on the Social Science Research Council delineated in Jay Schulman, Carol Brown, and Roger Kahn, "Report on the Russell Sage Foundation," *The Insurgent Sociologist*, 2 (Summer 1972), pp. 2–34.

50. O'Brien, "Modernization, Order, and the Erosion of a Democratic Ideal," p. 365. Richard Sandbrook, "The 'Crisis' in Political Development Theory," *Journal of Development Studies*, 12 (Jan. 1976), p. 179, makes the same point, noting the belief in the incontrovertibility of "a governing elite. Political development is seen as an evolutionary process which should take place under the aegis of incumbent political elites."

51. Francis X. Sutton, "American Foundations and U.S. Public Diplomacy," an address delivered before the Symposium on the Future of U.S. Public Diplomacy, Subcommittee on International Organizations and Movements, House Committee on Foreign Affairs, 22 July 1968, p. 9.

52. Indeed, there was some evidence to suggest just the opposite, that the masses in the Third World did *not* want to be "developed" along lines devised for them by Western social scientists and indigenous politicians who concurred in this theory. Barrington Moore, Jr., speaks to this point in his *Social Origins of Dictatorship and Democracy: The Making of Lord and Peasant in the Modern World* (Boston: Beacon Press, 1966), noting, p. 506, that "there is no evidence that the masses of the population anywhere has wanted an industrial society, and plenty of evidence that they did not."

53. Langer's quote comes from *Goals for Americans: The Report of the President's Commission on National Goals and Chapters Submitted for the Consideration of the Commission* (New York: Prentice-Hall, 1960), p. 301. This commission was administered by the American Assembly (about which more will be said in Chapter 5), and its work was funded by grants from several foundations, including Carnegie, Ford, and Rockefeller. In a letter dated 15 June 1953 to John S. Dickey, Ford Foundation Director of Research Cleon O. Swayzee wrote about discussions involving Langer and the foundation's sponsorship of a project in Indonesia. This was part of "the Langer recommendations for three studies on Russian [influence] abroad (India, Iran, Indonesia)." Swayzee to Dickey, 15 June 1953. Ford Foundation International Training and Research Papers, Administration, Board of Overseas Training and Research, Minutes of Meetings and Other Reports, 1953/54.

54. O'Brien, "Modernization, Order, and the Evolution of a Democratic Ideal," p. 372.

55. The full title is *The Crisis of Democracy: Report on the Governability of Democracies to the Trilateral Commission*; it was published by New York University Press. For an analysis of the book and some of its implications, see Alan Wolfe, "Capitalism Shows Its Face: Giving Up on Democracy," in *Trilateralism: The Trilateral Commission and Elite Planning for World Management*, ed. Holly Sklar (Boston: South End Press, 1980).

56. Additional evidence of foundation support for the viewpoints of these mainstream social scientists can be found in G. William Domhoff, *The Higher Circles: The Governing Class in America* (New York: Vintage Books, 1971), who notes the following on pp. 126–27: "The inter-relationship of corporate-controlled foundations, think factories, and university research institutes can be demon-

strated by studying the prefaces to leading books in the field of foreign affairs. For example, Gabriel Almond, of the very prominent Princeton Center for International Studies (publisher of *World Affairs*, which is second only to *Foreign Affairs* in this field), offers thanks to the Carnegie Corporation for the funds which made possible his study of *The Appeals of Communism*. Carnegie also supplied the funds for *The Civic Culture: Political Attitudes and Democracy in Five Nations*, co-authored by Almond and Sidney Verba. Thomas C. Shelling of the Center for International Affairs at Harvard wrote *The Strategy of Conflict* during a year-long stay at the RAND Corporation, and Herman Kahn did most of the research for *On Thermonuclear War*, published by the Princeton Center, while at the RAND Corporation. Lucien Pye's *Aspects of Political Development* was written while at the MIT Center for International Studies, with the help of Carnegie money."

57. Sandbrook, "'Crisis' in Political Development Theory," pp. 177–80.

58. The document was entitled *Investment in Education: The Report of the Commission of Post-Secondary School Certificate and Higher Education in Nigeria* (Lagos: Government Printer, 1960), but is generally referred to as the Ashby Commission report after its chairman, Eric Ashby. See Chapter 5 of the text for details on the commission's origins.

59. Not all Nigerians share the general enthusiasm for this theory that its sponsors and proponents exhibit. For an example of one voice of dissent, see Benji J. O. Anosike, "Education and Economic Development in Nigeria: The Need for a New Paradigm," *African Studies Review*, 20 (Sept. 1977).

60. Some details of the foundations' role in convening this conference and in supporting the manpower-planning approach can be found in E. Jefferson Murphy, *Creative Philanthropy: Carnegie Corporation and Africa, 1953–1973* (New York: Teachers College Press, 1976), pp. 86–87. Support for the McGraw-Hill Series in International Development, of which the first volume was *Education, Manpower and Economic Growth*, was provided by the Carnegie Corporation and the Ford Foundation. Harbison and Myers's *Manpower and Education: Country Studies in Economic Development* was published in the same series the next year, as was Myers's study entitled *Education and National Development in Mexico*. Professor Harbison, in a recapitulation of his ideas on this topic in his *Human Resources and the Wealth of Nations* (New York: Oxford University Press, 1973), acknowledged the generous and extended support of the Carnegie Corporation and the Ford Foundation, which over the years enabled him to work out his theories.

61. Karabel and Halsey, *Power and Ideology in Education*, p. 15.

62. Martin Carnoy, "Education and Economic Development: The First Generation," *Economic Development and Cultural Change*, 25 (supp. 1977), pp. 437–38.

63. See, for example, Ivar Berg, *Education and Jobs: The Great Training Robbery* (Boston: Beacon Press, 1971), for an explication of this domestically; and Philip J. Foster, *Education and Social Change in Ghana* (London: Routledge & Kegan Paul, 1965), for an example in a Third-World setting. Interestingly, this significant foundation support for an approach which fails to fulfill its promise is not an isolated episode. A recent favorite area of foundation support has been the so-called nonformal approach to educational development in Third-

World nations. Yet, despite increasing evidence of the ineffectiveness of such an approach in achieving its stated goals, the foundations (and the international and national funding agencies) continue to support nonformal education at a high level. One can only surmise what foundation personnel must think after they read such critiques of their programs as the following: ". . . as long as employers look to formal school credentials as indices of the attainment of elite cultural attributes, it is likely that nonformal education will do little more than prepare non-elites to be more productive workers while relegating them to relatively inferior status positions." And what raises even more questions regarding the motives behind continuing foundation support for this approach is the opinion that "nonformal education is unlikely to have a significant impact on socioeconomic status without concomitant changes in the values and institutions which support the stratification process." Thomas J. LaBelle and Robert E. Verhine, "Nonformal Education and Occupational Stratification: Implications for Latin America," *Harvard Educational Review*, 45 (May 1975), p. 179.

64. See pp. 000–00 of the text for more on nonformal education.

65. Cf. Immanuel Wallerstein's comment, *The World Capitalist-Economy* (Cambridge: Cambridge University Press, 1979), p. 134, that "what was primarily wrong with all the concepts linked to the paradigm of modernization was that they were so ahistorical."

66. The foundations can call upon numerous scholars like Havighurst to articulate viewpoints supportive of their own. A recent example of this can be found in Havighurst's laudatory exposition of the foundations' role in American education during the twentieth century. See his "Foundations and Public Education in the Twentieth Century," in *Private Philanthropy and Public Elementary and Secondary Education: Proceedings of the Rockefeller Archive Center Conference*, ed. Gerald Benjamin (NP: Rockefeller Archives Center, 1980). Havighurst was an officer of the General Education Board during the 1930s.

67. Robert Havighurst and J. Roberto Moreira, *Society and Education in Brazil* (Pittsburgh: University of Pittsburgh Press, 1965), p. 109. Yet a further indication of how such "value-free" social scientists draw their conclusion *before* collecting their data is demonstrated by the authors' Foreword to the book, written after the 1964 Brazilian coup had ousted the democratically elected government, in which they comment, p. ix: "It seems clear that the new government is more conservative than the one it overthrew. Yet it is probably not a reactionary government." If only the wish were mother to the facts!

68. Ford Foundation, Fox, Oral History Transcript.

69. Packenham, *Liberal America and the Third World*, p. 298.

70. Myrdal, *Asian Drama*, p. 12. Benjamin R. Barber has put this somewhat differently: "Despite pretentions to objectivity, the ideological biases of many western social scientists have become embarrassingly transparent. Democracy becomes the only 'scientific' form of government, capitalism shares with science the 'open-market,' models of development and modernization turn out to bear a remarkable resemblance to the evolution of American industrial capitalism." See his "Science, Salience, and Comparative Education: Some Reflections on Social Scientific Inquiry," *Comparative Education Review*, 16 (Oct. 1972), p. 428.

71. O'Brien, "Modernization, Order, and the Erosion of a Democratic Ideal," p. 372. For a minianalysis of the manner in which these technological and bureaucratic elites impede meaningful development in an African setting, see Joel Barkan, "Some Dilemmas of Higher Education in Africa: (why African university graduates won't develop Africa)," *Conch*, 10 (1978), pp. 176-90.

72. Packenham, *Liberal America and the Third World*, p. 132.

73. Joseph H. Willets, "Preliminary Conclusions from the Study of Crete," 8 Mar. 1949. RFNYC: folder 900, Pro-Unar 2.

74. David Halberstam, *The Best and the Brightest* (New York: Fawcett Crest, 1973). Godfrey Hodgson, *In Our Time: America from World War II to Nixon* (London: Macmillan, 1976), comments at length on the widespread nature of this consensus.

75. Robert I. Rhodes, "The Disguised Conservatism in Evolutionary Development Theory," *Science and Society*, 32 (Fall 1968), p. 385. For an incisive critique of the ideological nature of some of the mainstream literature on development, see Irene L. Gendzier, "Modernity and Development," *Theory and Society*, 8 (1979).

76. Moore, in his *Social Origins of Dictatorship and Democracy*, analyzes the efficacy of the revolutionary as opposed to the evolutionary path of development.

77. See pp. 000-00 and 000-00 of the text for additional comments on this theme.

78. For an important discussion that questions the validity of the assertion that the Soviet Union's objectives during the Cold War were any more expansionist than they had ever been, see Daniel Yergin, *Shattered Peace: The Origins of the National Security State* (Boston: Houghton Mifflin, 1977).

79. Quoted in John Merrington, "Theory and Practice in Gramsci's Marxism," in *The Socialist Register, 1968*, ed. Ralph Miliband and John Saville (London: Merlin Press, 1968), p. 154.

80. Susanne J. Bodenheimer, "The Ideology of Developmentalism: American Political Science's Paradigm-Surrogate for Latin American Studies," *Berkeley Journal of Sociology* (1970), pp. 98, 122.

81. Ibid., p. 103.

82. Ibid., p. 109.

83. Joseph DiBona, "The Development of Educational Underdevelopment in India," *Asian Profile*, 5 (Dec. 1977).

84. Francis X. Sutton, "American Foundations and Public Management in Developing Countries," p. 16. Reprinted from "Education and Training for Public Sector Management in Developing Countries," Rockefeller Foundation, Mar. 1977. Available in a Ford Foundation reprint.

85. "Kissinger's Critique (con't.)," *The Economist*, 10 Feb. 1979, p. 3.

86. Francis J. Method, "National Research and Developmental Capabilities in Education," in *Education and Development Reconsidered: The Bellagio Conference Papers*, ed. F. Champion Ward (New York: Praeger Publishers, 1976), p. 137.

87. John A. Smyth, "Equity Criteria in Educational Planning," in *Education and Development Reconsidered*, p. 116.

88. Eric R. Wolf, *Peasant Wars in the Twentieth Century* (New York: Harper Colophon Books, 1969), p. 276. The quotes in this section are from this source.

89. Ali A. Mazrui, "The African University as a Multinational Corporation," *Harvard Educational Review*, 45 (1975), p. 200.

90. Thomas E. Weisskopf, "Capitalism, Underdevelopment, and the Future of the Poor Countries," in *Economics and the World Order from the 1970s to the 1990s*, ed. Jagdish N. Bagwati (London: Macmillan, 1972), p. 50.

91. Mazrui, "African University as a Multinational Corporation," p. 194.

92. Ralph J. Miller, "The Meaning of Development and Its Educational Implications," in *Education and Development Reconsidered.*

93. Richard R. Fagen, "A Funny Thing Happened on the Way to Market: Thoughts on Extending Dependency Ideas," *International Organization*, 32 (Winter 1978), p. 295.

94. A work in progress indicates the role of the Ford Foundation in institutionalizing in Chile during the 1960s the domain assumptions of Western sociology, and raises questions regarding the beneficiaries of the transplantation. See Edmundo F. Fuenzalida, "Consequences of the Reception of 'Scientific Sociology' on the Social Organization of the Production of Sociological Knowledge in Chile: Transnational Integration/Disintegration," a paper presented at the Conference on the Origins and Operations of Educational Systems, organized by the Research Committee on Sociology of Education, International Sociological Association, Paris, 6–9 August 1980.

Chapter 5. Foundation Influence on Intermediate Organizations, International Forums, and Research

1. F. C. Ward to Messrs. Gant, Kingsley, Stone, and Wilhelm, 5 Feb. 1965. Ford Foundation, International Training and Research Papers, Administration, Institute of International Education folder, 1965.

2. Ford Foundation, John B. Howard, Oral History Transcript.

3. Details on the early history of the Institute of International Education come from Stephen Mark Halpern, "The Institute of International Education: A History," Ph.D. diss., Columbia University, 1969.

4. Ibid., p. 189.

5. Quoted from draft memorandum from Melvin J. Fox to C. H. Faust, 3 Aug. 1965. Ford Foundation, International Training and Research Papers, Administration, Institute of International Education folder, 1965.

6. Halpern, "Institute of International Education" p. 220. See also the institute's *Annual Reports*, 1954–1968.

7. M. J. Fox to F. Champion Ward, 4 Feb. 1965. Ford Foundation, International Training and Research Papers, Administration, Institute of International Education folder, 1965.

8. E. Jefferson Murphy, *Creative Philanthropy: Carnegie Corporation and Africa, 1953–1973* (New York: Teachers College Press, 1976), p. 29.

9. The magnitude of the support is indicated by the following partial figures: in fiscal year 1956 the institute's total income was $1,531,000, of which $350,000 came from a Ford Foundation grant for general support and $280,000 from other foundation grants for the same purpose. Comparable figures for fiscal 1964 were: total institute income, $3,227,000, Ford Foundation grant $350,000;

other foundation grants, $517,000. The bulk of the remaining income during these years was realized from fees for contract services, and in this context the comment of Ford's F. C. Ward is instructive. After noting that the foundation had used IIE's services heavily since 1951, he commented that "we [the Ford Foundation] run the U.S. Government a close race as contractor for IIE services (in the neighborhood of $2.7 million of project funds in recent years). . . . the fees for these services [being approximately] $350,000 annually." F. C. Ward to Messrs. Gant, Kingsley, Stone, and Wilhelm, 5 Feb. 1965. Ford Foundation, International Training and Research Papers, Administration, Institute of International Education folder, 1965; and M. J. Fox to C. H. Faust, draft memorandum, 3 Aug. 1965. Ford Foundation, International Training and Research Papers, Administration, Institute of International Education folder, 1965. In his memorandum to Faust, Fox estimated that between 1951 and 1965 the Ford Foundation's general support grants totaled approximately $5.5 million.

10. Ford Foundation, Melvin J. Fox, Oral History Transcript.

11. For details on the history of the African-American Institute, see Evelyn Jones Rich, "United States Government-Sponsored Higher Education Programs for Africans, 1957-1970, with Special Attention to the Role of the African-American Institute," Ph.D. diss., Columbia University, 1977.

12. Quoted in ibid., p. 97. Corroboration of this has come also from William Cotter, AAI's president during the 1970s. Personal interview, 14 May 1976, New York City.

13. Rich, "United States Government-Sponsored Higher Education Programs for Africans," p. 98.

14. Ford's John Howard, among others, was quite explicit on this point. See, for example, p. 00 of the text.

15. Murphy, Creative Philanthropy, pp. 87-88, comments on the ties between the Carnegie Corporation and the African-American Institute, on how corporation officers "Stackpole and Pifer maintained frequent contact with Institute staff and officers, and were able to obtain informal assistance from the Institute's offices in Africa from time to time," and on corporation grants for practicular projects.

16. Ford Foundation, Melvin J. Fox, Oral History Transcript, p. 205.

17. Rich, "United States Government-Sponsored Higher Education Programs for Africans," pp. 158, 251.

18. Melvin Fox to John Howard, 2 Sept. 1960 Ford Foundation, International Training and Research Paper, John Howard, Africa-Educational Exchange.

19. James P. Grant to John B. Howard, 30 Sept. 1960. Ford Foundation, International Training and Research Papers, D-246, African-American Institute folder.

20. The institute's total attributable income in 1960 amounted to $546,350, of which 15 percent came from foundation grants. In 1963 total income was $3,942,155, 50 percent of which came from government sources. By 1968 government support accounted for 90 percent of the institute's budget of $7,732,903. Rich, "United States Government-Sponsored Higher Education Programs for Africans," p. 99.

21. By 1973 the level of this Carnegie Corporation support had reached $588,000. Murphy, Creative Philanthropy, p. 88.

22. Carnegie officials in particular were concerned about this. See for example, correspondence in Carnegie Corporation Archives (CCA): American Council on Education.

23. Details on the evolution and work of the Africa Liaison Committee can be found in Murphy, *Creative Philanthropy*, chapter 7; and Richard D. Heyman, "Carnegie Corporation and African Education, 1925-1960," Ed.D. diss., Columbia University, 1970. See also CCA: file, American Council on Education, 1; and Ford Foundation, Minutes of the Anglo-American Conference on Aid to Higher Education in Africa, 19 Jan. 1959, a meeting between Foundation Representatives and Members of the British Delegation, John Howard, International Training and Research Papers, African Conference.

24. The initial Carnegie grant of $12,500 for work of the Africa Liaison Committee was made in 1959. By 1962 this figure stood at $90,000, and was increased to $247,000 the following year. The level of support remained high into the 1970s; for example, in 1972 the committee received a Carnegie grant of $200,000, an amount over and above the annual appropriations made by the American Council on Education. Figures culled from Murphy, *Creative Philanthropy*, Appendix B, pp. 259-62. Early organizational problems are noted in correspondence in CCA: file, American Council on Education—Committee for Educational Liaison with African Countries.

25. Ford Foundation, James L. Morrill, Oral History Transcript, p. 20.

26. The other charter members of the committee were President Harvie Branscomb of Vanderbilt University, President Cornelis W. deKiewiet of the University of Rochester, and President Arthur Adams of the American Council on Education. DeKiewiet's association with the Carnegie Corporation dated from 1946, when the corporation's president commissioned him to visit South Africa on behalf of the corporation to ascertain program possibilities there. He was to play a central role in the fortunes of the committee and, through it, of the Carnegie Corporation.

27. Arthur A. Adams to Alan Pifer, 2 May 1960. CCA: file, American Council on Education, 2.

28. Docket memorandum entitled "The American Council on Education," 5 May 1960, prepared by Alan Pifer. CCA: file, American Council on Education, 2.

29. A roster of participants can be found in CCA: file, American Council on Education, 3.

30. Murphy, *Creative Philanthropy*, pp. 107-12, discusses this Princeton meeting.

31. On Bigelow's earlier contacts with Carnegie Corporation, see pp. 000-000 of the text. The Karl W. Bigelow papers, Teachers College Archives (TCA), contain details of the Afro-Anglo-American Program in Teacher Education. Also, CCA: file, Columbia University-Teachers College, Afro-Anglo-American Program in Teacher Education, 1959-60, 1961-63, 1964-65.

32. These details are drawn from Murphy, *Creative Philanthropy*, p. 94; and from memorandum from John B. Howard to McGeorge Bundy, Board of Trustees Docket Item, 11 May 1966. Ford Foundation, International Training and Research Papers, John B. Howard, Education and World Affairs grants file.

33. Ibid., pp. 2-3.

34. Murphy, *Creative Philanthropy*, p. 94. Among the works completed under the auspices of Education and World Affairs were (1) a study of relations between the Agency for International Development and American universities, requested by AID director David Bell (who subsequently became Ford Foundation vice-president) and Carnegie Corporation president John W. Gardner; (2) a study of the role of the United States Office of Education in the international field, which ultimately resulted in a reorganization of the office; (3) a study of professional schools and international affairs.

35. Proposal to the Ford Foundation, n.a., Dec. 1965. Ford Foundation, International Training and Research Papers, Education and World Affairs grants file. Also, *The University and World Affairs*, The Ford Foundation, 1960, p. 77.

36. Particulars on some of these, e.g., the work undertaken by Education and World Affairs Committee on Human Resource Development for AID in Nigeria, can be found in TCA: Karl W. Bigelow papers.

37. For more on these conferences, see pp. 000–000 of the text.

38. Among the major works are Philip Coombs, with Roy C. Prosser and Manzoor Ahmed, *New Paths to Learning for Rural Children and Youth* (Essex, Conn.: ICED, 1973); Philip Coombs with Manzoor Ahmed, *Attacking Rural Poverty: How Nonformal Education Can Help* (Baltimore and London: Johns Hopkins University Press, 1974); Manzoor Ahmed and Philip H. Coombs, eds., *Education for Rural Development: Case Studies for Planners* (Essex, Conn.: ICED, 1975).

39. Rolland G. Paulston and Gregory LeRoy, "Strategies for Nonformal Education," *Teachers College Record*, 76 (May 1975), p. 587.

40. Much of this discussion is drawn from material in Steve Weissman, "Foreign Aid: Who Needs It?" in *The Trojan Horse*, ed. Steve Weissman (San Francisco: Ramparts Press, 1974).

41. See the council's statement of purpose, as it appears, for example, in ODC's 1980–81 publications bulletin.

42. Weissman, *Trojan Horse*, pp. 16–17.

43. Ibid., p. 17.

44. For example, May Rihani, *Development as If Women Mattered: An Annotated Bibliography with a Third World Focus*, ODC Occasional Paper no. 10, 1978. Jere R. Behrman, *International Commodity Agreements: An Evaluation of the UNCTAD Integrated Commodity Program*, ODC Monograph no. 9, 1977. Gordon W. Smith, *The External Debt Prospects of the Non-Oil Exporting Developing Countries*, ODC Monograph no. 10, 1977. On alternatives to orthodox development models, see Denis Goulet, *The Uncertain Promise: Value Conflicts in Technology Transfer* (New York: IDOC/ODC, 1977).

45. See, for example, Denis Goulet, *Looking at Guinea-Bissau: A New Nation's Development Strategy*, ODC Occasional Paper no. 9, 1978.

46. For a perspective on the Overseas Development Institute, see Teresa Hayter, *Aid as Imperialism* (Harmondsworth: Penguin Books, 1971).

47. Jason Epstein, "The CIA and the Intellectuals," *New York Review of Books*, 20 April 1967, p. 16.

48. For an explication of this point, see Christopher Lasch, "The Cultural Cold War: A History of the Congress for Cultural Freedom," in his *Agony of the American Left* (New York: Knopf, 1969).

49. These materials are drawn from Ford Foundation grant file PA56-340.

50. My emphasis. The Ford Foundation was so concerned with the continuance of and the valuable role performed by the congress that it began to increase its level of support when the CIA began to withdraw its funding after the revelations of such linkages in the mid-1960s.

51. The outbreak of World War II brought Carnegie's African programs to a virtual standstill. In 1945 Corporation president Deveraux Josephs (an influential member of the Council on Foreign Relations) asked the Department of State to suggest contacts to help Carnegie develop its African programs. Little came of these efforts, other than a continuation of the pre-1939 Visitors' Program, which brought to the United States for study tours carefully selected colonial officials and Africans.

52. Pifer had spent several years with the U.S. Fulbright Commission in London before joining Carnegie Corporation. Heyman, "Carnegie Corporation and African Education," p. 160, quotes Pifer as saying in 1952 that "education is, of course the key. There is no aspect of African life which is not affected by it. Ordered growth and continual stability depend on it. The United States . . . has already made an immense contribution in Africa, but it can and must do far more."

53. Grant approval document entitled "The American Assembly, Columbia University," n.a., n.d., but c. early 1957. CCA: file, Columbia University-American Assembly, Africa.

54. Alan Pifer, Background Paper for Conference on "The United States and Africa," 14 May 1957. CCA: file, Columbia University-American Assembly on "The U.S. and Africa."

55. American Assembly, *The United States and Africa* (New York: American Assembly, 1958).

56. Quotes are from the unpaged "Final Report of the 13th American Assembly," 4 May 1958, typescript copy in CCA: file, Columbia University-American Assembly, Africa.

57. For details, see pp. 00-00 of the text.

58. Murphy, *Creative Philanthropy*, p. 60. A complete list of conference participants can be found in CCA: file, Greenbrier Conference, 1958. Much of the discussion that follows comes from this source as well.

59. Heyman, "Carnegie Corporation and African Education," pp. 177-78.

60. Pifer, Background Paper for Conference on "The United States and Africa," 14 May 1957.

61. Andrew Cohen, Harris Lecture, Northwestern University, April 1958. Copy filed in Ford Foundation, International Training and Research Papers, file Africa, Greenbrier Conference on, 1958.

62. Details on these subsequent meetings can be found in Murphy, *Creative Philanthropy*, pp. 62-65. Also, CCA: file, Conferences, 1959.

63. Details on the background to the Ashby Commission study are drawn from a memorandum from Alan Pifer to staff, 29 Sept. 1958. CCA: file, Nigeria, 1.

64. The most important study on the expansion of schooling in western and eastern Nigeria at the time is David Abernethy, *The Political Dilemma of Popular Education: An African Case* (Stanford: Stanford University Press, 1969).

65. The document was entitled *Investment in Education: The Report of the Commission of Post-Secondary School Certificate and Higher Education in Nigeria* (Lagos: Government Printer, 1960), but is generally referred to as the Ashby Commission Report, after its chairman, Eric Ashby.

66. The manner in which this was accomplished is the subject of Barbara A. Rhodes, "The Genesis of the Ashby Commission Report on Education in Nigeria," Ph.D. diss., University of Southern California, 1973. A 1961 internal Carnegie document further illustrates this. A docket excerpt dated 5 April 1961, prepared by Alan Pifer for the trustees' consideration, noted that "like the Ashby Commission the present project was conceived by the Corporation's officers but has been completely taken over by local interests, in this case by the University College [of Rhodesia and Nyasaland]." CCA: file, Rhodesia, 3.

67. Murphy, *Creative Philanthropy*, p. 80.

68. Interoffice memorandum from Bryce Wood, 10 Mar. 1948. Rockefeller Foundation Archives, New York City: folder 900, Program and Policies, Under-developed Areas.

69. Details on the planning for this and other Rockefeller-sponsored conferences can be found in materials at the Rockefeller Archives Center.

70. F. Champion Ward, ed., *Education and Development Reconsidered: The Bellagio Conference Papers* (New York: Praeger Publishers, 1974). Parts of several of the papers in this collection raise questions concerning developmental orthodoxy. See, for example, Ralph M. Miller, "The Meaning of Development and Its Educational Implications," and Francis J. Method, "National Research and Developmental Capabilities in Education."

71. Kenneth W. Thompson and Barbara R. Fogel, *Higher Education and Social Change: Promising Experiments in Developing Countries, vol. 1, Reports* (New York: Praeger Publishers, 1976), p. 3. The second volume, edited by Thompson, Fogel, and Helen E. Danner, was published by Praeger in 1977.

72. Thompson and Fogel, *Higher Education and Social Change*, 1:4.

73. For details on Soedjatmoko's career and his links to U.S. foreign policy and corporate interests, see David Ransom, "The Berkeley Mafia and the Indonesian Massacre," *Ramparts*, 9 (Oct. 1970), pp. 27–29, 40–49. See also my discussion of the Ford Foundation's role in Indonesian development planning after 1965, in Chapter 3.

74. This "networking" principle is discussed in the last section of Chapter 3.

75. Thompson and Fogel, *Higher Education and Social Change*, 1:9.

76. Ibid., 1:49.

77. Among, the task force members were Duncan Ballantine, education advisor, World Bank; F. Champion Ward of the Ford Foundation; Alfred Wolf, program advisor to the president of the Inter-American Bank and formerly a Ford Foundation official; Michael Todoro of the Rockefeller Foundation. Included among the corresponding members were Carl Eicher, chairman of the Overseas Liaison Committee of the American Council on Education; Robert Goheen, former president of Princeton University and president of the Council

on Foundations; J. George Harrar, former Rockefeller Foundation president; Father Theodore Hesburgh, chairman of the Rockefeller Foundation board of trustees; Arthur Porter, vice chancellor of the University of Sierra Leone, formerly vice-principal of the University of Nairobi, and collaborator in the Rockefeller and Ford foundations' East African university program; Cranford Pratt, former principal of University College, Dar es Salaam, and Ford Foundation consultant; Herman Wells, Chancellor of Indiana University and formerly head of the board of trustees of Education and World Affairs.

78. Miller, "The Meaning of Development and Its Educational Implications," p. 83.

79. James A. Perkins, Memorandum on the Council on Foreign Relations, 18 Mar. 1953. CCA: file, Council on Foreign Relations, 1943–56.

80. William A. Marvel, draft agenda sheet, 17 Dec. 1959. CCA: file, Council on Foreign Relations—Regional Councils and Fellowships.

81. William Greenleaf, "The Ford Foundation: The Formative Years," unpublished manuscript, c. 1959, typescript copy in Ford Foundation Archives. The following material comes from the same source, chapter 5, pp. 30–35.

82. For details on foundation support for the Institute of Defense Analysis and other centers of national security research, see Gene M. Lyons and Louis Morton, *Schools for Strategy: Education and Research in National Security Affairs* (New York: Praeger, 1965).

83. Edited by William A. Hance and published in 1968 by Columbia University Press.

84. Waldemar A. Nielsen, *African Battleline: American Policy Choices in Southern Africa* (New York and Evanston: Harper & Row, for the Council on Foreign Relations, 1965), p. 143.

85. Waldemar A. Nielsen, *The Great Powers and Africa* (New York: Praeger Publishers, 1969), p. 358.

86. Rich, "United States Government-Sponsored Higher Education Programs for Africans," p. 2.

87. Ibid., p. 124.

88. Murphy, *Creative Philanthropy*, p. iii.

89. Carnegie Corporation provided significant funding for the Center for Education in Africa at Teachers College. Through 1975 Teachers College Press had published sixteen monographs dealing with various aspects of African education in an arrangement with the center.

90. Murphy, *Creative Philanthropy*, p. iv.

91. Murphy acknowledged as much in a conversation with the author on 3 Nov. 1976 in Boston.

92. Murphy, *Creative Philanthropy*, pp. 87–88, explains the increased foundation support as follows: "In 1963 the Corporation joined with Ford Foundation and Rockefeller Brothers Fund to provide the Institute with a base of private funds for general administration, leavening somewhat its heavy dependence on the Department of State and Agency for International Development, for whom it administered contracts for educational assistance to Africa." There is no mention of the CIA's long involvement in the fortunes of the institute. Melvin J. Fox, long-time Ford Foundation program officer, notes the foundation response to the public disclosures that the African-American Institute was supported by

the CIA as follows: "And the question emerged around this time of the desirability of trying to put it on a sounder footing. We participated, and I think it was about 1965, in an effort which was a joint Foundation effort; the Rockefeller Brothers Fund was a participant in this and the Carnegie Corporation and Rockefeller itself, and we, in making it possible for AAI to shift its operations on to a private footing." Ford Foundation, Fox, Oral History Transcript, p. 205. It is perhaps significant that part of this transcript dealing with the relationship linking the institute to the CIA has been deleted.

93. A recent Carnegie-supported study of the Inter-University Council, with which the corporation's overseas programs have long been intertwined, is only the latest manifestation of such sponsored research. See I. C. M. Maxwell, *Universities in Partnership: The Inter-University Council and the Growth of Higher Education in Developing Countries 1946-1970* (Edinburgh: Scottish Academic Press, 1980).

94. Two important works that examine this contradiction are James O'Connor, *The Fiscal Crisis of the State* (New York: St. Martin's Press, 1973); and Erik Olin Wright, *Class, Crisis, and the State* (London: NLB, 1978).

95. Richard R. Fagen, ed., *Capitalism and the State in US-Latin American Relations* (Stanford: Stanford University Press, 1979), p. 8.

96. Ibid., p. 15.

97. Manuel Castells, *The Economic Crisis and American Society* (Princeton, N.J.: Princeton University Press, 1980), p. 70.

98. Ibid., p. 130.

99. For two in attendance at the 1974 Bellagio conference, see n. 70 to this chapter.

Chapter 6. Technocracy, Cultural Capital, and Foundation Programs

1. The foundation addiction to the "efficiency" criterion, a crucial component of a technocratic worldview, is discussed in Chapters 1 and 4 of the text.

2. Trent Schroyer, "The Need for Critical Theory," *The Insurgent Sociologist*, 3 (Winter 1973), p. 31.

3. Ibid., p. 34.

4. Ford Foundation, Melvin J. Fox, Oral History Transcript, p. 217.

5. For details, see Dennis Buss, "The Ford Foundation and the Exercise of Power in American Public Education," Ed.D. diss., Rutgers University, 1972; and Paul A. Woodring, *Investment in Innovation: An Historical Appraisal of the Fund for the Advancement of Education* (Boston: Little, Brown, 1971).

6. Joseph P. Farrell, "A Reaction to 'The Macro-Plannning of Education: Why It Fails, Why It Succeeds, and the Alternatives,'" *Comparative Education Review*, 19 (June 1975), pp. 208-9.

7. Joseph E. DiBona, "The Development of Educational Underdevelopment in India," *Asian Profile*, 5 (Dec. 1977), p. 617.

8. Thomas J. LaBelle and Robert E. Verhine, "Nonformal Education and Occupational Stratification: Implications for Latin America," *Harvard Educational Review*, 45 (May 1975), p. 179.

9. Ford Foundation grant file PA61-81, Request for Grant Action No. OD-773G.

10. For details on the American educational response, see Joel Spring, *The Sorting Machine: National Education Policy since 1945* (New York: David McKay, 1976).

11. For example, the *Ford Foundation Annual Report, 1962* lists grants of $95,000 and $39,000 to Educational Services, Inc.; the 1964 *Annual Report* lists a $218,000 grant.

12. Ford Foundation grant file PA 61-81, Request for Grant Action No. OD-773G, p. 1.

13. Farrell, "Reaction to 'The Macro-Planning of Education'," p. 209.

14. This is not to suggest, of course, that dependency theory alone can explain all the multitudinous problems of underdevelopment facing Third-World nations. The outright rejection of the theory's main tenets by the foundations and kindred organizations, however, calls into question the foundations' repeated claims about considering seriously all approaches to the alleviation of Third-World underdevelopment. On dependency theory and the development of underdevelopment thesis, see, for example, Andre Gunder Frank, *Capitalism and Underdevelopment in Latin America* (New York: Monthly Review Press, 1969); Samir Amin, *Unequal Development* (New York: Monthly Review Press, 1974); Paul Baran, *The Political Economy of Growth* (New York: Monthly Review Press, 1972); James D. Cockcroft, Andre Gunder Frank, and Dale L. Johnson, *Dependence and Underdevelopment* (Garden City: Anchor Books, 1972). The foundations and other international donor organizations have been equally dismissive of the ideas of world-systems theorists and of the theory's major proponent, Immanuel Wallerstein. See particularly Wallerstein's *The Modern World System: Capitalist Agriculture and the European World-Economy in the Sixteenth Century* (New York: Academic Press, 1974); *The Modern World System II: Mercantilism and the Consolidation of the European World System, 1600–1750* (New York: Academic Press, 1980); and *The Capitalist World-Economy* (Cambridge: Cambridge University Press, 1979). Cf. Amiya Kumar Bagchi, *The Political Economy of Underdevelopment* (Cambridge: Cambridge University Press, 1982). Dependency theorists and world-systems theorists are not without their critics, of course, even on the left. See in particular, for example, the critique of the perspectives of Frank and Wallerstein in Frederick Stinton Weaver, *Class, State and Industrial Development: The Historical Process of South American Industrial Growth* (Westport, Conn.: Greenwood Press, 1980), especially chapters 3 and 8.

15. See, e.g., the bibliographical references in Rolland G. Paulston, "Multiple Approaches to the Evaluation of Educational Reform: From Cost-Benefit to Power Benefit Analysis," paper presented at the International Institute of Education Planning Seminar on the Organization of Educational Reform at the Local Level, Paris, 27–30 Nov. 1979; and the *Comparative Education Review*, 22 (Oct. 1978), whose special theme was Evaluating Educational Reform.

16. One example among many will illustrate the point. In the mid-1960s the Fund for the Advancement of Education, organized by the Ford Foundation in the early 1950s to administer domestic educational activities, commissioned a study to determine the impact of the fund's massive expenditure on instructional television. Selected to conduct the evaluation were Judith Murphy and Ronald

Gross, respectively consultant to and staff member of the Fund for the Advancement of Education. For details, see Dennis Buss, "The Ford Foundation in Public Education: Emerging Patterns," in *Philanthropy and Cultural Imperialism: The Foundations at Home and Abroad*, ed. Robert F. Arnove (Boston: G. K. Hall, 1980); and Judith Murphy and Ronald Gross, *Learning by Television* (New York: The Fund for the Advancement of Education, 1966).

17. At least one Ford officer was concerned about the lack of meaningful evaluation of field projects. Melvin Fox recalled that "in Africa [there was] nil evaluation practically of the kind that one could call evaluation." Fox, Oral History Transcript, p. 232.

18. See Chapter 3 for details of Harris's involvement in the fortunes of the National School.

19. Ford Foundation Archives report 001382, p. 38.

20. Gaston V. Rimlinger, "Administrative Training and Modernization in Zaire," *Journal of Development Studies*, 12 (July 1976), pp. 364–82.

21. "Responses to Edward H. Berman," *Harvard Educational Review*, 49 (May 1979), p. 183.

22. This quotation and the following discussion are drawn from Paulston, "Multiple Approaches to the Evaluation of Educational Reform."

23. This discussion is drawn from Noel McGinn, Ernesto Schiefelbein, and Donald Warwick, "Educational Planning as Political Process: Two Case Studies from Latin America," *Comparative Education Review*, 23 (June 1979), pp. 218–39.

24. For a short study arguing that the graduates of these institutions will *not* lead demands for far-reaching structural changes, see Joel Barkan, "Some Dilemmas of Higher Education in Africa: (why African university graduates won't develop Africa)," *Conch*, 10 (1978). Cf. also my comments, pp. 000–00.

25. See, e.g., Pierre Bourdieu and Jean-Claude Passeron, *Reproduction: In Education, Society, and Culture* (Beverly Hills: Sage Publications, 1977), and *The Inheritors* (Chicago: University of Chicago Press, 1979); Basil Bernstein, *Class, Codes, and Control: Theoretical Studies towards a Sociology of Language* (London: Routledge & Kegan Paul, 1971); Michael F. D. Young, ed., *Knowledge and Control: New Directions for the Sociology of Education* (London: Collier-Macmillan, 1971); Michael W. Apple, *Ideology and Curriculum* (London: Routledge & Kegan Paul, 1979); and Michele Barrett et al., eds., *Ideology and Cultural Reproduction* (New York: St. Martin's Press, 1979).

26. Karl Marx and Friedrich Engels, *The German Ideology, Parts I and II* (New York: International Publishers, 1947), p. 39.

27. Altbach notes that although Third-World universities may be peripheral to metropolitan universities, they stand at the center of their nations' cultural and intellectual life. Philip G. Altbach, "The University as Center and Periphery," in *Universities and the International Distribution of Knowledge*, ed. Irving G. Spitzberg (New York: Praeger Publishers, 1980).

28. Many people have neglected the important role played by universities in the perpetuation of a particular ideology. Universities accomplish this because, as Noble notes, "the universities could do what no other research agencies . . . could do: they could reproduce themselves." David Noble, *American by Design: Science, Technology, and the Rise of Corporate Capitalism* (New York: Oxford University Press, 1979), p. 128.

29. Ali A. Mazrui, "The African University as a Multinational Corporation: Problems of Penetration and Dependency," *Harvard Educational Review*, 45 (May 1975).

30. Ibid., p. 200.

31. Ibid., p. 204.

32. The classic statement of this position remains Max Weber, *The Protestant Ethic and the Spirit of Capitalism* (New York: Charles Scribner's Sons, 1958).

33. See, e.g., Eric Ashby, *Universities: British, Indian, African* (Cambridge, Mass.: Harvard University Press, 1966).

34. Edward T. Silva, "Cultural Autonomy and Ideas in Transit: Notes from the Canadian Case," *Comparative Education Review*, 24 (Feb. 1980), pp. 67-68.

35. Philip G. Altbach, "The Distribution of Knowledge in the Third World: A Case Study in Neocolonialism," in *Education and Colonialism*, ed. Philip G. Altbach and Gail Kelly (New York and London: Longman, 1978), p. 307.

36. Mazrui, "African University as a Multinational Corporation," p. 194.

37. Thomas Eisemon, Yakov Rabkin, and Eva Rathgeber, "Collective Scientific Self-Reliance: Possibilities and Limitations," in Spitzberg, *Universities and the International Distribution of Knowledge*.

38. Altbach, "Distribution of Knowledge in the Third World," p. 317.

39. Robert F. Arnove, "Foundations and the Transfer of Knowledge," in Arnove, *Philanthropy and Cultural Imperialism*.

40. Ibid., p. 322.

41. Ibid., p. 323.

42. This discussion relies heavily on Laurence H. Shoup and William Minter, *Imperial Brain Trust: The Council on Foreign Relations and United States Foreign Policy* (New York: Monthly Review Press, 1977), pp. 254-84.

43. See particularly C. Fred Bergsten, "The Threat from the Third World," *Foreign Policy*, 11 (Summer 1973).

44. For example, Ford officer Melvin Fox noted that the foundation's "capacity to analyze problems of social change has increased by light years, but it is questionable whether we have made significant advance in the sense of how to apply that knowledge to improve the condition of the underprivileged." Ford Foundation, Fox, Oral History Transcript, addendum to Oral History Project Interview.

45. The fullest explication of these linkages can be found in Philip H. Burch, Jr., *Elites in American History: The New Deal to the Carter Administration* (New York: Holmes and Meier, 1980).

46. For an elaboration on this point, see pp. 000-00 of the text, and n. 60 to Chapter 3.

Index

Accountability, 10, 162, 177
Adams, Arthur, 57, 135
Africa, 15, 57, 154-156; capitalism and, 24; Carnegie Corp. in, 74, 88-93, 145-149; cultural dependence in, 172; educational exchanges and, 132-133; education in, 22-24, 61, 68; Ford Foundation in, 72. *See also* East Africa
Africa Liaison Committee, 57-58, 77, 133-136
African-American Institute, 131-133, 154, 155, 156
African Education Commission, 22-24
Agency for International Development, 48, 59-60
Agricultural commodities, 53
Agriculture, Rockefeller Foundation and, 59
Aid, multilateral, 140-143. *See also* Foreign aid
Altbach, Philip G., 172-173
Altruism, 2-3, 174-175
American Assembly, 146-148
American Council on Education, 57-58
Andreski, Stanislav, 107, 111
Anticommunism, 49-50. *See also* Communism
Area studies, 8, 61-62, 99-105, 110
Arnove, Robert F., 69, 80, 82, 105, 173, 174
Ashby Commission, 115, 148-149
Ashley, Walter E., 86
Asia, 150-151, 151-152, 182n10; communism in, 56; raw materials, 46
Asian Institute of Management, 97
Assumptions. *See* Bias; Values
Autonomy. *See* Dependence/autonomy

Baldwin, David, 44-45, 52
Barraclough, Geoffrey, 66
Bates, Thomas R., 13
Beard, Charles A., 17

Bechtel, Stephen, 33-34
Becker, Gary, 109
Beckmann, George, 103-104
Behavioralism, 107-108
Belgium, 85
Beliefs. *See* Ideology
Bellagio conferences, 149-152
Bias/objectivity, 18-19, 127-128, 142, 149-156, 158-159, 166-168. *See also* Value-free/apolitical approaches; Values/background assumptions
Bigelow, Karl W., 90, 91, 92-93, 136
Binder, Leonard, 114
Black, Eugene, 51, 52, 53-54, 55
Bodenheimer, Susanne, 121, 122
Bowie, Robert, 96
Bowles, Samuel, 39, 104, 109-110
Brazil, 97-98, 118, 139, 151
Bretton Woods conference, 51
British Dominions and Colonies Program, 74
British possessions/colonies, 74. *See also* Great Britain
Brown, E. Richard, 24-25, 25-26
Brown, William O., 72
Buchanan, Norman S., 70
Bundy, McGeorge, 4, 12, 63, 132
Bureau of Educational and Cultural Affairs, 155

Capitalism, 37-38, 174-175; advantages of, 64; Africa and, 24; hegemony of, 177-178; liberal, 5; progressive, 141-142; reforms and, 16-17; state and, 157. *See also* State capitalism
Capon Springs, 20-21
Carnegie Corporation, 61-62, 74-76, 78, 88-93; Africa Liaison Committee and, 133-136; Ashby Commission and, 115; bias/objectivity in, 155-156; Education and World Affairs and, 136-137; founded, 17; grants, 34-35; Institute of

221

International Education and, 130; international conferences and, 145-148; *Journal of Negro History* and, 27-28; Negro education and, 22, 23; in Nigeria, 75-76; objectives of, 57-58; South Africa and, 38; teacher education and, 68-69
Carnegie Endowment for International Peace, 95-96
Carnegie Foundation for the Advancement of Teaching, 17
Carnegie Institute, 17, 18-19
Castells, Manuel, 157
Central Intelligence Agency, 61, 86, 143; African-American Institute and, 131-132, 154, 156; Robert Bowie and, 96; Congress for Cultural Freedom and, 213n50; Indonesia, 83; William Langer and, 113; National Student Association and, 94
Centre for Applied Legal Studies, 38
Charity organizations, 19
Chile, 38, 139
China, 15, 25-26, 56, 94
Class. *See* Ruling class; Social class; Upper class
Clay Commission, 54, 55
Clay, Lucius, 54
Cleaver, Harry McBeath, Jr., 94
Cohen, Andrew, 147
Cold War, 6-7, 14, 28-29, 55-59. *See also* Communism; Union of Soviet Socialist Republics
Colleges. *See* Postsecondary education
Colombia, 71, 151
Colonialism, 14
Columbia University, 101; Teachers College, 88-89, 90-91, 91-93, 93-94, 136
Committee on Economic Development, 46
Communism: in Africa, 57-58, 87, 154-155; in Asia, 56; educational exchanges and, 132-133; raw materials and, 47; underdevelopment and, 111-112. *See also* Anticommunism; Cold War; Union of Soviet Socialist Republics
Concentration/specialization, foundations', 8
Conferences, 129, 145-152, 155
Conflict, development and, 168
Congo/Zaire, 68, 85-87, 97-98, 166-167
Congress for Cultural Freedom, 143-145
Consensus, 65-66; in foreign policy, 42, 63; on Third World development, 118-121

Conservatism/conservatives, 7; in developmental theory, 116-117; in social sciences, 109-110
Consultations among foundations, 8
Consumer culture, 170
Coombs, Philip, 12, 137-139
Cooption of radicals, 159
Coordination for universities, 133-137
Coordination of activities, 12
Corporations, 17-18, 42, 141, 170
Coser, Lewis, 13
Council on Foreign Relations, 35-37, 62; Carnegie Corp. and, 153; 1980's Project, 175-176; raw materials and, 47; War-Peace Studies Project of, 41-42
Cultural capital, 169-174
Culture, 5, 11, 12, 162

Defense. *See* Military
de Kiewiet, Cornelis W., 77
Democracy, development and, 144; elites and, 27-28
Dependence/autonomy, 169-174
Dependency theory, 165-166
Development Advisory Service, 83, 84
Development/modernization, 8-9; Cold War and, 28; elites and, 6; foundations' goals in, 26-27; reconceptualization of, 149-152; social scientists on, 111-118; theory of, 8, 121-125; undesired, 205n52; War-Peace Studies Project and, 43-46
DeVinney, L. C., 60, 69
Dewey, John, 17
DiBona, Joseph, 122-123, 164
Dickey, John, 36
Disagreements, foreign-policy, 65-66
Dissent, 92, 104. *See also* Radicals
Duggan, Laurence, 129, 131
Dulles, John Foster, 46, 47, 62

East Africa, 71, 76-79, 80, 81-82, 135-136
Eckes, Alfred E., Jr., 46-47
Economic growth, 44-45
Economics, 68, 80, 109-110; developmental theories of, 115-117
Education, 4, 129-140, 164-165, 168-169; African, 145-149 (*see also* Carnegie Corp.); economic development and, 116; evaluation of, 149-152; foreign policy and, 12; hegemony and, 30; in India, 122; Negro, 20-24; nonformal, 164
Education and World Affairs, 136-137
Educational Services, Inc., 165
Elites, 33-37, 113, 171; behavioralism and, 108; Chinese, 25; democratic,

27-28; development through, 15-16,
123-124; in foundations, 5-6, 7, 12-13;
Latin American, 122; nonformal
education and, 139. *See also* Leaders
El Salvador, 125
Engels, Friedrich, 42, 169
Epstein, Jason, 143
Europe, 45
Evaluation of projects, 9-10, 166-169
Evolution/gradualism, 48-50, 119, 120,
121
Experts, 9; elites and, 12-13; Ford
Foundation and, 73; as leaders, 14. *See
also* Elites; Technology

Fagen, Richard R., 124, 157
Fahs, Charles, 58-59, 69, 102
Failure of development, 138. *See also*
Evaluation of projects
Fairbanks, John K., 182n10
Farrell, Joseph P., 164, 165
Federal University of Bahia, 97-98
Fellowships, 8, 24, 68, 82, 93-96, 103-104
Finletter, Thomas, 36
Fisher, Donald, 108
Fisk University, 21-22
Ford Foundation: African-American
Institute and, 132-133; Asian Institute
of Management and, 97; Congo/Zaire
and, 85-87; Congress for Cultural
Freedom and, 143-145; Council on
Foreign Relations and, 153; education
and, 12, 60-61; Education and World
Affairs and, 136-137; fellowships and,
94, 103; foreign-policy establishment
and, 63; grants, 35; in higher
education, 72-74; Indonesia and, 83-84,
84; Institute of International Education
and, 130; left wing and, 39; Marxism
and, 31; C. Wright Mills and, 31; in
Nigeria, 75; objectives of, 56-57; project
evaluation by, 166-167; public
administration and, 85-87; research
availability and, 173; Dean Rusk on,
2-3; science education and, 165; social
sciences and, 80; Tanzania and,
193n78; teacher education and, 90-91;
technology and, 164; trustees of, 33-34;
universities and, 13-14, 100-103
Ford, Henry, 16, 17
Foreign Affairs, 47
Foreign aid, 8, 52-59; rationale for, 48
Foreign Area Fellowship Program,
103-104
Foreign Student Leadership Program, 94
Fosdick, Raymond, 106
Fox, Melvin, 72, 132, 164, 219n44
France, 14

Freire, P., 139
Fulbright, J. William, 136
Functionalism, 106-107, 117-118
Fund for the Advancement of Knowledge,
12, 217-218n16

Gaither, Rowan, 61
Gardner, John, 15, 57, 148
Gates, Frederick T., 17, 184n33
General Education Board, 12, 17, 20-22,
23, 25
Gintis, Herbert, 39, 104, 109-110
Gouldner, Alvin W., 87-88, 96, 106-107
Goulet, Dennis, 39
Gradualism. *See* Evolution
Gramsci, Antonio, 5, 8, 13, 32
Grant, James P., 140-141
Grants, 34-35, 38-39
Gray Commission, 54
Gray, Gordon, 54, 57
Great Britain, 14, 22-24, 89-91, 134, 148
Great Depression, 43-44, 106
Green Philip, 7
Green Revolution, 59

Haig, Alexander, 190n29
Halberstam, David, 64, 120
Halsey, A. H., 109, 116
Harbison, Frederick, 115-116, 148
Harrar, J. G., 71, 194-195n10
Harriman, W. Averell, 45
Harris, James T., 86, 166-167
Harvard University, 101
Havighurst, Robert, 117-118
Heald, Henry, 61, 136
Health, 24-26
Heaps, David, 86, 87
Hegemony: capitalist, 177-179;
determinants of, 29-32
Herter, Christian, 136
Higher Education and Social Change,
150-152
Higher education. *See* Postsecondary
education
Hodgson, Godfrey, 42
Hoffman, Paul, 47, 56, 63
Holland, Kenneth, 129, 130
Homogeneity, social, 32
Horowitz, David, 108
Howard, John, 56, 61, 72, 83, 128
Human capital/resources, 115-117,
122-123, 148. *See also* Manpower
planning
Huntington, Samuel, 114

Ideology, 11, 13, 15-18; agreement on,
64-65; of capitalism, 38-39;
foundations, 26-27; modernization and,

168; pluralism and, 40; of ruling class, 29-30; social sciences and, 84; technocracy and, 163. *See* Bias/objectivity; Orthodoxy
Import-Export Bank, 44-45
Independence/dependence, organizations', 127-128, 131, 137. *See also* Interrelationships
India, 56, 122-123, 164
Indonesia, 83-84, 150-151
Inequalities, 117-118
Influence, foundations', 1-2, 35-36, 127-128, 157-159. *See also* Independence/dependence; Interrelationships
Information, Third World, 141-142. *See also* Research
Infrastructures, 52-53
Injustices, 16
Institute for Medical Research, 17
Institute of Defense Analysis, 153-154
Institute of International Education, 128, 129-131
Intellectual network, 96-98
Intellectuals, 13
Intermediate organizations, 9, 127-143, 157-158
International affairs, study of, 99, 100-105
International Bank for Reconstruction and Development. *See* World Bank
International Cooperation Administration, 42
International Council for Educational Development, 47, 137-139
International Development Advisory Board, 54
International Education Board, 93-94
International grants, 34-35
International Health Commission, 24
International Institute of Tropical Agriculture, 76
International Monetary Fund, 51
Internationalization of staff, 167
Interrelationships, 5, 157-158; foundations-governmental, 5, 6-7, 35-37, 42, 62-63, 64; foundations-social scientists, 206-207n56. *See also* Independence
Inter-University Council for Higher Education, 90, 93
Investment: statist, 191n38; private, 51-52, 53
Iran, 123

Japan, 144-145
Jeanes, Anna T., 23
Jeanes teacher-training institutes, 23-24

Johnson, Lyndon B., 63
Jones, Thomas Jessee, 22-24
Journal of Negro History, 27-28

Kahnin, George M., 101
Kaldor, Mary, 66
Karabel, Jerome, 111, 116
Karl, Barry, 17, 18
Katz, Stanley N., 18
Kennedy, John F., 12, 53, 63
Kenya, 24, 198n60
King, John K., 47
Kissinger, Henry, 123
Knowledge, 169. *See also* Information; Research
Kristol, Irving, 42

LaBelle, T. J., 164-165
Langer, William, 113
Languages, European, 171-172, 173
Larsen, Roy, 33, 34
Lasch, Christopher, 14, 95
Latin America, 54-55, 82, 84, 121-122, 151, 164-165, 173-174
Lattimore, Owen, 46
Leaders/leadership, indigenous, 14-15, 48, 60, 67-68, 71-74, 124. *See also* Elites
Left wing, 39; Marx and, 31. *See also* Communism; Radicals; Socialism
Legitimation, 157-158
Lenin, Vladimir, 31
Lewis, W. Arthur, 144
Liberals, 7, 19-20, 26-27, 37-40; capitalism and, 5; evaluation by, 167-168; functionalism and, 107; philosophy of, 177-179; radical research and, 157
Life-style, 170
Linkages. *See* Interrelationships
Locke, John, 112

McCloy, John J., 32, 33, 34, 36, 51, 52, 63
McGinn, Noel, 168
McKenzie, Fayette, 21
McNamara, Robert S., 63
Magdoff, Harry, 48
Manpower planning, 80-81, 82. *See also* Human capital
Markets overseas, 66
Marshall Plan, 45
Marx, Karl, 29, 169
Marxists, 5, 18-19, 31, 84; critique by, 104-105; Great Depression and, 106-107; support for, 39
Massachusetts Institute of Technology, 165
Mazrui, Ali A., 124, 170-171, 172

Method, F. J., 123
Methodology, social-science, 111
Milibrand, Ralph A., 13, 50
Military, 63-64, 153-154
Miller, J. Irwin, 33
Mills, C. Wright, 31, 108
Mobutu, Sese Seko, 87
Models, educational institutions as, 70-71
Modernization. See Development
Moi, Daniel Arap, 196n60
Moore, Barrington, 120, 120-121
Morison, Robert S., 70-71
Morrill, James L., 86, 134, 136
Moseby, Philip, 55
Multinational corporations, 170
Murphy, E. Jefferson, 74, 155-156
Myrdal, Gunnar, 83, 111

National Institute of Political Studies, 85
National School of Law and
    Administration, 85-87, 166-167
National Student Association, 94-95
Nationalism, African, 154-155
Negroes, 20-24, 27-28
Nelson, Joan, 43
Netherlands, 14
Networks, educational/intellectual, 69,
    96-98
Neutrality. See Independence
Nicaragua, 125
Nielsen, Waldemar, 2, 49, 132, 133,
    154-155
Nigeria, 71, 75-76, 80, 148-149. See also
    University of Ibadan
1980's Project, 175
Nitze, Paul, 96
Nixon, Richard, 46
Nyerere, Julius, 193n78

Objectives, foundations', 1-3. See also
    Anticommunism; Bias/objectivity
O'Brien, Donal Cruise, 112, 113, 114
Oil industry, 188-189n11
Orthodoxy, intellectual, 92, 93, 95, 96,
    104, 178. See also Dissent, Radicals
Overseas Development Council, 140-143

Packenham, Robert A., 8-9, 48, 112, 118,
    119
Pakistan, 80
Papanek, Gustav, 84
Parsons, Talcott, 106-107
Paulston, Rolland G., 105
Peking Union Medical College, 25
Perkins, James, 36
Persuasion, 13
Phelps-Stokes Fund, 22-24, 93
Philippines, 26, 81, 97

Pifer, Alan, 57, 58, 62, 88, 89, 134, 135,
    145-147
Pluralism, 5, 39-40
Polarization, political, 163
Policy-makers, 28-29
Political science, 107-109
Politics, 163. See also Value-free/
    apolitical approaches
Postsecondary education, 42-43, 48-49,
    59-61, 70-93, 129-137 passim, 170-171;
    aid for, 8, 12-14; graduates of, 124;
    Negro, 21; Nigeria, 148-149;
    Progressive Era, 18; in U. S., 82,
    99-105. See also Teachers, education of
Power-elitist school, 108-109
Price, Donald, 58, 73
Private property rights, 49-50
Production, accumulation of, 157
Progressive Era, 16, 17-26
Propaganda, 143-145
Public administration, 85-88
Publishing, 172
Puey Ungphakorn, 150
Pye, Lucien, 114, 204n49

Radicals: critique by, 178; development
    theory of, 120-121; research by, 141,
    142, 159. See also Communists; Dissent
Ramparts, 2
Rationality, technology and, 161, 163
Raw materials, 41-42, 66
Reagan, Ronald, 49
Reality, sense of, 30, 40
Reform/reformers, 14-15, 48-50; in U. S.,
    16
Reproduction, cultural, 162
Research/scholarship, 172-174, 175-176;
    biased versus objective, 152-153;
    dissent/orthodoxy of, 104-105. See also
    Bias/objectivity
Revisionist historiography, 6
Revolution, 48-50, 124-125
Rimlinger, Gaston V., 167
Rockefeller, Foundation: Carnegie
    Endowment for International Peace
    and, 95; developmental strategy and,
    149-152; education and, 60, 69-71;
    founded, 17; grants, 34, 35;
    international studies and, 102;
    motivation of, 24-25; objectives of,
    58-59, 70-71; science and, 14;
    secretaries of state from, 62-63; social
    sciences and, 105-106; universities and,
    81-82; University of East Africa and,
    76-79; War-Peace Studies Project and,
    41-42, 43. See also University
    Development Program
Rockefeller, John D., Sr., 12, 17, 21

Rockefeller, John D., III, 58
Roosevelt, F. D., 44, 51
Rostow, W. W., 67, 112, 164
Ruling class, 30-31, 174-177; ideas/
    ideology of, 29-30, 169-170. *See also*
    Elites
Rusk, Dean, 2-3, 58, 60, 63, 64-65, 70
Russell Sage Foundation, 2, 19, 20

Sallah, David L., 30
Sandbrooks, Richard, 114
Saudi Arabia, 34
Schlesinger, Arthur, Jr., 112
Scholarship. *See* Research/scholarship
Scholarships, 131
Schroyer, Trent, 79, 163
Schultz, Theodore, 109
Science: learning of, 165; Rockefeller
    Foundation and, 14
Secretaries of state, 62-63
Seligman, E. R. A., 18
Seybold, Peter J., 31, 107-108
Shepardson, Whitney, 36, 43
Silva, Edward T., 19, 20, 171
Slaughter, Sheila, 19
Smyth, John A., 123
Social class: interests of, 162; in Latin
    America, 122. *See also* Elites; Ruling
    Class; Upper class
Social homogeneity, 32
Social Science Research Council, 105,
    107, 108, 113, 114
Social sciences, 79-84, 99-100, 105-125
Social work, 19-20, 20
Socialism, 16-17, 18-19, 20, 39, 64, 124
Sociology, 106, 117-118
Soedjatmoko, 150-151
South Africa, 38
South (U. S.), 20-22, 25
Southern African Student Program, 155
Southern Education Board, 21
Spaeth, Carl, 56
Specialization, foundations', 8; in social
    sciences, 115
Spofford, Charles, 36
Stackpole, Stephen, 78, 89, 145-147,
    199n86
Staff, foundations', internationalization
    of, 167
Stalin, Joseph, 31
Standard Oil Co., 16
Stanley, Manfred, 9
State capitalism, 2, 3, 4, 7, 29, 157. *See
    also* Capitalism
Statist development, 191n38
Stone, Shepard, 143
Structural change, societal, 116, 117,
    117-118

Structural-functionalist approach, 106-107
Students, critique by, 178
Studies. *See* Research
Suharto, 83
Sukarno, 83
Sutcliffe, R. B., 52-53
Sutton, Frank, 78, 97, 123, 167
Swayzee, Cleon O., 57, 205n53

Tanzania, 39, 193n78
Taxation, 17
Teachers College. *See* Columbia
    University
Teachers, education of, 68-69, 90-91
Technology/technocracy, 9; development
    and, 161-169; reform and, 16
Thailand, 71-72, 150
Theory of development, 121-125
Thompson, Kenneth, 67-68, 69, 71, 81,
    150, 195n20
Tipps, Dean C., 111-112
Trade, international, 184n33
Traditional societies: development in,
    123-124; nonformal education in,
    137-138
Transfer value, 70
Travel, 62
Trilateral Commission, 175-176
Truman, Harry S., 45, 49
Trustees, 32-33
Tuskegee philosophy, 20-24, 90, 93

Underprivileged, 176
Union of Soviet Socialist Republics, 6,
    41, 121, 143, 200n98
United States Advisory Commission on
    International Educational and Cultural
    Affairs, 14-15
U. S. Public Law, 480, 53
Universities. *See* Postsecondary education
University Development Program, 60, 75
University of Chicago, 12
University of Djakarta, 83
University of East Africa, 76-79, 80,
    98-99
University of Ibadan, 75-76, 82
University of London, Institute of
    Education, 89
University of Nairobi, 198n60
University of Valle, 151
University of Zaire, 97-98
Upper class, 66

Value-free/apolitical approaches, 80,
    110-111. *See also* Bias/objectivity
Values/background assumptions: in
    methodology, 111; propagation of, 30;
    in Third World, 113

Van Sickle, John, 106
Vance, Cyrus, 62-63
Vietnam War, 120, 163
Vincent, George, 26

Wallace, Schuyler, 96
Ward, F. Champion, 128, 130, 195n20
War-Peace Studies Project, 41-46, 50-51
Weir, John, 78, 116
Whitaker, Ben, 32-33
Whites, African regimes of, 154

Williams, Gwyn, 32
Williams, Raymond, 29-30, 92
Wolf, Alfred C., 195n20
Wolf, Eric R., 123-124
Wood, Bryce, 55, 112-113
Woodson, Carter G., 27-28
World Bank, 50-52
World-system theorists, 217n14

Yergin, Daniel, 43

Zaire. See Congo/Zaire